But Didn't We Have Fun?

But Didn't We Have Fun?

❖ ❖ ❖

An Informal History of
Baseball's Pioneer Era, 1843–1870

PETER MORRIS

Ivan R. Dee Chicago

www.ivanrdee.com

The paperback edition of this book carries the ISBN 978-1-56663-849-4.

Library of Congress Cataloging-in-Publication Data:
Morris, Peter, 1962–
    But didn't we have fun? : an informal history of baseball's pioneer era,
 1843–1870 / Peter Morris.
      p. cm.
    Includes bibliographical references and index.
    ISBN-13: 978-1-56663-748-0 (cloth : alk. paper)
    ISBN-10: 1-56663-748-1 (cloth : alk. paper)
    1. Baseball—United States—History—19th century. I. Title.
 GV863.A1M644 2008
 796.3570973'09034—dc22
                                                             2007024315

To my great friends, the Reslocks

Contents

Contents

But Didn't We Have Fun?

Introduction

❖ Many histories of baseball barely mention the nineteenth century, and those that do generally skip straight from the activities of the Knickerbocker Club of New York City in the mid-1840s to the undefeated season of the Red Stockings of Cincinnati in 1869. If a sentence or two is allotted to the intervening years, this generally consists of a few generalizations that are at best half-truths. Often more time is spent debunking the Abner Doubleday myth than describing the game's real pioneers. (Please see Appendix One for an explanation of what Doubleday didn't do.) The unfortunate result is that the story of the first generation of Americans to embrace a game recognizable as baseball has never been told.

Historians who have attempted to address this omission have faced a daunting task. To begin with, this forgotten era is so abundant with clubs, players, and games that it takes a long book just to map out the terrain. At the same time geographic impediments and primitive modes of transportation and communication made regions of the country far more isolated than they are today, so that a basic truth about baseball in one part of the country did not necessarily apply to another locale.

Works about baseball in this era have thus faced a dilemma. A number of painstakingly researched studies have provided us with a wealth of detail about how baseball was played during these years. Yet this very abundance of detail has made the resulting narratives extremely dense. Even experts on the period find them difficult to read, while the casual fan finds them overwhelming and impenetrable.

Those authors who have sought to overcome this problem have all too often fallen victim to the opposite defect. In omitting or summarizing the details, they have reduced these extraordinary years to little more than a series of oft-repeated anecdotes and shopworn generalizations. Worse, in trying to avoid losing readers in a labyrinth of detail they usually concentrate on the game's development in and around New York City, which has led to distorted versions that have little to say about the rich story of how baseball spread to other regions and became the national pastime.

Unfortunately this editorial predicament is easier to identify than to solve. Imagine a writer who comes to be stranded for several years on an alien planet populated with a rich variety of exotic terrains and inhabitants. He or she would return to Earth with a great story to tell but would find it virtually impossible truly to do justice to the alien world. Omitting any of its bounties would seem unforgivable, yet mentioning all of them would turn the narrative into a dreary catalogue.

The problem seemed insurmountable until I began to discover a rich array of accounts written by the men who played and watched baseball in the 1840s, 1850s, and 1860s. While these writings could not stand by themselves, it became clear to me that they provided the basis for a history of that era that captured what it was like really to be there. So my challenge has been to weave their fascinating reminiscences into a coherent narrative.

The result is certainly not the definitive chronicle of the era—many of the greatest players and clubs and most momentous games do not receive their due here. More important, memory distorts, and this is magnified by the egos, biases, and limitations of the men who are quoted in these pages. While demonstrably false statements have not been included, there can be no doubt of inaccuracies and exaggerations in their versions. The reader is forewarned.

Yet a healthy skepticism about some of the details should not blind us to the essence of these recollections. As one of the era's greatest writers said in response to critics of his novel *Oliver Twist,* "It is useless to discuss whether the conduct and character of the girl seems natural or unnatural, probable or improbable, right or wrong. IT IS TRUE." Read in that spirit, I hope this book will finally provide baseball fans with a ready means of access to the story of the pioneers who gave us the national pastime.

*   *   *

Most knowledgeable baseball fans are at least vaguely aware that the Knickerbockers of New York played a major role in the early history of the game, but comparatively few fans have sought to learn more about them. This is hardly surprising. The Knickerbockers are generally depicted as such stodgy figures that it becomes impossible to think of them as young men who had fun playing the game. For an analogy, imagine a youngster's reaction to a grandparent or great-grandparent offering to explain the facts of life.

This perception of the Knickerbockers as a sober bunch is not entirely without basis. Rather than inventing the game of baseball, the Knickerbockers *reinvented* it by burdening a child's game with an adult's seriousness of purpose. In order to do so and to be successful in persuading others to join them, the club had to stress adult concerns and make light of the elements of play and sheer enjoyment.

That being the case, the Knickerbockers made comparatively little mention of the pleasure they derived from the playing of the game. And since this emphasis on adult preoccupations was the club's most important contribution to baseball, historians have understandably focused on it. Yet seeing this as the essence of the Knickerbockers is a mistake.

A perfect example is one of the first instances of a ballplayer being fined for something that happened on a baseball diamond. At the bottom of the score sheet from one of the Knickerbockers' early games, we learn that one of the players was assessed six cents for saying "s—t." This surprising information serves as an excellent reminder of the club's desire to elevate baseball's moral and social status. But it is just as dramatic an illustration of the fact that the players continued to play the game in a way that was highly spontaneous and not always subject to societal restraints.

This, then, is the central paradox of the Knickerbockers. Yes, they unquestionably did what they are credited with doing—making key revisions to a rural child's game that enabled it to emerge as an acceptable activity for urban adults. And since that accomplishment is their claim to fame, it naturally gets most of the attention. This emphasis, combined with their relatively formal attire, their old-timey names like Ebenezer, and their preoccupation with creating a written record of their activities, can fool us into assuming that the Knickerbockers devised the rules of baseball at a committee meeting—and had about as much fun as the typical committee meeting produces.

But it is a mistake to assume this. There is, surely, a sense of mischief in specifying that a player was fined for saying "s—t" rather than just reporting that he broke a rule against cursing. And, if we look closely enough, we can discern this same sense of fun peeking out from behind the carefully erected façade of grown-up responsibility.

At heart the Knickerbockers were just young men who gained the same pleasure from ball-playing as any other generation. This was equally true of the generation of young men who succeeded them and turned baseball into America's national pastime. It was genuinely an innocent age for baseball and only by understanding this forgotten element can we appreciate how baseball has come to mean so much to Americans.

THE PIONEER ERA IN A NUTSHELL

This work is intended to be a history of baseball before 1870 but not a chronicle, so the accumulation of names, dates, and similar minutiae has been kept to a minimum. But naturally readers will need to keep a few of each in mind, so here is a convenient listing of some of the most significant ones. This is not remotely a complete list, nor should it be assumed that a club or player listed here is more important than others that are omitted. These are simply the names that figure most prominently in this narrative.

Timeline of Key Events

Before 1843: Bat-and-ball games with similarities to baseball are played in all regions of the United States. Regional variants abound, however, and no effort is made to standardize them.

1843 (approximate): The Knickerbockers of New York City form a club to play baseball.

1845–1846: The members of the Knickerbocker Club formally adopt rules and begin playing match games.

1853–1854: After a period of little growth, during which the Knickerbocker Club's existence is quite tenuous, multiple clubs around New York begin to adopt the Knickerbockers' rules.

1857–1858: The game's first governing body, the National Association of Base Ball Players (NABBP), is founded. In spite of the use of the word "national," almost all of the clubs that use the Knickerbockers' rules are in or near New York City.

1859–1860: Considerable spread of the Knickerbockers' game begins. The Excelsiors of Brooklyn embark upon the first important tour.

1861–1865: The Civil War slows the growth of the game and ends the career of many clubs and ballplayers.

1866–1867: A great boom of baseball enthusiasm occurs, with far more clubs participating than ever before. The National Club of Washington becomes the first Eastern club to tour west of the Alleghenies. Professionalism continues to be prohibited by the NABBP, but under-the-table arrangements become increasingly common. The Eastern cities begin to be plagued by troubles resulting from professionalism and a spirit of competitiveness.

1868: A troubled year brings an end to the amateur era. The problems that had previously been restricted mostly to the East become widespread.

1869: Professional play, increasingly common for several years, is reluctantly legalized by the NABBP. The Red Stockings of Cincinnati are one of about a dozen clubs to play openly as professionals. The club's undefeated record and gentlemanly conduct lead to short-lived hopes that the professional era can retain many of the characteristics of the era when clubs were ostensibly amateur.

1870: The decision to disband the Red Stockings after a tumultuous season leaves little doubt that the pioneer era of baseball is over. After the season the first professional league, the National Association, is formed. Amateur ballplayers form their own organization but never again receive anywhere near the attention given professionals.

Key Clubs

Knickerbocker Club of New York City: the club most responsible for baseball acquiring standard rules.

Olympic Club of Philadelphia: a "town ball" club that had been in existence since the early 1830s, its decision to switch to the Knickerbockers' game was an important development.

Tri-Mountain Club of Boston: the first New England club to switch from the "Massachusetts game" to the Knickerbockers' rules, a crucial step toward arriving at a set of standard national rules.

Excelsiors of Brooklyn: the first club to go on a prominent tour and act as ambassadors for the game of baseball. The Excelsiors were a national power before the Civil War and likely the first to hire a paid player, but they soon became disenchanted by postwar changes to the game and ceased to be a contender.

Pastimes of Brooklyn: a prewar club of gentlemanly, socially prominent young men. They symbolized the idea that a club didn't have to be very good at baseball in order to have a great time playing it.

Athletics of Philadelphia: the first national contender from outside New York, though chicanery by the New York clubs prevented them from ever being recognized as champions. The club had a troubled transition to professionalism, exemplified when their club president blasted them for turning their backs on the club's founding principles.

Nationals of Washington: the first Eastern club to tour west of the Alleghenies in 1867, the club enjoyed the generous support of the U.S. Treasury Department. Many looked the other way at the governmental backing the Nationals received, but others resented it.

Cincinnati Base Ball Club (universally but unofficially known as the "Red Stockings"): the club that took the country by storm in 1869, the first year of open professionalism. The club went undefeated and took on all comers, even traveling to California, while becoming synonymous with gentlemanly conduct. But the next season saw both losses and lapses in conduct, with the result that the Cincinnati Base Ball Club pulled its support for the professionals at season's end.

(Note: Club names during the era were generally rendered with the nickname preceding the city name; e.g., the Eckford Base Ball Club

of Brooklyn, or, for simplicity, the Eckfords of Brooklyn. Only as the era was ending did the order begin to be reversed.)

Key People

Daniel Adams: a founding member of the Knickerbockers. He was one of the men most responsible for keeping the club going during the late 1840s because he made sure that functional baseballs were always on hand—no easy task in those days.

Frank Pidgeon: one of the founding members of the Eckford Club of Brooklyn in the early 1850s, he wrote a memorable description of the club's early days. He was regarded as one of the top pitchers of the 1850s, but when professionalism began to change the game he was one of many who turned his back on it.

Jim Creighton: the game's first superstar. He was probably also the first paid player, and was certainly the man most responsible for increasing the pitcher's role. He died in 1862 at age twenty-one.

Henry Chadwick: pioneer sportswriter and influential voice in baseball development throughout the nineteenth century. Chadwick would come to view the early game condescendingly as primitive, but he never lost his fondness for its players.

Harry Wright: captain of the Red Stockings, his father's career as a professional cricketer left him with an intense conviction that there was nothing wrong with being paid to play baseball. It was shared by his younger brother George, shortstop of the Red Stockings and one of the era's greatest players.

CHAPTER 1

Before the Knickerbockers

❖ The Knickerbocker Club of New York City first took up baseball around 1843, and historians now unanimously credit this club's members with a major role in the game's development. Yet initially they could not possibly have had any sense they were doing anything particularly noteworthy, let alone historic. To begin with, there was nothing remotely novel about Americans playing bat-and-ball games. Nor was there anything out of the ordinary in the fact that the Knickerbockers changed some of the rules, since variants were played all over the country. As a result, it would have shocked the Knickerbockers had anyone suggested that their game might one day become America's national pastime—or indeed that any game would fill such a role. A review of the bat-and-ball games being played in this country before 1843 will help us understand why this was so.

If reconstructing the details of long-extinct forerunners of baseball doesn't sound like much fun, relax. This chapter will include descriptions of such early American bat-and-ball games as wicket, round-town, and town ball, because a general sense of how these games were played is useful to appreciating the contributions of the Knickerbockers. But there won't be any quizzes about these details, and indeed anyone who tries to commit the rules of each game to memory has missed the point. Bat-and-ball games of this era were played much as small children today play hide-and-seek or tag—a few general principles remain standard, but most of the rules can be adapted to specific conditions, number of players, or just a sudden whim. The essence of such games was and is their fluidity: their rules are flexible by design so as to allow variation from region to region, from site to site, and even from day to day.

Of course none of these traits was true of cricket, which had well-established rules by the time it first arrived on American shores. But cricket's stability did not prove to be an asset. As a writer explained in 1860: "Cricket we have always had, as an exotic. It has been played for years at Hoboken and other retired localities, but chiefly by Englishmen, and it is still regarded, even by American players, as an English game." It was precisely its inflexibility that made cricket a niche sport whose rhythms defied adaptation to the conditions of the New World. This in turn prompted Americans to devise bat-and-ball games that could be adapted to local climates and conditions.

Just as crucially, this country in 1843 was still very much the United *States* of America: a group of states that had agreed on certain general principles but had agreed to disagree on a long list of specifics. Even the country's name was still regarded as a plural entity; people said "the United States are" instead of "the United States is." The desirability of centralized legal and governmental systems was still a hotly debated topic, so the idea of a national pastime would have seemed bizarre. And even if Americans had perceived a national sport as a desirable concept, the notion would have been hopelessly impractical in a vast country with primitive transportation and communication. Just getting the staples of life and essential news from town to town was an ordeal; trying to disseminate the rules of a game would have seemed absurd.

As a result, regions developed their own bat-and-ball games, some of which had generally agreed-upon practices while others were so fluid that their rules and even their names changed constantly. Adding to the imprecision, most of the surviving accounts of these games were written long after the fact and use hindsight to impose more structure and consistency than seems plausible. Thus these reports are most valuable for the sense they give us of the spirit in which these pre-Knickerbocker games were played.

On a first examination of these descriptions, it is easy to feel overwhelmed by the baffling array of accounts of pre-1840 American bat-and-ball games. A large part of this confusion is the natural result of the nation's continued reliance upon oral communication. Word-of-mouth transmission creates imprecision in any endeavor, and this is especially true in the case of an ephemeral activity such as a game.

"The variants of tag have descended to us and are played today," explained the popular historian of colonial American customs Alice Morse Earle in 1899, "just as they were played when Boston and New York streets were lanes and cowpaths. The pretty game, 'I catch you without green,' mentioned by Rabelais, is well known in the Carolinas, whither it was carried by French Huguenot immigrants. . . . Stone-tag and wood-tag took the place in America of the tag on iron of Elizabeth's day. Squat-tag and cross-tag have their times and seasons, and in Philadelphia tell-tag is also played. Pickadill is a winter sport, a tag played in the snow. Another tag game known as poison, or stone-poison, is where the player is tagged if he steps off stones." Obviously, each of these versions can be treated as a distinct game, yet it is not misleading to refer to all of them as tag. Similarly, an impressive number of regional American bat-and-ball games thrived during the mid-nineteenth century, but their distinguishing characteristics should not cause us to overlook their underlying unity.

A good place to begin our survey is in Connecticut, with a game known as wicket. It originated in Bristol around 1830, soon spread to Litchfield, Hartford, and several rural counties, and remained popular for half a century. As its name implies, wicket borrowed extensively from cricket, with each side getting two innings during which the batsmen defended a wicket from a ball thrown by the bowler. But, as an 1880 account pointed out, "it is not cricket by any means," and each of the modifications gave wicket the flexibility that the British game lacked.

For starters, the wickets were placed only a few inches above the ground, while the ball was softer and nearly twice as big as a cricket ball. The bats were correspondingly larger and thicker; eventually they came to bear "a strong resemblance to a Fiji war-club, the material being well-seasoned willow," but in the early days it is likely that any large chunk of wood might be called into service. These features eliminated much of the finesse associated with cricket—as one observer explained, wicket "is a game for fun and exercise only, affording little scope for what is called scientific play."

Another distinguishing characteristic of wicket was that it could be played by as many as thirty players per side, with all the players except the two bowlers "swarming afield as 'bartenders,' 'close-tenders,' and fielders generally." While the score was tracked, it was done in far less detailed fashion than in cricket: "no record is kept of the fielding, nor are the achievements of the bowlers credited to them on the score-book."

A Hartford resident later recalled wicket's popularity in the late 1840s and early 1850s, when games were typically "played in Cooper Lane, now Lafayette street, at its northern end where the roadway meets Washington street. It was an ideal spot for the game because of the broad street and level ground. Very many matched games were here played with clubs from the towns around Hartford, and usually a great game was played on Fast day, although many good people objected to such sports on that day.

"Wicket was played in various locations in the city, for instance: Hill boys played at the junction of Garden and Myrtle streets where the old reservoir now stands. At the south end Buckingham Square was the rallying place; at the north end, where several streets meet near the tunnel, made a fine spot for the game; while over on the east side Prospect street between

Grove and Atheneum streets was used by lads living in that vicinity. But the best games of all in many respects were the early morning games, played by clerks who were employed in stores and banks about State House (near City Hall) Square. These games which were kept up for two or three years in the early '50's were played in the early morning for four or five months on Main street in front of the State House. The bats, balls and wicket sticks were kept in front of the cellar of Welles's drug store, next north of the Phoenix bank.

"As it was customary for the drug, jewelry, dry goods and some other stores, also for banks and insurance offices, to have one or more clerks sleep in the place of business there were probably two score young men in the vicinity, most of whom were glad of the sport and exercise. It was customary for the one who was first awake at 5 o'clock to dress, and make the rounds of the square, knocking on the doors and shouting 'Wicket.' By 5:30 enough would be out to begin playing, and soon with 15 to 20 on a side the game was in full swing.

"There was very little passing of teams and but little danger of breaking store windows, although cellar windows would occasionally be broken, and paid for. Most stores had outside shutters to the windows, so they were protected. These games would end about 6:45, in time to open the stores at 7 o'clock. It was good exercise, and very enjoyable, and I have no doubt that many of our older merchants and bankers will recall with pleasure the good old wicket games in State House Square in 1852-3-4."

While wicket was most closely associated with Connecticut, the increasing mobility of mid-nineteenth-century Americans enabled one region's game to surface in unexpected locales. The opening of the Erie Canal in 1825 created a steady flow of traffic between the Northeast and the Great Lakes states, with the result that toward the end of the 1850s wicket became popular in western Michigan. It enjoyed a brief vogue in Grand Rapids around that time, only to be outstripped by the arrival of the

Knickerbockers' game. Similarly, until the advent of "hard" baseball in the late 1850s, boys in Kalamazoo "played a form of cricket with a big soft ball as large as a modern football, but round and made at home of twine and leather and bowled over a level field to knock down wickets less than its own height from the ground." In equally unpredictable fashion, wicket made appearances in Brooklyn and Hawaii as well as in several New England states.

Massachusetts also had a game of its own, which was most commonly known as round ball at the time but which eventually came to be referred to as the Massachusetts game. (And, typically, other names such as "Massachusetts Run-Around" appear to have been used as well.) Stoughton native Billy de Coster later recalled: "We used to play what was called the Massachusetts game. That was where we had a square, instead of a diamond, and ran four bases. We had a small ball and a small bat, and the ball could be thrown at a base runner and if it hit him before he got to the base he was out." This element of fielders throwing the ball at base runners was, as we shall see, one of the most popular and best-remembered features of all these games. As with the games themselves, this practice was known by many names, but the most common one was "soaking."

In rural Virginia the ball game of choice was known as round-town, a sport that was "well understood and is much enjoyed by every country boy, though only a few of their city cousins know the first rudiments of it." According to a later account: "The game of round-town is played in this manner: two sides are formed, the number of players of the division being equal. Four bases are used and are placed in the same manner as if they were being fixed for a game of baseball, although men are only placed in the positions of the pitcher, catcher, and first baseman, the rest of the players being scattered in the field where they think the ball is most apt to be knocked. The first batsman on the opposing side takes his place at the plate, and he has in his hand a paddle an inch or two thick, and in which

This is the only known photograph of the Massachusetts game being played on the Boston Common. Space constraints were an ongoing problem for ballplayers at the Common, and this issue proved crucial in the eventual demise of the Massachusetts game. [Courtesy of Mark Rucker]

only one hand is used in striking. The pitcher delivers a solid gum ball with all the swiftness attainable, the use of the curve never being thought of, and it is therefore very seldom that a 'strike out' occurs. The batter hits the ball at the first opportunity and endeavors to drive it over the hands of his opponents, for if it is caught on the fly or the first bound the runner is called out, and also if it is gotten to the first baseman before the runner arrives at the base. Should the runner reach first base safely he can continue to run to the other bases if he wishes, but his opponents have the privilege of hitting him with the ball, and as it is very painful to be struck with a gum ball, the runner is very cautious, and if he is struck he is counted out of the game, although should he reach any of the other bases he is safe."

Obviously round-town was not a highly structured game. And in all likelihood these rules were even more flexible than is suggested by this account, with many of their components subject to modification as needed.

While wicket, round-town, and the Massachusetts game retained strong affiliations with a single state, the game known as town ball sprang up in a number of large cities without following any obvious pattern. It first came to prominence in Philadelphia, where it was closely associated with one of the country's pioneer ball-playing clubs. The Olympic Ball Club was formed in 1833 from the remnants of two groups of town ball players and lasted long enough to celebrate its golden anniversary in 1883 (though it had switched from town ball to baseball in 1860). As with the Knickerbocker Club, one of the secrets of this aggregation's longevity was a more formal structure than other clubs of the era. The Olympics' constitution was published in 1838 and suggests a high degree of organization.

But just as was the case with the Knickerbockers, this appearance is deceptive. The club's steps toward formal organization seem to have been a matter of self-preservation, as the Olympics were often battling to survive. One of their predecessors was able to convince only four men to attend their first outing, which forced them to play the simple game known as "Cat Ball" or "Two Old Cat." Nonetheless this foursome had so much fun that they "told some of their younger friends of the pleasure and advantage they found in resuming their boyish sports," and soon had a group of fifteen to twenty regulars.

Their fun, however, was soon menaced by new impediments. Philadelphia had a law against ball-playing, so the group began to take a ferryboat to Camden, New Jersey, on Saturday afternoons to play. The locale had much to recommend it, as Camden was still "a very small village, comparatively little resorted to by Philadelphians, the means of communication with the city limited, slow, and imperfect, consisting mainly of two or three small horse ferry-boats, which left the wharf at the north side of Market street at intervals of about half an hour, and occupied about fifteen minutes in crossing. The ground on which

The clubhouse of the country's pioneer ball-playing club, the Olympics of Philadelphia, which began playing town ball in the early 1830s and switched to the Knickerbockers' game in 1860. Clubhouses were a powerful symbol of the pride felt by early clubs and were decorated with flags, pictures, trophies, gilded game balls, and other mementos of the club's triumphs. [Courtesy of John Thorn]

the play began and continued for several years was common and open to the street on which it bordered: no rent was paid for it, and no permission given or asked to use it. The players made their own bats and balls, and kept them at one of the public gardens on Market street, the keeper of which sent out a pail of ice-water to the ground, and supplied the ball players at his garden when the game was over, about sunset, with a bowl of lemon-ade, etc., at a very moderate charge."

At first the isolated location enabled the Olympics to remain delightfully informal in their play: "Their first Association had no constitution or by-laws, or elected members, but the absence of these formalities was not felt, and was no disadvantage; for there were no quarrels or disputes among the players, who always found the principles of good-fellowship and gentlemanly intercourse a sufficient rule for their guidance, and what the Society of Friends [the Quakers] call the 'weight of the meeting' a sufficient authority to restrain any inclination to a breach of good order."

But they soon encountered another significant obstacle: "So great was the prejudice of the public against the game at that time, that the players were frequently reproved and censured by their friends for degrading themselves by indulging in such a childish amusement, and this prejudice prevailed to a great extent for many years." Eventually the club made concessions to those who took a dim view of adults playing ball games. Thus the adoption of a more formal structure appears to have been part of the price the Olympic Club had to pay to attain respectability, rather than something the club members perceived as innately desirable.

Town ball gradually spread to a number of other cities, with mixed results. The game was reported to have acquired "quite a footing in St. Louis" before the arrival of regulation baseball in the late 1850s. Meanwhile in Davenport, Iowa, it was reported in 1858 that "two 'Town Ball' clubs have been formed from the original one, and they are now proceeding to a regular organization. They will have a big list of members, a lot of their own for playing purposes, and a good time generally. They have their rules and regulations printed, and everything will be done on system."

Cincinnati also had a couple of town ball clubs, but according to one observer, "Town ball found more favor in those days than any other sport, yet the number who patronized it were very few. But two clubs of our city could lay claim to excellence, the Excelsior . . . and the Buckeye, a foster child of the Excelsiors composed mainly of teachers. Loafing had more attraction for the great mass of our boys than any active exercise. The orphan Asylum grounds, on Elm street, were the scene of operations for these clubs, whose performances failed to arouse the public to the point of assembly in numbers to witness them. Nothing like popularity could be claimed for the game, and the few who played, finally tired of it, and it was soon forgotten."

References to town ball are more plentiful than detailed descriptions of how the game was played. One of the better sketches was provided by Hiram Waldo of Rockford, Illinois, who recalled many years later that the game "consisted of a catcher, thrower, 1st goal, 2nd goal and home goal. The inner field was diamond shape: the outer field was occupied by the balance of the players, number not limited. The outs were as follows: Three strikes, 'Tick and catch,' ball caught on the fly, and base runner hit or touched with the ball off from the base. That was sometimes modified by 'Over the fence and out.'"

Note that even this account of how town ball was played in one specific locale suggests a very loose structure, with both the few rules and the number of players subject to change. Since town ball spread entirely by oral transmission, it is safe to assume that there were still greater variations from region to region. And it is quite conceivable that the game known as "town ball" varied so much from one locale to another that "town ball" itself was effectively a catchall term.

Lending credence to this possibility is the name "town ball." Most of the era's bat-and-ball games bore names derived from a distinguishing characteristic, whether it was a wicket or round ball or square ball. This is even true of the name "base ball," which became more common as stakes were replaced with flatter objects. In contrast, "town ball" is a vague phrase, suggesting that it may have been applied to a variety of different bat-and-ball games. And at least a couple of early ballplayers claimed that town ball received its name because it was played at town meetings, an origin that would suggest a high degree of fluidity in the rules.

While we cannot be entirely sure of the extent to which town ball was a generic term, it is almost certain that this was the case with some of the era's other bat-and-ball games. For example, longtime Detroit resident Henry Starkey reported that before 1857 "we played the old-fashioned game of round ball. There were no 'balls' or 'strikes' to that. The batter waited until a ball came along that suited him, banged it and ran. If it was a fly and somebody caught it, he was out and couldn't play any more in the game. If the ball was not caught on the fly, the only way to put a batter out was to hit him with the ball as he ran. There were no basemen then; everybody stood around to catch flies and throw the ball at base runners."

Yet across the state in Kalamazoo, another pioneer later recollected that that city's early residents played a game called patch ball, which "was played very much like pass ball is played today only instead of throwing a man out at first base we threw the ball at him as he was running between the bases. I see it has not altogether gone out of style yet, as this is the game often played by boys now when they can not get enough together to play the regular game." Based on these descriptions, there appear to be no significant differences between what the one man described as "round ball" and the other as "patch ball." Indeed these descriptions could just as easily have been provided by eyewitnesses to numerous other games.

The reality that multiple names were used to describe the same basic game can also be seen in other accounts. Robert S. Pierce, one of Cleveland's earliest baseball editors, reported that when baseball arrived in that city it displaced "what was known as 'long ball,' 'square ball' and 'sock ball,' in which a soft ball was used. One of the ways of getting a batter or base runner out was to hit or 'sock' him with the ball before reaching or while off his base." Major Julius G. Rathbun, an early Hartford ballplayer, made clear that he saw little distinction between "ballplaying, barnball, one, two or three-old-cat, and games with chosen sides, a larger or smaller number."

Other early ballplayers were later unable to recall any special name for the game they played. John McNamee, who became sheriff of Brooklyn and a well-known sculptor, reminisced in 1876 that, "years before the formation of the Atlantic Club, I used to get some of the 'boys' together on a good afternoon, and go in there and play the old game, where you used to 'sock' one another with the ball." Even the Knickerbockers, recollected an original member, Duncan Curry, evolved from a group who "would take our bats and balls with us and play any sort of a game. We had no name in particular for it." Another original member, William Wheaton, confirmed that the Knickerbockers were preceded by an aggregation that played by looser rules and used "no regular bases, but only such permanent agents as a bedded boulder or old stump, and often the diamond looked strangely like an irregular polygon."

No doubt some of these versions included specific rules now lost to history, but these accounts suggest that the rules were of little import. The essence of these games was a few basic similarities, especially a great deal of running, an inherent flexibility that allowed the game to be played on almost any field and by almost any number of players, and the use of a soft ball with which runners were "soaked," "socked," or "patched." As we have seen, this last aspect was the one that featured most prominently in memoirs, in large part because it was eliminated by the Knickerbockers' rules. As one early participant put it, "I forget now as to many points of the game, but I do remember that we used to run bases, and the opposite side to ours would try to get the ball, and you would have to be hit with it before out while running your base to get home."

One game that has not been mentioned thus far is rounders, which a number of sources have credited with being the forefather of baseball. The historian David Block, however, has effectively demolished that claim, showing that rounders is not of great antiquity and that much of its support derives from being the game that the influential sportswriter Henry Chadwick played as a boy in western England.

As Chadwick explained, rounders shared the same essentials as the games preferred by Americans: "This pastime was merely a source of fun and frolic with a bat and ball, the interesting feature to both sides being the chances afforded to 'plunk' a fellow with the ball when running the bases. No skill was required to

play the game, swift and accurate throwing being the main requisite, and any school boy could learn to play it in ten minutes."
And thus it clearly belongs to the family of games that helped
pave the way for the Knickerbockers' version.

But Chadwick's additional claim that rounders "was the
parent of America's national game of base ball" cannot be justified. At most, rounders is one of a family of games that shares
that distinction, and considering that its popularity in America
was limited, the game does not deserve precedence over the
other candidates. In addition, Chadwick's own description suggests that insofar as rounders differed from the multitude of
American bat-and-ball games, it did so by including elements
that did not become part of baseball, such as using a hole for
home base and aligning the bases into a circle.

So this leaves us with Americans of the early 1840s playing
an array of bat-and-ball games which were known by a variety
of names, and which exhibited significant rule variations from
region to region. "Significant" might not in fact be the best
word, because few if any of the participants seem to have viewed
the rules as being important enough to write down at the time
or to remember with much precision. By and large, the only
traits that early players could later recall about these early
games were the few recognizable features they all shared. As a
result, when the Knickerbockers introduced the way of playing
what we now consider baseball, no one failed to recognize it as a
modified version of a familiar American game.

Many, indeed, embraced the new version as an inherited
pastime because they saw it as pretty much town ball (or one of
the other games) without the soaking. An 1879 account in the
Cincinnati Enquirer conveyed this adroitly: "Base-ball sprang
entirely from the old game of town-ball, which our fathers,
when they were college boys and young business men, played
with as much excitement attending the sport as now attaches to
this latter-day game. Twenty years ago town-ball clubs existed
all over the country—regularly organized clubs like the clubs of

to-day. Many clubs had their exclusive grounds, and the greatest rivalry existed between certain clubs. There were town-ball teams which went so far in the excitement as to visit neighboring cities and engage in friendly contest with their neighbors. The balls which were first used were soft, light and harmless. It was necessary that they be soft, for in those days the runner was put out by being hit with the ball from the hands of some opponent. There were no basemen to whom the ball was thrown, but the sphere was hurled directly at the base-runner. As the excitement of the game intensified the ball began to be made harder and heavier to aid the throwing. This led to an unusual number of accidents, resulting from the players being hit by a too solid ball. It was this dangerous outgrowth of town-ball playing which first suggested to some Yankee mind (whom nobody knows) to put basemen on the bases and let the ball be thrown to them instead of at the runner."

Thus when the Knickerbockers arrived on the scene, America already was home to a number of bat-and-ball games that featured a man hitting a soft ball with a stick and running around bases while fielders tried to retrieve the ball and throw it at him. Many variations existed, based on how many players participated and on how well- or ill-suited the field and equipment were, with some calling the game by a different name when the conditions varied dramatically. But most of the players didn't attach much significance to changes in the rules or care very much what the game was called. After all, it was just a game.

CHAPTER 2

The Knickerbockers' Game Becomes the New York Game

❖ The historical legacy of the Knickerbockers is that they unified all the multiple strands discussed in the preceding chapter into a single "regulation game." By doing so, they made baseball ready for a nation transformed during the 1850s and 1860s by a series of breakthroughs in communication, transportation, and technology that changed how and where Americans lived. Yet while this is the Knickerbockers' legacy it is by no means how the club viewed its own activities. The players took themselves far less seriously than historians have, and had far more in common with their predecessors than with most of their successors.

Of course many of them lived long enough to see their efforts develop into the national pastime, and some reflected on those long-ago days. With their questioners interested in learning about the origins of baseball, these pioneers naturally concentrated on the more formal aspects of the Knickerbockers' activities. Historians have compounded this perspective by stressing what was new and unique about the club while neglecting their fun-loving, spontaneous side, often making it sound as if their recreation was about as enjoyable as a visit to the dentist. Nothing could be farther from the truth.

The Knickerbockers formally organized on September 23, 1845, a date that is deservedly recognized as a milestone in baseball history. The date, however, is also noteworthy because of how late it comes in the club's history. By then its members had already been playing bat-and-ball games for at least two or three years, and several early members report that a predecessor had been active in the late 1830s.

A simple explanation for this delay is that the club did not view its activities as being of any great moment. This interpretation is confirmed by the comments of club member Duncan Curry, who reported that in these years "it had been our habit to casually assemble on a plot of ground that is now known as Twenty-seventh street and Fourth avenue, where the Harlem Railroad Depot afterward stood. We would take our bats and balls with us and play any sort of a game. We had no name in particular for it. Sometimes we batted the ball to one another or sometimes we played one o' cat."

Even the steps the Knickerbockers did take toward organization and uniformity were made reluctantly. According to Curry, when Alexander Cartwright proposed standard rules: "His plan met with much good natured derision, but he was so persistent in having us try his new game that we finally consented more to humor him than with any thought of it becoming a reality." (Curry's claim that Cartwright devised many of the Knickerbockers' key rules in a single pass is dubious, but his recollection of resistance to formal rules seems far more plausible.)

During these years this same aimlessness was reflected in the club's lack of structure. Instead of having regular practice days, "It was customary for two or three players, occasionally during the season, to go around in the forenoon of a pleasant day and muster up players enough to make a match." Even though many of the players were well connected, the club allowed itself to be buffeted from one site to another. The Knickerbockers used no fewer than three headquarters in Manhattan before finally settling on the Elysian Fields in Hoboken.

The formal attire and detailed record-keeping of the Knickerbocker Club of New York City (shown here with the Excelsiors of Brooklyn) has led many to believe that the club viewed baseball as a highly solemn activity. In fact they were just a group of young men who were out to have fun and get some exercise. They made history purely by accident. [National Baseball Hall of Fame Library]

So why did this loosely structured group decide to organize formally in 1845 and, just as important, to create a written record of its activities? The journalist Charles Peverelly credited Cartwright with having "one day upon the field proposed a regular organization," but he gives no indication of Cartwright's reasons for doing so. William Wheaton was still more vague, saying only that "it was found necessary to reduce the new rules to writing."

Thus we must look to the club's rules themselves for the answer. (See Appendix Two for a list of all twenty rules.) There is no disputing that the significance of the Knickerbockers' twenty initial rules is enormous. Two of these rules—the one that abolished soaking and the one that designated a foul as a do-over—were revolutionary, while the others gave the game a new degree of uniformity.

Yet it is striking that no fewer than seven of the twenty rules have to do with administrative matters. In particular, a recurring theme was who would be allowed to play—whether nonmembers could participate, when latecomers could join in, and the like. Reading between the lines, we may infer that some disputes had occurred over these issues, and it is even possible that they were the motivation for drafting rules in the first place.

Just as noteworthy is that many crucial items are absent from the playing rules. Some of these omissions, such as the number of players per side, were left out because the club chose to keep things as flexible as possible. But other basic elements, including the direction of baserunning, the placement of fielders, and how a run was scored, are also left unspecified. Their absence strongly suggests that the Knickerbockers' rules were designed to clarify disputed points rather than to spell out all the rules of the game.

Finally, it must be remarked that the two most novel rules seem to have had practical origins. The decision to eliminate soaking was, as suggested in the *Cincinnati Enquirer* article quoted in the preceding chapter, most likely the result of injuries. And the designation of a foul as "no play" was probably motivated by the Knickerbockers' difficulty in finding a playing field. This new rule didn't make land any more plentiful, but it did make it much easier to play on a smaller piece of land.

The rules thus point us to a logical and, I believe, compelling explanation for why they were devised. The Knickerbockers' fun was being diminished by confusion about a few specific points of play, by physical obstacles, and by disputes about who could participate. The solution was to create rules that would settle these specific points while otherwise leaving things as they were.

Committing the rules and the club's activities to print was another step that signaled a new degree of seriousness. The Knickerbockers' second rule advised: "When assembled for exercise, the President, or in his absence, the Vice-President, shall appoint an Umpire, who shall keep the game in a book provided for that purpose, and note all violations of the By-Laws and Rules during the time of exercise."

It may reasonably be argued that this was the most important of all the Knickerbockers' rules, since without it their version might well never have spread. But again, it is important to be cautious about using hindsight to attach too much weight to this decision. There is no indication that these initial rules were printed or distributed, nor that the Knickerbockers made the slightest effort to publicize their version. Indeed, it probably never occurred to them to do so.

Instead, after taking the historic step of creating and writing down these rules, the club's own existence was soon in jeopardy. Over the next few years, recalled Daniel Adams later, "I had to employ all my rhetoric to induce attendance." Despite his best efforts, his success was sporadic: "I frequently went to Hoboken to find only two or three members present, and we were often obliged to take our exercise in the form of 'old cat,' 'one' or 'two' as the case might be."

The Knickerbockers' survival was also threatened by a practical dilemma. Adams originally made the club's baseballs but found the covers troublesome. "I went all over New York to find someone who would undertake this work," he later recollected, "but no one could be induced to try it for love or money. Finally I found a Scotch soldier who was able to show me a good way to cover the balls with horsehide, such as was used for whip lashes." Adams continued to make the covers himself until "some time after 1850" when "a shoemaker was found who was willing to make them for us."

This may seem like a rather trivial issue to modern readers, but as we shall see from later accounts it was a grave one at the time. Had Adams not located the soldier and the shoemaker or, even more crucially, had he not shown such dedication in the intervening years, the club well could have died for lack of a functional baseball.

Thus, instead of the new rules of 1845 leading to a higher level of commitment and dedication, the club headed in the opposite direction. Between 1846 and 1851 the Knickerbockers played no known matches with outsiders, and it was not until 1854 that such contests occurred with any frequency.

In addition, the club added no significant new rules during those years. The few advances seem to have been ad hoc responses to specific problems that arose. The biggest of these was the introduction of the shortstop, a position that Adams himself first played. He explained that he was stationed there because a more resilient ball had begun to be used that could be hit and thrown farther, which made it necessary for someone to relay the balls from the outfielders to the basemen.

Similarly unromantic reasons explain the Knickerbockers' 1849 decision to adopt a uniform of blue woolen pantaloons, a white flannel shirt, and a straw hat. According to one early ballplayer, the fashion statement was a pragmatic one; in a previous game the players had found "that trousers impeded their movements and that the wearing of linen shirts was a handicap."

Why the Knickerbockers exhibited so little outward activity in the eight years after the unveiling of the first rules in 1845 is unclear. Perhaps many of the members were simply losing interest in baseball. No doubt the lack of other clubs to compete against also contributed. But it also seems reasonable to assume that many of the club's members never bought into the formality suggested by the 1845 rules and that they continued to treat the game as a lark.

If that sounds unlikely, consider the case of the historic 1838 constitution of the Olympics of Philadelphia. According to Horace S. Fogel, "Little or no attention . . . was paid to [the constitution], and it fell into disuse. It was signed by a few of the original Camden party, but its existence was unknown to many of them." So it is quite plausible that many of the Knickerbockers felt little attachment to their landmark rules.

In any event, it was not until 1853 that the game began to spread, and by then some members of the Knickerbockers were ready to assume a prominent role. When the club's rules were printed in 1856, their dissemination brought the new way of playing to many parts of the country. The club also helped form the game's first central body, the National Association of Base Ball Players (NABBP), and many of its members assumed leadership roles in that organization. In the years to come, the Knickerbockers lent their authority to many of the key issues faced by the NABBP.

The importance of these accomplishments is undeniable, but presenting them in isolation creates a distorted picture of this pioneer club. After initially being involved in organizing and popularizing the game, the Knickerbockers receded into the background and acted primarily as the voice of moderation.

And the club's membership changed significantly between the early 1840s and the late 1850s, so that the club's actions in the latter years do not necessarily reflect the intentions of the original members.

When the NABBP was formed it naturally looked to the Knickerbockers for input on the rules. Club members did their best to oblige, but all indications suggest that their aim was to be helpful rather than to impose their rules on others. Adams prepared a set of rules for the NABBP in 1857, but his account of the process suggests diffidence and even reluctance. For example, he established the historic distance of ninety feet between the bases, but instead of taking credit he modestly explained that the earlier decision to measure the length in paces had been "rather vague."

The Knickerbockers were even more reluctant to embrace the competitiveness that soon became part of the game. While other clubs began to accept members on the basis of ball-playing skill, the Knickerbockers made no such concessions. In 1866 Charles Peverelly observed: "The same [membership] standard still exists, and no person can obtain admission in the [Knickerbocker] club merely for his capacity as a player; he must also have the reputation of a gentleman; and hence arises one of the causes of its not being what is called a match-playing club."

The Knickerbockers instead became synonymous with efforts to "foster, encourage, and promote the pleasure of all who were desirous of enjoying the game." Or, to put it more simply, with having fun.

Fun doesn't always get recorded for posterity, but there are plenty of indications of the good times that the members of the Knickerbockers shared. A member named William Vail, for instance, became known as "Stay-where-you-am-Wail," for reasons that can readily be surmised. Another, Charles DeBost, was recalled as being "full of good-humor, always creating much amusement upon the ball field." And, as noted in the introduction, when a player earned a six-cent fine for swearing, someone waggishly recorded in the club's scorebooks that he had said "s—t."

Their fun-loving natures were most apparent at the feasts that brought two or more clubs together. When the Knickerbockers joined with the Eagle and Gotham clubs at Fijux's for a grand dinner following the 1854 season, "The utmost hilarity prevailed, and everything passed off in a happy manner. A song, composed for the occasion by J. W. Davis, of the Knickerbocker Club, was so well received that the Eagle Club had it printed. It was entitled 'Ball Days,' and abounded in witty allusions to the principal players of the three Clubs." Thus while the Knickerbockers are now thought of as stodgy, formal figures, that simply wasn't the case. And, far from being men who sought to create a national game for Americans, it is probably more accurate to view the members as accidental trailblazers who revised a familiar game to fit their own needs and were shocked when it swept the country.

So how did this club's game spread so rapidly and become so permanent a part of American culture? In the years between 1845 and 1853, as we have seen, the spread of the Knickerbockers' way of playing ball was almost nonexistent. And so too, in other regions, the local versions continued to be firmly entrenched. As a 1905 account explained, "Previous to the year 1854 the game of bat and ball was played in a 'scrub' way, and there were too many differences of opinion on rules to allow the game to proceed smoothly."

In the mid-1850s the first harbingers of change began to emerge. The Knickerbockers' rules began to spread throughout New York City, with new clubs springing up in each of the cities that would later become boroughs. The most imposing obstacle to the game remained the shortage of land, which was now more severe than when the Knickerbockers had been forced to relocate to Hoboken. But where there was a will there was a way, as Henry Chadwick explained: "Hamilton Square, a plot covering some ten acres at 63rd street and 3rd avenue—now covered

The "cradle of the game"—the Elysian Fields in Hoboken, New Jersey, where the Knickerbockers finally settled after being evicted from three different sites in Manhattan. This 1853 drawing shows the natural beauty that caused one early player to recall the site as "an opening in the 'forest primeval.' The open spot was a level, grass-covered plain, some two hundred yards across, and as deep, surrounded upon three sides by the typical eastern undergrowth and woods and on the east by the Hudson River. It was a perfect greensward almost the year around. Nature must have foreseen the needs of base ball, and designed the place especially for that purpose." [Collection of Tom Shieber]

with a solid mass of residences and warehouses—was every day the scene of numerous matches, while on Saturday afternoons it was covered with youthful devotees of the new game. Wheat Hill, a similar spot in Williamsburgh, was likewise swarmed, while the Elysian Fields—the cradle of the game—was occupied by the Knickerbockers, Empires, Gothams, and clubs of that class."

Before long the "vacant fields then existing in South Brooklyn" became the center of activity. The result was that in 1854 and 1855 Brooklyn's sandlots played host to an influx of ballplayers from throughout the surrounding area. Brooklyn's youth joined in to such an extent that the city eventually became known as the cradle of ballplayers. "Base ball," one of the city's leading newspapers later proudly announced, "practically received its first start in this city." Another native son would boast: "Virginia was the mother of presidents, Brooklyn of ball players."

By 1857 a national publication observed, "Verily Brooklyn is fast earning the title of the 'City of Base Ball Clubs,' as well as the 'City of Churches.'" Yet despite the dramatic upswing in the game's popularity in Brooklyn and throughout greater New York, there was little reason to imagine it would spread farther afield.

The obstructions, after all, seemed as formidable as ever, and the success of the Knickerbockers' game in and around New York City did nothing to remove them. To begin with, it was difficult to communicate the new rules. More daunting, there was no reason to think that young men in other regions would prefer the new game to those their fathers had taught them.

The problem was not so much that the Knickerbockers' rules were new and different. What was disturbing was that their version imposed rules and restrictions where before there had always been flexibility. A Hartford resident nicely conveyed the sense that the new game seemed rigid: "Along in the late '50s we began to hear of baseball, a new game with nine players on a side, a new set of rules, a regulation ball, etc." It is no coincidence that the Knickerbockers' version was often referred to as the "regulation game."

Not surprisingly, many Americans resisted giving up their more casual approach to playing bat-and-ball games. Having flexible rules, after all, allowed them to adapt to however many players showed up, to whatever field was convenient, and to any ball (or reasonable facsimile) that was handy. Why give up this freedom in order to conform to some rules formulated by a bunch of New Yorkers?

Just as important, the New Yorkers didn't seem to much care whether anyone outside their metropolitan area took up their version. The Knickerbockers had long appeared unconcerned about whether others adopted their rules, and the rash of new clubs showed a similar lack of interest. Quite possibly such rules as the introduction of foul territory were merely a concession to their own space limitations, and they would have thought it silly for rural clubs to adopt such a rule.

For example, Frank Pidgeon gave this description of the early days of the Eckford Club of Brooklyn, destined to become one of the country's dominant clubs: "A year ago last August, a small number of young men of that part of the city known as the Island, formed themselves into a club, for the purpose of enjoying this noble and manly game. Being shipwrights and mechanics, we could not make it convenient to practise more than once a week; and we labored under the impression that want of practice and the small number from whom to select our nine, would make it almost impossible for us to win a match if we engaged in one. However, we were willing to do the best we could, if some club would give us an invitation to play. But, alas, no such invitation came, and we began seriously to doubt if we were worth taking notice of. Still, we had some merry times among ourselves; we would forget business and everything else on Tuesday afternoons, go out in the green fields, don our ball suits, and go at it with a perfect rush. At such times, we were boys again. Such sport as this brightens a man up, and improves him, both in mind and body." For clubs like this, baseball was clearly still a diversion, not a movement.

While a few New Yorkers had begun to refer to baseball as the national game by the mid-1850s, this was, to put it mildly, a stretch. The 1858 efforts to form the "National Association of Base Ball Players" struck the *New York Clipper* as preposterous: "the convention seems to be rather sectional and selfish in its proceedings, than otherwise, there having been no invitations sent to clubs in other States. . . . National, indeed!

Why the association is a mere local organization, bearing no
State existence even—to say nothing of a National one." Despite the dramatic increase in interest that occurred between
1853 and 1857, baseball seemed no closer to becoming a national game.

CHAPTER 3

The New York Game Becomes America's Game

❖ Astonishingly, the game that had belonged strictly to the Knickerbockers as late as 1853, and that was still almost exclusively confined to the New York metropolitan area as late as 1858, was well on its way to becoming the national pastime when the first volleys of the Civil War were fired in 1861. The most important factor in this development was the entire country's long familiarity with games that incorporated most of the key elements of baseball. Nonetheless this rapid transmission and acceptance of a single region's version of the game is a striking accomplishment that demands an explanation.

Two basic questions need to be answered: How did the game spread, and why was it able to supplant its rivals? The latter question is a complex one that historians continue to debate, so let's start with the more straightforward issue of how the Knickerbockers' version spread and gained momentum.

One of the developments that helped was the appearance of the club's rules in a national publication called *Porter's Spirit of the Times* on December 6, 1856, and in the *New York Clipper* a week later. This was an important step for a country that was still making the transition from oral communication to print. The historian Tom Melville has argued that "baseball was the first game Americans learned principally from print," noting that town ball was "handed down from generation to generation orally" but that baseball was transmitted by reading "printed regulations."

As we shall see, Melville overstates the extent to which players actually learned the game of baseball from printed sources. Even so, the game's association with the printed word spurred its growth. For starters, print was ideally suited to communicating the changes made by the Knickerbockers. As anyone who has struggled with an instruction manual can appreciate, print is not a medium that is well suited for explaining something to someone who is entirely unfamiliar with it. But as we have seen, that was not much of a problem in the 1850s because the country knew the rudiments of the game. More important, print was effective for the task at hand: listing changes, updates, and revisions to an already familiar activity and thereby creating the uniformity that American bat-and-ball games had lacked.

An added bonus was that mass printed communications were to the 1850s what television was to the 1950s and the internet was to the 1990s: a new medium crackling with excitement and potential. This was particularly true of the burgeoning American newspaper industry, which had been revolutionized by the introduction of the penny paper in the 1830s and the spread of telegraph lines. Americans were awed by the speed with which news from the other side of the country, or even the world, could land on their doorsteps. In short order, newspapers had become affordable, accessible, and a vital part of the lives of an increasingly literate American population. Hitching the game to this rising star was to prove highly beneficial.

The publication of the Knickerbockers' rules was directly responsible for the game's introduction in at least one state. Detroit's Franklin Base Ball Club was organized in 1857 and became the first club west of New York that is known to have used the Knickerbockers' rules. In an 1884 interview, founding club member Henry Starkey explained, "There was an old fiddler here in the city named Page. . . . He used to take the *New York Clipper*, and one day he showed me a copy in which there

was quite a lengthy description of the new game of base ball.
. . . There was quite a number of us who felt an interest in the
game, and we came to the conclusion that the new way must be
an improvement over the old. Anyway, we decided to try it, so
I wrote to the *Clipper* for a copy of the new rules, and paid $1
for it. After we got the rules we organized a club—the first in
Detroit."

This method of introducing the game was, however, far from
universal. While a printed listing of the rules could single-hand-
edly introduce the new version, it appears to have been more
typical for it to be accompanied by instruction from someone
who had witnessed the game firsthand. Albert G. Spalding, for
example, offered this description of how baseball was introduced to Rockford, Illinois, around 1863: "One of our young
townsmen, while in the east, had seen several games of ball
played by New York clubs at the Elysian Fields, Hoboken, N.J.,
then the home of the game; and becoming interested in it, on his
return home to the west he brought with him some base ball
materials, and a copy of *Beadle* [sic] *Dime Book of Base Ball*, the
standard book of the game at that period. . . . From the pages of
this book, aided by personal instructions by our teacher, we
were initiated in the mysteries of base-ball, and of course we became infatuated with the sport."

Baseball offered a number of attributes that specifically
appealed to a rising new generation. The Knickerbockers'
rules made it more acceptable for adults to play while at the
same time giving young participants the sense that the game
they were playing was not entirely their fathers' game (always
a selling point for youths on the verge of adulthood). Its pace
was also well suited to youth. While we now think of baseball
as a leisurely activity, just the opposite was the case in the late
1850s. "Cricket has its admirers," noted an 1859 article, "but
it is evident it will never have that universality that base ball
will. The latter named game is essentially 'fast,' is easily
learned, affords all the exercise demanded, and occupies no

unnecessary time in preliminaries and parliamentary rules and discussions."

As this account suggests, in addition to being fast-paced the new version could be quickly learned. This accessibility worked in tandem with the game's ties to the vibrant print medium to convince a new generation that baseball was their game. In particular, students were drawn to the new game's cutting-edge status and became its most prominent exponents. "Base ball," remarked the New York correspondent for a Pennsylvania newspaper in 1855, "is quite national; the boys learn it in school." And soon these boys were taking the game they learned in school all over the country.

A Cincinnati writer explained: "The 'rage' moved Westward slowly. It is undoubtedly to college boys that the West owes its early indebtedness for the introduction of base-ball. In Cincinnati the first game was instituted by two young men from Rochester College in the fall of 1860. One of these was Theodore Frost, and the other is now a prominent druggist of Cincinnati. They worked hard to substitute the new game for town-ball, and in the fall of that year succeeded in organizing the Buckeye Base-ball Club. This was the first Base-ball Club gotten together in Cincinnati. The players were selected from the Woodward and Hughes High School scholars and young business men of the city. The Buckeyes laid out a ground and played that fall on Potter's field, now Lincoln Park."

Students were similarly responsible for introducing baseball to Decatur, Illinois: "The first baseball ground laid out in Decatur was in 1866. It was laid out on [the] site of [the] Wabash freight house. W. C. Johns, then a student at Ann Arbor [at the University of Michigan], had come home for vacation and brought baseball with him. He borrowed A. T. Risley's surveying instruments and laid out [the] diamond assisted by the late Tom C. Heaton of Springfield who was then bookkeeper for Hinkle & Priest's mill and C. M. Allison who drove the stakes. Allison was in the high school."

Robertson Fisher, one of the pioneers of baseball in Fort Wayne, told a similar story: "It was in 1868, just after I had come to Fort Wayne from Elizabeth, New Jersey, where I attended school, and I was chock full of the game which was enthusing the sport-loving fans of the east. I felt lonesome without the game, and began to work up an interest among the young fellows who had the time for practice. One day Charley [Taylor] and I were sitting on the north steps of the old court house. We discussed the proposition to organize a team, and before we left the spot finished the preliminaries. Soon the team was organized. It was the first in the state, as far as I have been able to find out. We played local 'scrub' teams and after a while the other towns caught the fever and we met them either in Fort Wayne or on their diamonds."

Likewise the "regulation game" arrived in Essex County, New York, in 1866 when Malcolm N. MacLaren moved from LeRoy to Elizabethtown to study law in the office of a judge named Robert S. Hale. MacLaren soon taught the new game to his fellow students, who formed the county's first club.

Even when students didn't specifically introduce the Knickerbockers' game, they often played a key role in popularizing it. High school students formed the Union Club, one of St. Louis's first and most important organized clubs, in 1859. In Cleveland, too, many of the most prominent early players "engaged in the game after school."

Students took to the new game with an infectious enthusiasm and devoted every spare moment to it. Their passion was nicely captured by the narrator of Clarence Darrow's autobiographical novel *Farmington*: "At school we scarcely took time to eat our pie or cake and cheese, but crammed them into our mouths, snatched the bat, and hurried to the ball-grounds, swallowing our luncheon in great gulps as we went along. At recess we played until the last tones of the little bell had died away, and the teacher with exhausted patience had shut the door and gone back to her desk; then we dropped the clubs and

[*43*]

hurried in. When school was out, we went home for our suppers and to do our few small chores, and then rushed off to the public square to get all the practice that we could."

At many schools the zeal of the students was enough to gain at least the tacit support of their instructors. At Wisconsin's Beloit College, for example, "the faculty of the college . . . was in heavy sympathy with the boys, and cheered them with their presence as well as by their voices. The grave, sedate, dignified President was an habitué of the ball ground, and it is reported that he would become so enthused at times that he would rise in his carriage and wave his silk hat, in a very dignified manner, of course, to cheer the boys."

In addition to gaining momentum from students' enthusiasm, baseball's spread also owed much to Americans' mobility. New railroads were springing up across the country and, together with the openings of the great canals and the various gold rushes, prompting rapid relocations on a mass scale. As new areas opened up, baseball rushed in, and its path became inextricably linked to the era's great population thrusts. Following the Erie Canal, it coursed through Erie, Buffalo, Rochester, and Syracuse in 1858, then wended its way through Michigan and into shipping ports such as Chicago and Milwaukee. In the wake of the California Gold Rush, it arrived in San Francisco in 1858 and Sacramento in 1860. Yet another torrent brought baseball clubs to Baltimore, Washington, and Richmond before the Civil War.

Baseball's success in moving into most of these areas was greatly aided by the absence of well-established rival versions. This created tremendous momentum for the Knickerbockers' game, but it also meant that the "regulation game" still had to surmount an important hurdle in order to become the national pastime. Would the new way of playing ball catch on in Boston and the other regions of New England that played the Massachusetts game? How would it do in town ball strongholds such as Philadelphia, Cincinnati, and St. Louis? And what would happen in other regions and towns that already had their own way of playing?

The regional variants did not go down without a fight. As a Cincinnati writer recalled, "The old town-ball clubs merged themselves gradually into base-ball clubs and, slowly but reluctantly, one by one fell in with the new system. It required time and much persuasion to accomplish the revolution. The old love fought hard against invasion, but the new love, by force of reason and persistency, won its way gradually into the town-ball sport, and finally superseded the old game entirely."

Important resistance was also encountered in other cities, but one by one the regional variants fell by the wayside. When a man named Merritt Griswold moved from Brooklyn to St. Louis, he had no easy time convincing a town ball club to try to learn the rules that he'd played by as a member of the Putnam Club. Eventually, "after considerable urging and coaxing on my part they passed a resolution at one of their meetings that they would try the national rules for one morning if I would . . . teach them, which I consented to do if they would agree to stick to it for the full hour without 'kicking,' for as I told them they would not like it until after playing it for a sufficient length of time to be familiar with some of its fine points, all of which they agreed to and kept their words like good fellows as they were, but in ten minutes I could see most of them were disgusted, yet they would not go back on their word and stuck to it for their hour's play. At the breaking up of the game to go home they asked me if I would coach them one more morning as they began to 'kindy like it.'"

A similar response occurred in Kalamazoo, when another student returned home with the new version. According to eyewitness Jerome Trowbridge, "John [McCord] used to play the old game of patch ball with us when he was here, but he went down to Poughkeepsie to school and when he came back to Kalamazoo he told us of the other game and prevailed upon us to try it. We tried it and were thoroughly disgusted with the whole thing and wanted to go back to the old game, but John kept at us telling us that this would soon be the only game that would be played and he was right. We kept at it but there were a great many things that we could not get used to. We still wanted to patch a man and some way we could not get used to this new way of putting a man out."

Frank L. Smith provided a virtually identical description of the 1866 introduction of the New York game to his hometown of Janesville, Wisconsin. Smith returned home after attending school in Connecticut, anxious to "astonish the natives with my knowledge of the new game," and found that a transplanted New Yorker named W. J. Doolittle had already begun the process. But winning acceptance for the new game did not prove easy: "It was certainly up-hill work inducing a sufficient number of apt pupils to learn the game. Some promising players who had played the old high school game could not break themselves of the habit or resist the temptation to throw the ball at the base runner, which, while amusing to the spectators, was rather annoying to the party who was hit."

The new version appears to have met with far less resistance in Philadelphia. While that city's first baseball clubs were not formed until 1859 or 1860, their enthusiasm was so infectious that by the end of 1860 the venerable Olympic Club had switched from town ball to baseball. The new sport experienced a few wobbles, but after the Athletic Club established itself as one of the nation's best in 1862, baseball became a fixture in the Quaker City.

The "New York" game might have been expected to have an especially difficult time in Boston, but there too its triumph was decisive. The Tri-Mountain Club adopted the New York version in 1857 and was joined by the Bowdoin Club, but these clubs remained in the minority until 1861. Then a man named John A. Lowell persuaded some students at Boston's Latin and English and Chauncey Hall high schools to try the new version by promising to instruct the scholars and, perhaps decisively, "also to give them a set of implements."

[46]

The new club, named the Lowells in honor of its sponsor, helped popularize the New York game during the years when older clubs were losing members to the Civil War. In 1864 the club's namesake offered a silver ball to the champion club of New England, again specifying the use of the New York rules. The trophy remained the subject of heated competition for several years, leaving no doubt that the New York game had made another conquest. By the 1867 season a national publication reported that every single club that had played the Massachusetts game had either switched to the New York game or disbanded.

Not all clubs embraced the new game—naturally, we tend to have the histories of only those that persisted. The Excelsior Club of St. Louis, for example, tried the new version for a single season, "that period of time being long enough to tire the boys out in carrying the old style sand bag bases back and forth the long distance to the grounds. Another feature of the game that added to the disheartening of this mis-named club was the round shape of the bats, whereby they were unable to hit the ball so frequently as with the old paddles."

But while some clubs gave up, and many more were done in by the Civil War (as we shall see later), those that did persevere were almost exclusively playing "regulation" baseball. By the war's end every major urban area had made the switch, and soon afterward the few remaining holdouts were eliminated by enthusiasts who brought baseball to Connecticut, to sparsely populated regions, and to the South.

Cricket endured, but more than ever it was perceived as a foreign import. As noted earlier, by 1860 a journalist described cricket as "an exotic. It has been played for years at Hoboken and other retired localities, but chiefly by Englishmen, and it is still regarded, even by American players, as an English game." Just as important, cricket came to be perceived as an older man's game, increasing baseball's connection with the younger generation. Thus, a few scant years after the very idea of a national game would have been inconceivable, the 1860s began with baseball well on the way to attaining that distinction.

While printed rules, students' enthusiasm for the game, and the mobility of Americans helped "regulation" baseball spread, there remains the more perplexing question of why the new version was so successful at driving out well-established rivals. Even the firsthand accounts excerpted above are vague on this matter, generally having more to say about the absence of soaking than about any features of the new game that proved appealing. What would cause so many Americans to willingly abandon a familiar way of playing ball in favor of a method preferred by faraway New Yorkers?

There does not seem to be a single answer to this question. Rather, a number of key factors combined to create this remarkable outcome.

Practical considerations played a crucial role. The Knickerbockers' decision in the 1840s to designate a foul ball as a nonevent appears to have been primarily designed as a concession to the scarcity of land in Manhattan. For the next decade, such an accommodation would have seemed unnecessary and even peculiar in most other American cities. But by the end of the 1850s the same land crunch was occurring elsewhere, giving the New York version a major advantage.

This was especially true in Boston, where the scarcity of land meant that the Boston Common became "the scene of nearly all of the important base ball contests in this vicinity." Yet the Common was too small to be convenient even for baseball. According to the early ballplayer Jack Chapman, even at the most suitable location "The left-fielder had about the hardest position to field and he was compelled to chase the ball up a hill." Obviously a site that was barely large enough to accommodate the New York version would have been a terribly tight squeeze for the space-demanding "Massachusetts game."

Having one standard version of playing baseball also made it far easier to arrange competitions between clubs. As long as the rules were fluid and variable, the fun of matching skills against the best players from another club or neighboring city was likely to be overshadowed by confusion and even arguments. The adoption of uniform rules eliminated such troubles and thereby proved another boon to the spread of the New York game.

Even the elimination of soaking ended up contributing to the ascendancy of the Knickerbockers' version. While soaking was beloved by many players, it also demanded the use of a soft, often pillowlike ball. Such a ball could not be hit very far, making the game revolve around running and chasing. This in turn reinforced the stigma that the games were childish activities.

More than anything else, this association of the older games with child's play spelled their doom. Even the proponents of these games began to recognize that their very pliability meant they would always be viewed as childish. "Base ball," commented one observer in 1860, "has been a school-boy's game all over the land from immemorial time, but it was, until recently, considered undignified for men to play at it, except on rare holidays, and then they were wont to play on some out-lying common, where they would be unseen of their more staid associates."

By contrast, the Knickerbockers' version was not really that different from its rivals, yet it offered the prospect of a new beginning as an adult activity that could proudly be played in the center of town. This sense increased as reports suggested that the new game was gaining favor among the socially prominent. Many of the Knickerbockers themselves came from well-to-do backgrounds, though the extent of this social position is sometimes exaggerated. As their game spread to other cities, it quickly found acceptance among those of similar status.

In St. Louis, for example, the club that was formed as the result of Merritt Griswold's persuasive skills included "some of the brightest young men of St. Louis, among them a number of whom have left the impress of their handiwork in almost every honorable calling." Cleveland's earliest ballplayers "were nearly all scions of the best families in Cleveland, and the games always attracted a good turnout of fathers, mothers, sisters, sweethearts and the usual following of ardent and admiring supporters. All contests took place in the open field with no seating accommodations except the green grass." Malcolm MacLaren's success in introducing regulation baseball to Elizabethtown, New York, was no doubt aided by the fact that his father was a minister and that he himself had arrived in town to study law. And these are but a few examples of the many young men whose status and backgrounds made them ideal ambassadors for the new way of playing.

As the New York game spread, so too did an appreciation of its advantages—that the "regulation" version made it easier to find an acceptable locale and to compete against rival clubs, and that, instead of having to play in secrecy, they might be watched by the town's most respected citizens. These benefits convinced most ballplayers that at least they had to give the new way of playing a chance. As Michigan pioneer Henry Starkey matter-of-factly put it, "Anyway, we decided to try it." And many of them, like the St. Louis town ball players, eventually decided that they "kindy like it."

The more the players got used to the harder and livelier baseball, the more benefits they found in this change. The old soft balls could not be hit very far, and the absence of foul ground in the Massachusetts game encouraged batters simply to deflect the pitched ball off behind them. Both these features understandably struck many onlookers as childish. They also made the game rather monotonous to watch. The practice of deflecting pitched balls could in addition be hazardous to catchers; according to one early Boston player, "there is no doubt that catchers were sometimes intentionally disabled that way."

By contrast, the New York version allowed batters to try to hit the ball out of sight, especially when a rubbery ball was used. Many players raved about this new aspect. When the new baseball was introduced in Luzerne, Pennsylvania, for instance, players marveled: "We used the 'lively' ball and when it left the bat after being hit square, came at one as though shot from a cannon . . . a good batsman could drive the ball almost to kingdom come."

Boston ballplayers found that the New York game had several advantages over their local game, but they too were most enthusiastic about the possibility of the long ball: "The pitching, instead of swift throwing, looked easy to hit, and the pitcher stood off so far, and then there was no danger of getting plugged with the ball while running bases; and the ball was so lively and could be batted so far!"

Spectators were just as enthralled, and before long almost every town had its legendary stories of long-ball hitters. In Boston old-timers related stories about a brawny lad "who used bats four feet long, and his score averaged more than ten per cent of home runs. He struck a ball considerable over the vane of Park Street Church, 225 feet up, and would repeatedly send a ball to that height without moving from his position." In another game he "sent the ball to the face of the clock on the Congregational Church. The following Sunday the choir remained later than usual at rehearsal, and at 1 o'clock the clock struck thirty-seven times. . . . The boy had to quit using those bats for fear of pitchers becoming cross-eyed dodging between the ball and the broken end of the bat."

In 1865 the *Brooklyn Eagle* gushed that Boaz Pike had "struck the longest ball yet batted on the field, not less, perhaps, than 600 feet straight ahead." Boaz's younger brother Lipman soon succeeded him as Brooklyn's most feared power hitter. And in Ann Arbor, Michigan, when the distinguished University of Michigan Professor of Greek Albert H. Pattengill died in 1906, his obituary reported: "To this day the students relate a tradition as to how he batted a home-run once from a point 100 feet south of North University avenue, so that the sphere landed on the skylight on top of the old medical building." Who said Babe Ruth invented the long ball?

The increased potential for walloping baseballs out of sight had important side benefits. Where speed had formerly been a batter's primary weapon, in the new game strength and hand-eye coordination became valuable. This was important because strength was a skill far more likely to be associated with grown men, which helped convey the message that this was no child's game. Yet the new emphasis on these skills did not diminish the role of baserunning, since the heavy hitting meant all the more running. Baseball had inadvertently hit on an ideal balance between speed and power, one that broadened the game's appeal by giving men with either skill a chance to excel. The balance accidentally struck between these two skills has proven so popular that ever since, whenever one or the other becomes too dominant, the result is dissatisfaction and a concerted effort to restore the equilibrium.

All these factors combined to make switching to the New York game a relatively easy decision for most of the players of the era. To be sure, they were making a few sacrifices, but these were far outweighed by the new game's improved prestige, convenience, sophistication, and balance between speed and power.

Abandoning cherished rules like soaking was the most conspicuous of these sacrifices, but an equally important sacrifice was adopting the formal structure of a serious adult activity. Ball clubs began to hold structured meetings and to produce gravely worded minutes that made topics such as practice times sound weighty. Yet from time to time, in reading the accounts of these doings of early ball clubs, there's an unmistakable sense that these men didn't take themselves that seriously. It's almost as if we're being winked at across the gulf of history by men who knew full well that they were holding these solemn meetings only because it gave them license to play what was still essentially a child's game.

In 1854, for example, a group of young Brooklyn men decided "to 'get up' a Base Ball Club, and accordingly on Thanksgiving Day in November of that year they met for practice, but under no especial organization. They styled themselves the 'J.Y.B.B.B.C.'s' (Jolly Young Bachelors' Base Ball Club)." But then the following month the members held a formal meeting at which they heard a report from a Committee on Constitution and By-Laws and adopted it, elected a slate of seven officers, and voted to adopt the more dignified name of "Excelsior."

Had the young men who "styled themselves" the "Jolly Young Bachelors" and practiced with "no especial organization" suddenly begun to take themselves very earnestly? Perhaps. Yet it seems far more likely that while they recognized the need for this new degree of formality, they also shared quite a few belly laughs over the incongruity of applying such practices to an activity like baseball.

This lighthearted approach is more readily apparent in the later recollections of the game's pioneers. In 1884, when a reporter interviewed Henry Starkey about the formation of Detroit's first baseball club, Starkey kept interrupting the narrative with silly jokes and anecdotes. Similarly, when early ballplayer John McNamee was interviewed in 1876, he seemed a bit taken aback as he acknowledged: "Why, I suppose some might say I was one of the originators of the game." He was vague about the organization and members of the Pastimes, but he did say that "we had a good time while the organization was going." This conveys, I think, a key to the charm of early baseball: nobody took it too seriously.

Once the New York version of baseball had spread and driven out other games, it gathered still more momentum. In 1860 an observer marveled: "B. B. Clubs outnumber the debating societies as much as they surpass them in enthusiasm. The infection seems to have seized all classes of people—intellectual youth, corpulent gentlemen, lawyers, butchers, dry goods clerks, doctors, every one, in short, if possessed of sound limbs and tolerable wind, must play one or two afternoons in each week, or be voted 'slow.'"

In particular it soon became apparent that interclub competition was the greatest benefit of adopting standard rules. This was most strikingly exemplified by Frank Pidgeon's enchanting description of the first match of the Eckford Club of Brooklyn.

As readers may recall from the preceding chapter, during this club's early days the members began to practice and "had some merry times among ourselves" but "began seriously to doubt if we were worth taking notice of." Finally, however: "After longing for a match, yet so dreading (not a defeat—we were sure of that) a regular 'Waterloo,' we finally, through sheer desperation, expressed a wish to play the winners in the match between the Baltic and Union Club of Morrisania. The Union won, and signified their willingness to play us. Well, we had got what we wanted—a match; and then, what? —why, we would have to do the best we could. The day came at last, on which we were to meet the conquerors of the Baltic; and nine determined, but badly-scared men, whistling to keep up their spirits, might have been seen wending their way to the Red House. It would be difficult to describe the sensations we felt that day—such an intense desire to win, and such a dread of defeat! We knew that, if badly beaten, we could never succeed in building up a club. Many of our friends would not go to see the match, because they did not wish to witness our defeat. . . .

"But, to the game. We pulled off our coats, and rolled up our sleeves; we stood up to the rack, but were very nervous—first appearance on any stage! Our first man took the bat, tipped out, great dependence placed on him. Good heaven! how unfortunate! Next man got scared; caught out. No use trying to win; do the best we can, however. Steady! boys, steady! Third man gave the ball a regular crusher. One desperate yell burst from eight throats, and I am not sure that the striker did not yell with the rest. First base, go it! Second base, come up! go again! Stay there, stay there! Another fortunate strike; man on the third base got home. Glory! One run. Ah! How proud the Eckford Club were of that run. Some ran to the Umpire's book to see how it looked on paper.

"The Innings ended with three runs for the Eckford. The Unions took the bat and made two runs—could it be possible! We could scarcely believe it. We did the best we could to keep our end up, and by that means we overdid the matter, and the result was: Eckford, 22; Union, 8. About seven o'clock that evening, nine peacocks might have been seen on their way home, with tail-feathers spread. Our friends were astonished, as well as ourselves, and all felt rejoiced at the result, except one old croaker, who insisted that 'it was all luck, and the next match would prove he was right, and that the Unions would bring out a stronger team in the next match.' We consoled ourselves, however, with the idea, that if we did not beat their team, we would send them along a pretty fast gait. On the 15th of October, we again met our gentlemanly opponents at the Red House. If we lost this match, then indeed they might say the first was all luck; but if we could only win! Every pulse beat quicker at the thought. Where there is a determination to succeed, there is seldom failure. We won, and the score stood: Union, 6; Eckford, 22. I don't exactly remember about the peacocks coming home that evening; all I know is, that the Unions fraternized with us, and we got home safe and happy, and, like true Christians, forgave the croaker. We look back with pride and pleasure to our first base ball matches, and hope that in all our future matches, whether we are the victors or vanquished, the same spirit of kindness and friendship may exist between our opponents and ourselves as now exist between the Union Club, of Morrisania, and the Eckford, of Manhattan Island."

A similar euphoria surrounded one of the first match games in St. Louis, held in the spring of 1861 and umpired by Captain Merritt Griswold, the man who had brought baseball to St.

Louis from Brooklyn. The two opponents, the Empire and Morning Star clubs, were so anxious to play that the match was scheduled for 5 A.M.: "The fact of it being the first match game entered into by either club caused every effort to be made to win it and so deep was the interest of the Empire boys that they sat up all night so as to keep the appointment in time. The night was spent at a fire engine house on Third Street, from whence they marched out to the grounds, carrying bats and bases, the latter being square bags of sand with leather straps around them by which they were buckled into iron rings fastened into wooden stakes that were driven about two feet into the ground, such being the style of those days. Some two or three carried bats over their shoulders so as the more easily to convey the demijohns which did not contain arnica, but some other 'soothing syrup.' Shortly after their arrival the Morning Star drove onto the grounds seated in two of Ubsdell, Pierson & Co.'s wagons attired in their handsome uniforms of heavy white flannel. As they alighted they made a fine impression, as they were all strong, well-built athletes, quick of action and all wide awake for business and somewhat in contrast to the Empire boys, whose all night vigil had not improved their personal appearances in the least and though the first sight of their fresh-looking opponents was calculated to somewhat dishearten them, they pulled themselves together in quick time and through good hard work pulled out victorious. This achievement 'set up' the Empires immensely and it was fully a week before the celebrations terminated."

This newfound relish for competition, more than anything else, made it unthinkable to return to the days when the wide assortment of rules made such matches impractical. Clubs that weren't up-to-date on the rules began to be chided or even mocked. An early Boston player, for instance, recalled: "There were a number of young men, principally cartmen from the vicinity of Pearl street, who styled themselves the Green Mountain Boys, but we did not recognize them as an organization.

They furnished much merriment to bystanders from their disregard of rules, which was inexcusable, to say the least."

And while matching talents with rival clubs added to the pleasure of belonging to an early baseball club, much of the fun was still derived from the camaraderie shared by the players. This is naturally the hardest part of the charm of early baseball to capture, but sportswriter Henry Chadwick did it nicely in 1889 when he recollected: "Thirty years ago last Spring a right merry party of amateur ball tossers 'might have been seen wandering their—anything but weary—way' toward the then open fields adjoining the Jamaica turnpike road, about half a mile east of old John Holder's hostelrie at Bedford, to the field of the then existing Long Island Cricket Club. The party in question were members of the old Pastime Base Ball Club, which flourished in 1858 and 1859, a club which at its organization went in for healthy, enjoyable exercise on the ball field. At that period the furor for base ball was just springing up, and old boys as well as young ones were struck down with the fever. . . . What jolly fellows they were at that time, one and all of them, and how fully they entered into the sport of the game. And truly were those meetings on the ball field in those days occasions well adapted to inspire good humor and gay spirits, for if there is any one thing more than another calculated to produce this kind of natural, happy feeling among kindred spirits it is to take to bright, green fields of a warm Spring day and enter into a lively game of base ball, just for the fun of the thing, you know. It was for just such enjoyment on the ball field that the old Pastime Club of 1858 was organized."

When there were joyful moments such as these to be experienced from the new game, sitting through a few dreary meetings to make them possible must have seemed a small price to pay.

CHAPTER 4

How the Game Was Played

❖ The Knickerbockers, as we have seen, made a number of changes to baseball that proved highly significant because they nudged the child's game toward acceptability among adults. During the late 1850s and the early 1860s, as the Knickerbockers' game became America's game, more new elements were introduced and still others began to appear on the horizon. Nonetheless the game remained at heart a simple one, not fundamentally different from the versions it supplanted.

As soon as the batter got a pitch that suited him, he whacked it with all his might. It was, as one observer recalled, "the sturdy, hard-hitting game of men, a sport that in itself ranked with the sturdiest of the sturdy." Once the batted ball was put in play, the real fun began. If a fielder caught it on the fly or the first bounce, the batter was out, though the base runners might try to advance. If the ball was not caught, the fielders ran as fast as they could to retrieve it while the batter and any base runners tore around the bases, hoping to be safely perched upon one of them before the ball made its way to the fielder who was responsible for covering the base.

The core of the game, then, was a contest between one side's fielders and the other side's batter and base runners. Observers differed in assessing the balance of power. Clarence Deming, captain of the Yale University nine, later recalled: "The heavy hitter, rather than the good fielder, was the Nestor of the game," especially when a rubbery ball was used. For support, Deming could point to the fact that scores of sixty or seventy runs by one side in a nine-inning game were not uncommon, and that even the century mark was topped from time to time.

Yet others reasoned that the advantage held by batters was precisely why fielding was the more important skill. Henry Chadwick believed that "Batting ought never to be placed upon the same scale as fielding. Every 'muffin' [an inexpert player] almost, can bat well; indeed, for that matter we have seen as fine batting in muffin matches, as we ever did in any other, with one or two exceptions. Fielding is the true criterion of excellence in base ball."

Whichever side observers took in this debate, they all agreed that the fundamental conflict was between fielders on one side and hitters and base runners on the other. Moreover it was taken for granted that this was the essence of baseball. In order to preserve this simple yet elegant conflict, the roles of all the other participants and onlookers were strictly limited.

This started with the spectators and the players who were not involved in the action. As an early ballplayer later recalled: "In those days the player's bench was the grass, a short distance back of the umpire. The grand stand and bleachers were also the grass—standing room only. The crowd was kept back by ropes strung a certain distance from the foul lines."

Even attempting to encourage the home side was unacceptable. The teammates of the base runners made no formal attempts to coach them. Spectators were expected to applaud good plays by either side and under no circumstances to boo. By the late 1860s spectators occasionally hissed, but it was assumed that they would do so only to express disapproval for unsporting play; booing a misplay, or in order to show animosity toward the opponents or the umpire, was considered a serious breach of decorum.

Scorekeepers for the respective sides were treated as dignitaries, but they too had highly circumscribed roles. Some clubs continued to keep track of the score by making notches on a stick, though most had scorebooks for this purpose. Yet even on these clubs there was little effort to achieve uniformity; scoring, as Clarence Deming explained, was "the subject of personal opinion rather than of formal rule."

The restrictions placed on spectators and scorekeepers should not come as a great shock, but today's fans may be more surprised to learn that the roles of early umpires were almost as limited. The earliest umpires typically were distinguished members of the community with no special knowledge of the game or its rules.

The treatment of these men befitted the largely ceremonial nature of their position. "The old time umpires," explained Jimmy Wood, "were accorded the utmost courtesy by the players. They were given easy chairs, placed near the home plate, provided with fans on hot days and their absolute comfort was uppermost in the minds of the players. After each of our games in the early '60's, sandwiches, beer, cakes and other refreshments were served by the home team. The umpire always received the choicest bits of food and the largest glass of beer—in case he cared for such beverage. If he didn't, he needed but to express his desires in the thirst-quenching line before the game started—and he got it."

Clarence Deming confirmed that "The umpire's place was usually a point even with home plate and about twenty feet away. There an armchair was set for him and, on sunny days, he was entitled to an umbrella, either self-provided or a special one of vast circumference, fastened to the chair and with it constituting one of the fixtures of the game. He had freedom of movement, but the prerogative was rarely used. In his pocket was a copy of 'Beadle's Dime Baseball Book,' then the hornbook of the game, and often in requisition. In his airy perch, shielded by his mighty canopy, the umpire of those days made an imposing figure, bearing his honors with Oriental dignity, though hardly with Oriental ease."

This dignified posture reflected the fact that the umpire was expected to ensure compliance with the spirit, not the letter, of the rules. He did not make judgment calls; there were no balls and called strikes, and the players were expected to be honest about whether they had caught a fly ball or been tagged by a fielder. Instead the umpire's primary role was to make sure the players did not breach the club's rules by acting in an ungentlemanly fashion.

The umpire was also consulted on questions about the rules, but that was why he had the rulebook in his pocket—in many cases he was a mere novice in the game's rules. In a game in Stoughton, Massachusetts, for example, one batter walloped a ball clear out of sight and over a house. But when the outfielder ran back clutching the ball, the umpire, a local minister, called the batter out. Similarly, an 1865 game between the Empire Club of St. Louis and its namesake from Freeport, Illinois, prompted this account: "Mr. S. Hoyt, of the Garden City Club, umpired the game and learned more that day than he had picked up in all his prior experience. The possibility of putting out three men at once was there demonstrated by the St. Louis team, though the umpire gave the credit for two outs only after having the triple play explained to him thoroughly, his original decision having been one out!"

Although these instances were extreme, they illustrate that there was still a very loose relationship between the rules of baseball and how the game was actually played. Thus, although the umpire had a rulebook handy just in case, his more usual functions were to ensure that decorum prevailed and to render judgments in situations that were not covered by the rules.

In one early game, for example: "Mr. Henry of the Tri-Mountains caught a ball in the pocket of his sack coat, and called on the umpire for judgment, because the rules did not specify that the ball should be caught by a hand." Nowadays we would feel such an omission to be a loophole in the rules and immediately try to close it. But in the 1850s that was what umpires were there for: to decide things according to the spirit of the rules on the not infrequent occasions when the rules did not cover the circumstance. And if an umpire in one town ruled differently from an arbitrator in another town, no one thought much of it. For that matter, umpires sometimes improvised even when the rulebook was crystal clear.

Eventually the rulebook was expanded and made more comprehensive, and umpires were expected to be familiar with all its provisions. The umbrellas and the largest glass of beer vanished, and instead of selecting a distinguished citizen to officiate, "The umpire was chosen by the captains of the two nines from some neutral club just before the game." But there remained for some time the assumption that the umpire would intervene in the action only when a player hollered "Judgment!" to request a decision. Of course this could only work if the game was played in a spirit of forthright honesty, and by and large it was: frivolous appeals were at first deemed a serious breach of etiquette.

The same spirit of honor infused other elements of the game. Players were not encouraged to look for loopholes in the rulebook to exploit; after all, the rules were so limited that it would be simple to do so. Similarly, new tactics gained acceptance only if they struck observers as being ethical. As one early player commented dismissively, "In the scrub games tricks were often resorted to for advantage. . . . These antics prevented the exercise for which the game was instituted and had no good effect."

Even a seemingly innocuous technique like sliding into bases raised concerns. Slides were extremely rare in early baseball; the few recorded instances seem to have been either accidental tumbles or desperate and spontaneous efforts by a base runner to avoid overrunning a base and being put out. When evasive slides made their first appearance, they were greeted with amazement and amusement.

In an 1859 game, when Moses E. Chandler of the Tri-Mountains of Boston dove for a base, "the feat fairly astonished the natives, who at first roared with laughter." After a slide in an 1867 game "the large crowd roared in glee, as seven-eighths of the spectators thought he had slipped and by accident beat out the play."

And, according to an account written many years later, a slide by William Stryker Gummere of Princeton in the late 1860s evoked like astonishment. Gummere, who later became chief justice of the New Jersey Supreme Court, "threw himself feet first at the bag" and successfully avoided the tag of the surprised baseman, who demanded, "What kind of damned fool trick is that?" The account concludes: "'That,' said Mr. Gummere with a dignity fitting to one destined to grace the Supreme Court, 'is a device to evade being put out when running bases.'" While this version of events sounds suspiciously like one that has been "improved" over the years, it is consistent enough with the other responses to slides that it seems reasonable to assume it had some basis in fact.

The laughter that greeted these slides was undoubtedly at least in part the result of genuine mirth. But it may also have been a nervous laughter from observers who were troubled by whether such an evasive action was legitimate. As late as 1884 one fan wrote to his local paper that "we should like to see the abolition of sliding. It is really a measure to dodge the baseman and not to gain time. It is not fair, manly, square work." And, whether due to moral scruples or just because the fields were strewn with pebbles, slides did not become common until the 1880s.

The absence of sliding contributed to early baseball's delightfully uncomplicated feel, as too did the lack of equipment. As will be discussed at greater length in the next chapter, fielder's gloves and protective equipment of any sort were almost unheard of, and catchers positioned themselves well back of the plate. The homemade bats and the rubbery balls similarly conveyed the message that baseball was still a very simple game.

Henry Chadwick is the only sportswriter enshrined in the Baseball Hall of Fame, a fitting tribute to his influence on baseball's development throughout the nineteenth century. Chadwick would come to take a rather condescending view of the pioneer era, but he never lost his fondness for early clubs such as the Pastimes and Excelsiors of Brooklyn, and wrote poignant tributes to them. [National Baseball Hall of Fame Library]

Adding to the game's spare elegance was that the importance of the nine defensive players was fairly evenly balanced. Pitchers, as we shall see, had begun to inch to the foreground by the end of the 1850s, and a club's catcher was typically its best athlete. Yet although these two players were arguably the most important, they remained just two of the nine fielders and did not yet have the outsized roles they would assume in the 1870s. Looking backward in 1884, George Wright lamented that pitchers and catchers had come to dominate the game, and fondly recalled that in the 1860s "the pitcher was of no more importance than any other man in the team."

The game of the late 1850s and early 1860s thus had the essential qualities of ritual: a showdown between two central antagonists in which every participant has an assigned role to play. But as with any example of minimalism, some see beauty in simplicity while others see only crudeness and primitiveness.

Henry Chadwick, the game's premier early sportswriter, became the leading spokesman for the latter perspective. In 1904 he wrote: "the existing code of 1850 [was] of the crudest character. In the first place, the ball was too large and too elastic. . . . Then, too, the pitcher could take a run in delivering the ball and the batsman could wait until he got a ball sent in to suit him. Base runners never touched bases in running round on a long hit and called strikes for not hitting at fair balls were almost unknown. The baby catch of the bounding ball was a fair catch; and, in fact, the rules were wanting in every essential of what the game was capable of under a more perfect code."

Chadwick was almost as dismissive of the game at the end of the decade: "In 1859 a ball weighing ten ounces and measuring ten inches in circumference, with two and a half ounces of rubber in its composition, was in use. Only pitching or tossing the ball to the bat was allowed and no throwing of any kind. A batsman was out if balls were caught on the bound, fair or foul. Players running the bases seldom or never touched them. Though strikes were in the rules they were rarely called, and the reason was that there was formerly no penalty for wild pitching. It was frequent to see a pitcher deliver 50 or 60 balls to the batsman before the latter selected one to strike at. There was no rule governing the delivery of the ball beyond that which required it to be pitched or tossed to the bat and as near as possible over the home base. The pitcher had to pitch behind a line twelve feet in length, and in its delivery he had the option of running up to the line from a point ten or twelve feet back of it. In fact the base ball of that period was a game for enjoyable exercise only, and in no sense was it the experts' game of the present day."

Chadwick's perspective is the one that historians have largely accepted, but it is important to recognize that he intertwined fact with opinion. While he must be credited with avoiding misty-eyed nostalgia (by which the imperfections of the present are compared to the supposed perfections of the past), he may reasonably be accused of falling into the opposite extreme: a bias sometimes known as presentism or Whig history, by which the imperfections of the past are compared to the supposed perfections of the present.

Moreover Chadwick's view that the early rules "were wanting in every essential of what the game was capable of under a more perfect code" is not merely biased but self-interested. Chadwick played a major role in revising the rules of baseball, and the above comments were prologues to lengthy disquisitions in which he credited his own modifications with saving the game. He typically reinforced such comments with references to "scientific baseball," a phrase that subtly invoked social Darwinism to imply that baseball had progressed from a lower to a superior form. In a 1904 article he even engaged in some uncharacteristic personal sniping at those who doubted the value of the rule changes he favored: "The 'fans' of [the 1850s] were opposed to any and all changes. They wanted to have the game 'played as their daddies did.'"

Chadwick's perspective is not without its validity. In comparing the crudeness of the early game to what it "was capable of under a more perfect code," he makes the undeniable point that the way the game was played in the 1850s could not last. Yet the equally clear implication that the game of the 1850s was inferior to the later game must be treated as simply Chadwick's perspective.

And it is important to recognize that his viewpoint was a minority one among the men who, like Chadwick, had watched baseball come of age. Indeed, for most members of that generation, baseball as it was played in the 1850s was the perfect game; subsequent changes were a source of regret.

Whether the changes to baseball were hailed or lamented, there can be no dispute that they were inevitable or that they began while the game was still confined primarily to New York

City and environs. One of the first was the elimination of the bound rule, by which a batter could be put out by catching his hit on the first bounce.

This rule change was brought up at the annual convention of the National Association of Base Ball Players no fewer than six times before being finally adopted after the 1864 season. The Knickerbockers led the campaign for the new rule, believing that it was necessary to complete the game's transition to an adult activity. Accordingly, as Warren Goldstein has documented, advocates of the change used the potent device of characterizing the bound rule as a childish custom unworthy of men.

They also found other ways to demean the opponents of this change. In 1860 the rules committee of the National Association of Base Ball Players unanimously recommended the "fly game," only to have the delegates vote it down. The result prompted this bitter commentary: "One of our best ball players remarked to us that if the clubs would send players to the convention instead of talkers the rules of the game would be made more satisfactory to the practical members of the Base Ball fraternity. It looked to us at times very much as though the delegates were selected with a view of their peculiar knowledge of parliamentary tactics, and not as practical ball players."

Henry Chadwick, typically, assigned himself a large role in the elimination of the bound rule and maintained that the repeal succeeded when the recalcitrant clubs finally "became ashamed of the boyish rule of the bound catch." In retrospect it is easy for us to agree that those who resisted such changes were shortsighted or ignorant. But in fairness, the proponents of the bound rule had some very good reasons.

The side in the field already had a devilishly hard time recording an out—after all, the ball was rubbery and the pitching underhand, the batter was allowed to select a pitch to his liking, the field conditions were poor, and the sun made things still more difficult. Fielders had only their bare hands with which to record an out, so their resistance to a proposal that would take away one of the few ways to do so was understandable. Indeed, in the years after the bound rule was eliminated, there are many accounts of clubs whose fielders became "demoralized" as their opponents posted twenty or thirty runs in an inning. No doubt these men felt that, while this new version of the game might be more "scientific," it wasn't much fun.

The elimination of the bound rule affected how baseball was played, as did some other new rules and tactics, but all these changes were minor compared to the revolution that was brought about when pitchers announced they were no longer content with the role they had been assigned in the ritual, and seized a far larger one. Or at least that was how many outraged nonpitchers saw it. From their perspective, it was as if the actor playing Rosencrantz in a production of *Hamlet* had decided that he didn't have enough lines and began to deliver his own soliloquies, or as if a coach in a coach-pitch league had suddenly begun hurling fastballs past the startled youngsters.

In the very early days, as noted earlier, the pitcher had the relatively minor role of tossing the ball to the batsman with an underhand motion and a stiff elbow—his "pitch" was, in the words of one early pitcher, "about the same motion as is used in pitching quoits." He was essentially just another fielder, and his ability to field his position and keep runners close to their bases often earned him more praise than his deliveries to the plate.

But pitchers very quickly began to carve out a larger role for themselves. In 1854 the Knickerbockers added a rule that the pitcher had to be at least fifteen paces from the batter, which strongly suggests that the fastball had begun to emerge. An 1856 account remarked that Knickerbockers pitcher Richard F. Stevens "sends the ball with exceeding velocity, and he who strikes it fairly must be a fine batsman." As it happened, the Knickerbockers had little choice in tolerating Stevens's offerings since his uncle, John Cox Stevens, owned the Elysian Fields where the club played.

There were also efforts to disrupt batters by putting spin on the ball, but both those endeavors and the experiments with greater speed seem to have been only minimally effective. Some pitchers were able to generate impressive speed while using the underhand, straight-arm delivery. A Portsmouth, Ohio, observer, for example, maintained that a pitcher named Joe Jarvis was able to "split heavy boards with the balls he pitched" without breaking the rules. Yet strikeouts remained rare occurrences, suggesting that batters were able to deal with speedy pitching, perhaps because the restrictions on deliveries still prevented pitchers from crossing them up with curveballs.

As the early pitcher Jimmy Williams later explained, in the days when the rules required that the pitcher deliver the ball with the "arm swinging perpendicular and the hand passing below the knee . . . the only way of outwitting the batsman was by a change of pace. A few pitchers—notably [Dick] McBride of the Athletics, [Asa] Brainard of the Cincinnatis, and [George] Zettlein of the Atlantics—were able to pitch with considerable speed by an imperceptible whip-like motion of the arm. [A. G.] Spalding of Chicago was perhaps the best exponent of this school of pitching, he having so well disguised the change of pace that he was very effective."

Thus the art of pitching primarily consisted of techniques designed to make it a wee bit harder for the batter to hit the ball out of sight. Chadwick later wrote condescendingly of the 1850s: "Frank Pidgeon, Tom Van Cott, Matty O'Brien and Tom Dakin were the strategic pitchers of the period and they tossed in good balls for that time." And on another instance he recalled: "Prior to [Jim] Creighton's day, slow, strategic pitching was the order, and the sharp 'points' and the beautiful fielding displays now characteristic of the game were unknown. 'Sloggy' batting was then the rule against the pitching of Tom Van Cott of the Gothams and Frank Pigeon [sic] of the Eckfords, the model pitchers before Creighton introduced the disguised underhand throw."

The term "underhand throw" was significant. As Chadwick notes, earlier pitchers had made incremental changes, but Jim Creighton was the first man to turn the pitcher into a dominant force. After the 1859 season the teenaged Creighton spent the winter throwing an iron ball of the same size as a regular baseball; by the spring his "speed was blinding." At the same time he mastered a lethal delivery in which he released the ball from only a few inches above the ground but caused it to rise "above the batsman's hip, and when thus delivered, the result of hitting at the ball is either to miss it or to send it high in the air." He thus complied with the delivery restrictions but managed to propel the ball with as much force and movement as if it had been thrown.

Creighton's delivery frustrated batters and prompted many complaints. Yet Chadwick pointed out in 1860 that by a strict reading of the rules it was a "fair square pitch." In vain others protested that it violated the intent of the rules—that the ball be tossed or pitched, not thrown. If so, they were told, the rules needed to be changed.

In the years to come the rules-makers would make almost annual efforts to do just that, and would fail miserably. They tried requiring that pitchers keep both feet on the ground, that they take no more than one step, and that they stand within a square enclosure, but none of these approaches succeeded in bringing back the days when pitchers played a minor role.

As it happened, long before they abandoned these efforts, Creighton was dead. And although he had inspired imitators, only a few of them had much success. (Joe Sprague, for example, learned to throw what some considered to be a curveball— a pitch that "took a sharp twist, sometimes turning in and sometimes turning away from the batter." Alphonse "Phonney" Martin developed a delivery that "was so long and drawn out that it tired the spectators and so slow that it maddened the batsman so that he tried to kill it. Instead of doing that he usu-

ally drove the ball high and generally to the left field where Al
Gedney, the Eckfords' speediest and best outfielder, generally
took good care of it.") Despite the fact that few of these deliveries were effective, the rules-makers continued their relentless
efforts to devise restrictions that would end them. For by then,
there was a far more pressing reason for wanting to end the experiments of the Creighton wannabes. Even when these deliveries did little to hinder batters, they damaged the game by
prompting tedious arguments.

This was true because efforts to duplicate Creighton's delivery were accompanied by an even more dramatic increase in the
use of another of Creighton's legacies: the tactic of trying to get
batters to chase bad pitches. By no means had Creighton invented this device, which in a sense was as old as the game. The
Knickerbockers' initial rules made no provisions for either balls
or called strikes, taking it for granted that pitchers would try to
pitch the ball accurately and that batters would swing at the
first good offering. By 1855 there were reports of pitchers trying
to tempt batters to offer at wayward pitches and of batters re-
taliating by standing at the plate and refusing to swing at any
pitch. At first this was viewed as a passing trend. Pitchers generally stood to gain little by this tactic, since any capable batter
could tell if a pitch was off course and refrain from swinging.
Batters had a little more to gain, since they could try to wear a
pitcher out. As an early player named G. Smith Stanton later
explained: "Those were the days that tried pitchers' bodies as
well as their souls. A batsman was not obliged to strike at a ball
until he got one to suit him."

This seemed neither fair nor sporting, so in 1858 umpires
were given the authority to call strikes on a batter who didn't
swing at good pitches. (Strikes for a swing and a miss had always
been part of the game, which is where the term came from—a
batter struck and missed.) Most observers assumed that this
threat alone would be enough to eliminate the undesirable tactic, and few umpires appear to have actually called strikes. The

presumption was that peer pressure to play the game as it ought to be played would take care of things.

There was just one small flaw: batters who indulged in the so-called "waiting game" could be punished, but pitchers couldn't. Initially this didn't seem to be a major shortcoming, since it was still fairly easy for batters to discern that a pitch was off target. But that changed when Jim Creighton's deliveries began to combine great speed with considerable movement, as is clear from this 1862 description: "Suppose you want a low ball and you ask him to give you one, you prepare yourself to strike, and in comes the ball just the right height, but out of reach for a good hit. You again prepare yourself, and in comes another, just what you want save that it is too close. This goes on, ball after ball, until he sees you unprepared to strike, and then in comes the very ball you want, and perhaps you make a hasty strike and either miss it or tip out. And if you do neither and keep on waiting . . . being tired and impatient you strike without judgment, and 'foul out' or 'three strikes out' is the invariable result."

Although none of his contemporaries could match Creighton's skill, it was far easier for them to imitate his penchant for errant offerings. Indeed, the harder they tried to duplicate the deceptive movement of his pitches, the more likely they were to test the batter's patience. This was dramatically illustrated by an 1862 game in which the pitcher "seized the ball, and swinging his hand behind him as if in an effort to dislocate his shoulder, put his head between his legs—almost—and running furiously, discharged the ball some yards away from the home base. . . . After repeating this action an indefinite number of times, our worthy Captain, who was batting, at last got a ball that suited him, and set a good example by a fine hit."

Helpless batters had little choice but to play the "waiting game," and umpires were equally powerless to intervene. Games ground to a virtual standstill; in one 1860 game, Jim Creighton delivered 331 pitches and his opposite number tossed 334 pitches—in just three innings!

Inevitably, in 1864 the concept of called balls had to be introduced to complement the earlier addition of called strikes. (A complicated warning system was also added but eventually scrapped.) At the same time a set of restrictions on pitching motions was added to the rulebook, and this led to premature declarations that the problem of uppity pitchers had finally been solved. In mid-season the *New York Clipper* wrote: "Last season, McKever's [Billy McKeever's] pitching, like several others, was made effective by his skill in what is called 'dodgy delivery,' that is, the balls he pitched, though apparently for the striker, were not such as he would strike at with any chance of hitting fairly. This style of pitching, and likewise the inaccuracy resulting from efforts to excel in speed, it was that led to the introduction of the new rules in reference to pitching, and hence McKever's style is this season deprived of all its effect."

Yet this optimism proved unfounded. Almost annually the rules-makers tweaked the number of balls and strikes or placed new restrictions on pitchers' deliveries, or both, but they were unable to restore the pitcher to being just another fielder. If anything their efforts had the opposite effect, as all the tinkering with the rules sent the message that the letter of the rules now mattered more than their spirit.

Although the introduction of called balls and strikes probably signaled the death knell for the vision of baseball as a conflict between batters and fielders, it was years before this reality was conceded. Rules-makers spent two more decades feverishly experimenting with ways to restrict the role of pitchers while it slowly but surely became clear that the battle had already been lost.

It had been lost for a couple of simple reasons. First, the introduction of called balls and strikes, more than anything else, rent the fabric of baseball as a gentleman's game. Until this time a player's honor was at stake, and this was all that was necessary to prevent a fielder from falsely claiming to have tagged a runner or to have caught a batted ball on the first bounce.

This worked because these were fairly cut-and-dried questions; a man almost always knew whether he tagged a runner or whether he caught a ball before it hit the ground. Balls and strikes, however, were much more subjective matters, since two men might reasonably differ on whether a ball was close enough to be a fair pitch. This rendered self-policing impractical.

Second, the various attempts to hamper the pitcher had forced another man to enter the action: the umpire, who was suddenly expected to make judgment calls instead of enforcing decorum. Instead of restoring baseball to a simple conflict between batters and fielders, the game now included *two* additional participants. What had been a spare ritual between two adversaries had been transformed into a murky mess that now also involved both the usurping pitcher and an umpire who was compelled to offer his often highly subjective opinions.

By the close of the 1860s this reality led to a barrage of new tactics that would earlier have been deemed unsporting. Instead of acknowledging an adverse result, players began automatically to appeal to the umpire for a decision, prompting complaints about "the constant cry of 'judgment on that,' 'how's that,' etc." Base runners, instead of touching or rounding the bases, began to cut in front of them. (Since early bases were often hard objects, early base runners didn't generally touch them. But by the early 1860s some were getting "in the habit of" cutting in front of them, prompting one reporter to complain: "it should be stopped at once by the Umpires. It is absolutely requisite that the bases should be touched in running round, unless the player passes outside of them, and when this is not done he should be made to return to the base he left.") Batters, instead of trying to hit the ball out of sight, tried new tactics such as place hitting and the deeply subversive bunt. They even discovered a dastardly play that became known as the "fair-foul"—taking advantage of the rule that a ball was fair or foul based on where it first landed, they struck down on the ball so that it landed in fair territory but then veered off into foul ground. Meanwhile fielders began deliberately to trap catchable balls in order to start double plays.

These new tactics had become increasingly evident in the big Eastern cities by the end of the 1860s and had begun to affect play elsewhere as well. Yet in most of the country these were still minor annoyances, and some clubs simply ignored new rules they didn't like.

Even in the Eastern hotbeds where it was harder to ignore such developments, there was still considerable optimism that a few minor rule adjustments would restore the pitcher to his proper place, reduce the role of the umpire, and thereby bring back the simple game envisioned by the Knickerbockers. Baseball still appeared to most observers to be a game, and a relatively simple one at that, albeit one that was suffering from growing symptoms of discontent.

CHAPTER 5

Bats, Balls, Bases, and the Playing Field

❖   As the preceding chapter made clear, during the first flourishing of baseball the rules were intended to be far more flexible than they are today. In particular, they were tailored to the available equipment and the playing field, not the other way around. And although the equipment generally consisted only of bats, balls, and bases, this very simplicity meant that these items assumed great significance. Similarly, the playing fields that were often roughly hewed out of nature affected the game in a multitude of ways.

BASEBALLS

As the central objects in games that are tinged by ritual, balls have always been potent symbols, a point thoughtfully explored in Robert Henderson's *Bat, Ball and Bishop*. Baseball is no exception.

Out of necessity, early baseballs came in a variety of colors, but white soon gained preferred status. It attracted special attention no doubt in part because of the contrast to the red ball traditionally used in cricket. But the reverence with which it was regarded suggests that the ball's whiteness was also seen as a symbol of the pureness and innocence of the game itself.

Clarence Deming, for example, recalled "the orthodox 'white' ball being used only for match games," with necessity often requiring the same ball to be brought forth for two or three matches. When a club in Rochester, New York, "ordered the first white horsehide ball, just one" from Brooklyn, it was treated with awe: "What a host of the boys came to see it and to have a kindly handling."

As soon as it became possible for a baseball to be spared, matches culminated with the losers presenting the game ball or a brand-new one to the winners. The obvious ritual undertones of this action were enhanced by the ceremony that accompanied it; as described in an account of an 1862 game, "the ball was delivered in a very manly speech [and] the customary things were said on both sides."

Yet while the ritual elements surrounding the early baseball are undeniable, it is a mistake to emphasize them at the expense of more practical ones. Although the symbolic significance of the baseball is often implicit in early accounts, it is the difficulty of replacing it that is always explicit. As had been the case with the Knickerbockers, early clubs were deeply conscious that their very existence was imperiled by the tremendous difficulty of creating or purchasing a usable ball.

When the ball had to be created from scratch, as was the case in most parts of the country during the early days of baseball, its manufacture involved a series of tricky processes. First, rubber, yarn, and leather had to be obtained, and someone had to be found who could transform the leather into an effective cover. The scarcity of critical components and budgetary constraints made scrounging for secondhand materials common, with the result that the finished baseball was often noticeably imperfect. But these earliest baseballs were treasured all the more for the struggles that went into assembling them.

At one of the first match games ever played in San Francisco, for instance, a field had been found and the two sides arranged before someone pointed out that no suitable ball was available. A committee had to be formed, and the problem was not solved until one of its members "came across a German immigrant who was the possessor of a pair of rubber overshoes. These he bought, after much dickering, for $10, and with the yarn unraveled from a woolen stocking and a piece of a rubber overshoe the first ball ever used in this city was made."

According to an account published nearly a century after the fact: "An old rubber shoe, melted down, became the core of the first ball manufactured [in Rockford, Illinois]. Around it, yarn was wrapped. An orange peel was quartered and used as a model for the leather cover which was sewn by George Lane, harness maker."

An 1890 piece in the *Chicago Herald* summed up the sacrifices that were typically involved: "Most men of to-day remember the time when they shinnied around and found a smooth old boot leg and a ball of yarn which they carried to the good mother with a request that she take her shears and needle in hand and fabricate a ball. In doing this the good mother cut the leather in much the same form that an orange peel takes on when neatly prepared for dessert, and then she wound the ball of yarn rather tighter than usual, boy patiently (for a wonder) holding his arms outstretched to do service as a reel. Next she sewed the leathern flaps together with shoemaker's thread, breaking many needles and losing a little temper during the operation, but finally turning out a very acceptable sort of ball— somewhat inclined to rip, it is true, and quick to lose its perfect sphericity, but still a mighty handy thing to have in one's pocket when ante-over or town ball or rounders was proposed."

An early Boston ballplayer recalled that in his youth a different part of the baseball's innards was in shortest supply, yet he had similar recollections of the rummaging that ensued: "it was not difficult to procure an old rubber shoe for the foundation of a ball. Many a dear old grandma or auntie of today will remember having stockings and mittens being begged of them, which were knit at home by hand, to be unraveled for ball stock." He also remembered that leather could not always be obtained, which forced another form of improvisation: "When leather was not to be had, a cheap and easy way to cover a ball was with twine in a lock stitch, called quilting."

Henry Chadwick later recollected that the baseball of the 1850s "weighed over six ounces and was over 10 inches in circumference and had 2½ ounces of short strip rubber over yarn in its composition." But it is important to realize that even these somewhat vague guidelines could not always be followed. In Chadwick's hometown of Brooklyn, a couple of enterprising club members used their experience in related trades to begin manufacturing baseballs around 1855, which brought far greater uniformity to the baseballs used in and around New York City. But in most regions, beggars couldn't be choosers; clubs felt lucky just to have a functional ball, and no one worried much about its exact specifications.

The result was that clubs around the country played with baseballs that varied enormously in every particular. Although unintentional, this variability was one of the many ways in which the game of baseball retained the defining characteristics of its predecessors—flexibility and unpredictability—in the years after the Knickerbockers' rules had begun the movement toward standardization.

It was in the cores of baseballs that this unevenness was most apparent, as sizable variations in the quantity and quality of rubber had predictable results. In Mansfield, Ohio, an early ballplayer later described "the great hit of the day" as one that resulted in the ball ending up 195 feet from home plate, which speaks volumes about the liveliness of the ball being used. But in Fort Wayne, Indiana, another pioneer recalled that in "those good old days of the game . . . we used what were called 'lively' balls—a baseball with a small rubber ball in the center. A batter could send one of them nearly a mile." And Clarence Deming claimed that balls were sometimes used in Boston with such "persistency of bound and roll" that "in a game on the hard soil of Boston Common . . . it is related that a batted ball striking inside the diamond was caught on the first bound by the left fielder standing in his normal place." Even Chadwick acknowledged that games were sometimes played with a ball that was so soft that pitchers who were hit square in the forehead with batted balls escaped uninjured.

Treatment of the rubber could introduce yet another variable. Occasionally the strips of rubber that made up the core "were put in a vessel of hot water and boiled until they became gummy, when they would adhere together and form a solid mass of rubber."

The shortage of baseballs meant that a good one would literally be used until someone knocked the stuffing out of it. This scarcity affected how the game was played in several ways. For example, if a ball wasn't lost or dispossessed of its cover, it would be gradually transformed from lively to dead, and of course this had a dramatic effect on scoring. Another consequence was that practice time was severely restricted or even rendered impossible. "There was only one base ball in the town at the time," an account of the first game in Whatcom County, Washington, pointed out bluntly, "and as this was in the possession of the Wide Awakes, all the Black Diamonds could do was to sit and wait for the day set apart for the game."

Sometimes another substance was substituted for rubber. "In the lake regions and other sections of the country where sturgeon were plentiful, base balls were commonly made of the eyes of that fish," recalled an 1884 article in the *Brooklyn Eagle* about the early days of baseball. "The eye of a large sturgeon contains a ball nearly as large as a walnut. It is composed of a flexible substance and will rebound if thrown against a hard base. These eyeballs were bound with yarn and afterward covered with leather or cloth. They made a lively ball, but were more like the dead ball of the present than any ball in use at that time."

In 1858 a country club visited a Boston nine for a match of the "Massachusetts game" and brought a still more unusual ball: "It was understood that balls for this game were to be made of rubber and yarn, but in the absence of this particular mention the visitors produced a ball of minimum weight made of yarn wound as loosely as possible over a bullet to secure the proper size, and insisted on using it. The bats provided by the home club were of little use with such a ball, but the guests had been equal to all contingencies and brought flat sticks, not for striking the ball to the foreground, but to touch it merely and direct it from its course to the rear." Gloves had to be used for self-preservation, but the "bullet ball" still took quite a toll on the fielders' hands: "Whenever this game was afterward mentioned in the presence of anyone who took part in it, there was a show of fingers as 'relic' of that game."

Because baseballs were so precious and irreplaceable, clubs went to extraordinary lengths to preserve them. Most of these efforts centered on the covers, since it was generally taken for granted that the ball would continue to be used as long as the cover remained intact.

An early Boston ballplayer recalled that some pioneers responded to the problem of baseballs that "would not last through a game" by swaddling the innards in two covers. Gradually, however, ball makers learned how to make the covers tough enough to endure a beating by covering them "with alum-dressed horse hide, that being the strongest leather known, being very elastic when water soaked, in which way it was used. The body of the horse being smoother, rounder and harder than that of other animals it follows that the skin would be more even throughout. The alum makes the leather white and may add some strength."

Considering the precious status of the baseball, players went to extraordinary lengths to avoid losing one. "We used but one ball then," remembered one early ballplayer, "and when some strong batter would lose it, the whole gang, including the spectators, would set out to find it. Occasionally some scamp would run away with it, and then there would be all kinds of trouble."

Harry Wright, according to the recollections of one of his contemporaries, once waded across a creek and climbed a bluff to retrieve a ball batted by the legendary slugger Gat Stires.

These searches created a golden opportunity for some young fans. One such youngster who grew up in Port Henry, New York, later recalled that games were played on a lot known as the Mineral Ground, which was "situated on a flat piece of ground at the edge of a mighty ravine down which to the waters of Mill Brook there was a regular stream of 'lost balls' rolling on match days, and we boys thought no small beer of ourselves when we had hunted a fine 'bounding rock' out of the hollow and presented same to some great man player like 'Doc' Austin, Mr. Yale, our Principal at the School, Johnny Mack or some other hero of our boyhood days."

Not until 1877 was the syntax of the rulebook changed and the phrase "the base ball" replaced with its plural. Even after it became common to have enough baseballs on hand for games to continue after one was lost, they still represented a considerable expense to ball clubs. The Detroit ballplayer Joe Weiss recalled the situation when he began playing in the 1870s: "When we played a match an agreement was entered into that each club pay for half the ball, which necessitated the levying of an assessment of about six cents on each player."

As scarce commodities, early baseballs were often preserved long after being retired from use. Many decades later, pioneer Milwaukee resident Elisha W. Edgerton presented the city's Old Settlers' Club with "a baseball which the young fellows of Milwaukee used to play with in 1836 on a flat field north and east of the postoffice about where the southeast corner of Milwaukee and Mason streets now is. Mr. Edgerton made the ball himself, and the cover was sewed on by Mrs. Edward Wiesner, wife of the first shoemaker in Milwaukee."

The Knickerbockers' preference for a hard, lively ball proved a key step toward establishing the game as an adult pursuit. At first, as we have seen, the practical difficulty of making and preserving a functional baseball ensured wide variations. But when manufacturing processes improved to the point that greater consistency was possible, the new ball's form added two new complications to the once-simple game.

One was the reality that with a hard ball and no protective equipment, serious injuries could result. Catchers were especially vulnerable, as they had begun to creep closer to the plate to deter opposing base-stealers. A few experimented with gloves, but the typical catcher "had no protection against a foul, excepting sometimes he would hold a slab of India rubber between his teeth to prevent the knocking out of his teeth, if struck in the face." There were reports of catchers being knocked cold by foul balls or of one having to "work through a game with the blood dripping from his bruised hands." Players at other positions were more fortunate, but many of them sported "crooked fingers [that] testify to many a hot grounder and difficult fly." At first such injuries were viewed as badges of courage, but their charm wore off fairly quickly, and by the 1870s players sensibly began to don protective equipment.

The hard, lively balls also brought threats of broken windows and injured passersby, which forced many clubs to move outside the city centers. In Kalamazoo, Michigan, for instance, as soon as the local club switched to harder balls, they were forbidden to play downtown; other similar examples are described later in this chapter. Broken fingers and broken windows thus served as symbols of a more irrevocable break: a break with the simpler days of the past.

BATS AND BASES

The only other essential implements during the game's early days—the bats and the bases—were not the subject of nearly as much toil or worry as the baseballs, but they were also emblematic of the presiding spirit of resourcefulness and adaptability.

The sportswriter and historian John H. Gruber nicely captured the analogy with frontier life when he explained that batters "selected the wood and whittled their own bats . . . there are stories told of enthusiasts who faced the pitcher with bats five feet long and nearly as thick as wagon tongues. It was a happy-go-lucky crowd, those pioneers of the national game, and quite as much in earnest as were their fathers who cleared the forests to erect homes, and spoiled many a good bat in doing so."

With the aim being to swat the ball out of sight, many batters approached the plate with what George Wright described in 1888 as "logs of wood, some of them three and a half feet in length, and fanned the air in a way that would seem perfectly ridiculous for the average player today." Rules were gradually adopted to restrict their length and thickness, but they could still be very large, and it is safe to assume that even these guidelines were not closely followed.

The choice of wood was just as haphazard. Through trial and error, ash soon became the favorite, but others remained common. Clarence Deming recalled, "A hard wood bat was barely or never seen. The regulation stick was long, thick, and of the 'pudding-stirrer' shape, made of spruce, bass, chestnut, and the lighter woods." Necessity dictated that bats were made of many different types of wood and occasionally led to radical improvisations. On October 20, 1865, the Athletics of Philadelphia scored 101 runs in a morning game and 165 runs in an afternoon game, in the process breaking so many bats that "they were compelled to use the handle of a shovel as a substitute for a bat at the finish."

Bats were originally viewed as just another of the implements of the game, rather than as a player's personal possession. John H. Gruber explained that early batters selected any bat they fancied, whether a teammate or even an opponent had brought it to the grounds. This free-and-easy approach slowly gave way to a more proprietary one, and in 1872 a rule was passed that "The striker shall be privileged to use his own private bat exclusively, and no other player of the contesting nines shall have any claim to the use of such bat, except by the consent of its owner." It was another sign of the end of an era.

Early bases, even more than the bats of the era, were the subject of improvisation. Any available object that was unlikely to blow away or impede play might be pressed into service.

In bat-and-ball games of the early nineteenth century, it had been common for participants to designate some of the many natural impediments on the playing field as bases. William Wheaton, one of the original members of the Knickerbockers, later recalled that in the late 1830s the club's predecessor used "no regular bases, but only such permanent agents as a bedded boulder or old stump." The result was that the concept of a standard distance between the bases was slow to emerge.

When a game was played on a field that was clear of such obstacles, stakes were most commonly used as bases. According to Frank G. Menke, a practical issue caused this to change between 1835 and 1840: "Because so many players were injured by collision with them, the four-foot high stakes were discarded and flat stones were substituted at the stations. [The] expression 'run to your stake' was abandoned for 'run to your base.' Stones soon were found impracticable for bases because many boys stumbled over them, and this brought sacks filled with sand into existence. These were referred to as 'bases,' and the game came to be known, for the first time, as 'baseball.'"

This appears to be a basically accurate version of what happened, but, as after-the-fact accounts often do, it includes oversimplification and some telescoping of events. The term "base ball" dates back to the eighteenth century, but like the game itself its use was not uniform. So the change from stakes to bases may well have helped the new name spread to new regions and become standard. Similarly the change from stakes to stones and then to bases did not follow an even trajectory; instead, as with virtually every element of the game's early development, it occurred by trial and error at staggered intervals as new regions adopted the game.

As usual, standardization came to New York far earlier than to the rest of the country. The New York–based National Association of Base Ball Players (NABBP) adopted a requirement in 1857 that the bases be "canvas bags, painted white, and filled with sand or sawdust." Clubs in other regions largely ignored the rule, and they sometimes found out the hard way why it had been implemented.

The first club in Kalamazoo, Michigan, formed around 1860, found that "much of the danger of the game lay in the rocks which were used for bases and gave Mr. [Oscar] Coleman, among others, a badly sprained ankle." Across the state in Detroit, Dexter M. Ferry (the founder of what is still one of the world's largest seed companies) learned a similar lesson. One of that city's pioneer ball players, David Peirce, later recollected: "D. M. Ferry played with us and he was a great hitter. He had an ankle sprained in one game and it laid him up for a long time. We had some new bases, fastened to stakes in the ground. Mr. Ferry made a long hit that proved to be a home run, but on the way around the bases he stepped on one of the posts, and turned his ankle severely. He kept on, and made the run, but it was his last for a long time."

At the same time, however, Eastern clubs were finding that the 1857 rule was flawed. Two injuries in an 1858 game between the Niagaras of Buffalo and the Flour Citys of Rochester led to the use of sand bases being denounced as "a dangerous practice." Perhaps more important, sand made the bases too heavy to conveniently transport to the ball field. As noted earlier, the demise of one of St. Louis's earliest baseball clubs was in part blamed on the ordeal of "carrying the old style sand bag bases back and forth the long distance to the grounds."

As a result, the 1866 rules required only that the bases be "filled with some soft material." Even with this increased flexibility, clubs continued to improvise. In an 1871 game in Kalamazoo, for instance, the bases were denoted by "stakes driven in the ground or bits of board."

The shift to using low-lying objects as bases also created an unforeseen difficulty. Since the lone umpire stood behind the plate, he had a hard time telling whether a runner had beaten the ball to a base. This tempted both runners and fielders to stray from the honesty they were expected to display by accepting the umpire's judgment even when they knew him to be wrong. Base runners also began to cause controversy by cutting in front of the bases.

This was another instance of a disturbing problem. Seemingly minor alterations to the game, when accompanied by changes in the spirit in which the game was played, were a major threat to the increasingly delicate fabric of baseball's pioneer era.

THE PLAYING FIELD

The attempts of early ball clubs to locate acceptable playing fields had every bit as large an effect on baseball's rules and customs as did those clubs' efforts to find functional balls, bats, and bases. Before the Knickerbockers, Americans who played bat-and-ball games other than cricket merely looked for a location that could be accommodated to their needs, and wouldn't have dreamed of trying to create a ball field. Indeed, as George Kirsch has suggested, the availability of a flat, well-manicured field was a critical factor in determining what game was played: those with ready access to such a site were likely to choose cricket, but many others played the various games that coalesced into baseball.

The Knickerbockers' choice of a harder yet lively ball soon changed things. Within a few years almost all the prominent clubs in the vicinity of New York City had moved to the outskirts of town or even farther afield. The Knickerbockers, as noted, moved several times before settling at the Elysian Fields in Hoboken, New Jersey, and they were far from alone.

The Knickerbockers' first rivals were a group called the New York Club, and this club's history is instructive for the telling influence of the playing field. Charles Commerford, the son of one of the era's best-known labor leaders, later recalled: "I first played baseball in the forties, and the first game I saw played was by the old New York Club, the predecessors of the Knickerbockers, which club had its grounds on a field bounded by 23rd and 24th streets and 5th and 6th avenues. There was a roadside resort nearby and a trotting track in the locality."

So at least one eyewitness declared that the New York Club preceded the Knickerbockers (and Commerford repeated this claim in another article based upon his recollections). In addition, the members of the New York Club were far superior at the new game, thrashing the Knickerbockers 23 to 1 on June 19, 1846, in the first game played by the Knickerbockers' own rules. So why are the Knickerbockers now credited with being the pioneers of baseball while the New York Club generally warrants at most a footnote? (There is also strong evidence that the Eagle Club was organized by 1840, meaning that this club too has grounds to claim precedence over the Knickerbockers.)

One of the few nineteenth-century writers to address this issue observed: "From all the information the writer has been able to gather, it appears that this was not an organized club, but merely a party of gentlemen who played together frequently, and styled themselves the New York Club." But this only tells us *what* happened, not why this "party of gentlemen" took a different course from the Knickerbockers and thereby relegated themselves to the dustbin of history.

It appears that several factors worked in tandem. One of the few facts we know about the New York Club's baseball players is that most of them were also cricketers. (Indeed, it is likely that the club was part of, or overlapped significantly with, the New York Cricket Club.) Commerford, who saw the club play, recalled that the New York Club "had its headquarters and grounds within an enclosure of a trotting park located where the Fifth

This 1853 rendering of a cricket game in Harlem illustrates two of the key factors that enabled baseball to emerge as America's national pastime. Note the vast amount of flat land that was required—a reality that made a cricket field very expensive even when the site was still "considered far out of town" and would soon make it virtually impossible to obtain a suitable site in New York City. Just as important, the spectators are situated far from the action. The New York Club, one of the participants in this game, played a brief but decisive role in the development of baseball. [Collection of Tom Shieber]

avenue hotel now stands. This place was a roadside inn and was under the management of a man by the name of Thompson and was in those days considered far out of town."

The New York Club gradually gave way to the Gotham Club, whose grounds, according to Commerford, "were located at Harlem—Second avenue, 104th and 105th streets. This was another roadside inn, with a half mile trotting park, and was under the management of a man named Brown. It was indeed a beautiful and level spot. A cricket club also occupied the grounds occasionally and they were kept in fine shape."

These descriptions suggest the fate that most likely befell the New York Club. The members initially found the new game of baseball a very appealing alternative to cricket because it could be played closer to town and on almost any surface. Once baseball's development made urban sites too small, leading the club to find a new refuge on a field suitable for cricket, the members probably rethought their decision, and many of them chose to return to playing cricket. Alternatively, having a field suited for either game, the club members may have gone back and forth between baseball and cricket. This would account for the cricket club that Commerford recalled sharing the Gothams' grounds: it was composed of the members of the New York Club who preferred the older game.

This raises yet another question. We have already seen that the Knickerbockers became so apathetic about the game that Daniel Adams claimed to have "had to employ all my rhetoric to induce attendance." So why didn't the Knickerbockers face a similar problem of members being torn between baseball and cricket?

The answer to that question is probably simple: the site at the Elysian Fields used by the Knickerbockers was poorly suited for cricket. The trees that ringed the field were in such close proximity to the diamond that even baseball games were significantly affected. Batters learned to "bat most of their balls" into them, "rendering it almost impossible to catch them, even on the bound." Other obstacles were still more directly in the way. It was not until 1866, after years of pleading, that the ballplayers received the welcome news that "The old tree to the left of the home base—always an eye sore to the players—has been removed."

Further rendering cricket difficult at the Knickerbockers' home on the Elysian Fields was the erratic care given the field. There are accounts of baseball games there during which unmowed grass impeded the fielders. After another game, a journalist complained, "There were not enough members, either, on the ground committee, the work falling upon three or four,

This 1858 drawing shows a cricket match between Canada and the United States in Hoboken in front of a large crowd. Note again the vast amount of impediment-free ground that is required for cricket. [Collection of Tom Shieber]

when all should have been engaged in keeping the field clear on such occasions."

In the departure of the New York Club from the baseball scene there may well be other factors that are lost to history. Perhaps its members had even more trouble creating functional baseballs than the Knickerbockers did. Possibly the fact that the Elysian Fields were owned by the uncle of one of the Knickerbockers' players played an important role. (If Richard F. Stevens had joined the Gothams instead of the Knickerbockers, would we today be playing the Gothams' game?) In any event, there can be no doubt that the availability of an appropriate site was a huge factor during this era in determining what ball game was chosen and how it was played.

Other New York City clubs joined the Knickerbockers and the New York Club in heading out of town. One of the most popular sites was the Union Field in Tremont, Westchester County, located a full fourteen miles north of the city. The field was surrounded by railroad tracks and also offered convenient transportation by boat and horse-car. Even so, the distance remained daunting.

The result was that, as noted earlier, the mid-1850s saw most of the area's clubs choose the "vacant fields then existing in South Brooklyn." One early Brooklyn ballplayer later looked back with fondness on the days "when base ball was a bucolic pastime . . . when the old Atlantics had their grounds on the old corn field adjoining the old Long Island Cricket Club's Field . . . and how we played on the old sand lots where the Prospect Park Place now stands."

Another old-timer named Captain John Brennan reminisced in 1894 about "the days the old Atlantics used to play on their grounds in front of the Clover Hill hotel, located on the corner of Marcy and Gates avenues. This old hostelry—then kept by the genial old Jimmy Wilde—still stands on the same corner, though it is now a grocery store. The old sign was on the building within the past three years. Captain Brennan still remembers the days when the old players marshaled their forces on the field lying between the boundary line of what is now Gates, Bedford, Putnam and Marcy avenues, which at that time was the old Decker farm, from which the space for the old Capitoline ground was afterward taken."

But farmland and vacant sandlots soon began to vanish from the outskirts of Brooklyn as well, forcing clubs to scramble to find new homes. In 1858 the Niagara Base Ball Club had to obtain written permission to use "the vacant ground on the block between Douglass, Degraw, Hoyt and Smith streets." John McNamee recalled playing ball on the "old York street lot, near the station house . . . until the principal of the school (No. 7) complained to the mayor that we interfered with the progress of the scholars in some way, and we had to stop playing there."

These images of cricket (above) and baseball (below) being played in Hoboken appeared in the same issue of *Harper's Weekly* in 1859. It is apparent that the games are being played at different locations—note how closely the baseball field is surrounded by trees while the cricket pitch is clear of such obstacles. The captions also differentiate the locations, with the baseball field being described as being at "the Elysian Fields, Hoboken," while the cricket locale was listed only as Hoboken. [Collection of Tom Shieber]

The game's arrival in new towns across the country led to renewed efforts to situate it in city centers. In many of these new markets, initial success in finding an appropriate site downtown proved a great boon. Nor did this occur only in less-developed cities.

Baseball took off in Cincinnati after the City Council granted permission to two local clubs "to play twice a week on the Orphan Asylum lot . . . corner of Central avenue and Twelfth street." The game received its impetus in Cleveland because local clubs were able to use Case commons, "a wide stretch of cow pasture, near the corner of Case and Woodland avenues." And baseball's success in supplanting wicket in Hartford after the Civil War was greatly aided when the city granted aficionados of the new game permission to use the west end of Bushnell Park.

It was not long, however, before the same pattern of being crowded out of city centers recurred. In Kalamazoo, Michigan, as noted, the village council reluctantly allowed ballplayers to use Bronson Park, but the village president regularly stopped by to warn them, "go on and have a good time, boys, but don't hurt the trees!" As soon as the players switched to a harder ball, their permission to use the park was revoked. Likewise the ballplayers of Washington, Iowa, were chided in 1859: "Boys! Boys! Playing ball is nice sport—it is healthful and invigorating—and we like to see you enjoying yourselves in that way. But there is a place as well as a time for everything. Now the County Judge and other citizens have gone to a great deal of trouble and expense to plant trees in the court yard and sow it in grass seed, so that it may look pleasant and nice and be an ornament to the town. But don't you see the trees will all be killed, and the grass can't grow at all, if it is made a playground for all the boys in town? Certainly you do, though perhaps you didn't think of it before, and now we are sure you will find some other place to play ball."

In one city, ballplayers successfully fought back. The Boston Common had been "the scene of nearly all of the important base ball contests in this vicinity" from 1857 to 1869 and had played a crucial role in the change from the Massachusetts game to the New York game. When the city's aldermen prohibited baseball there in 1869, the ballplayers retaliated by running a "Red Ball" ticket of candidates who promised to "grant our youth some spot for recreation" in that December's elections. Eight of the twelve men on the "Red Ball" slate were victorious, and baseball soon returned to the Common.

But Boston ballplayers appear to have been unique in successfully fighting an eviction notice. Most clubs had little choice but to hunt for new grounds, and often the process repeated itself several times. Pre–Civil War baseball in Rochester, New York, for example, was played at two prime locations known as the Babbit tract and Brown Square. But these sites proved too valuable to devote to baseball, and before long "the

Babbit tract had been divided into building lots and Brown Square planted with trees." After being driven out of the downtown area, the city's clubs set up bases in locations so wild that one game was interrupted by a flock of plovers.

Even after being relegated to the city's outskirts, Rochester's clubs were not safe from the relentless march of progress. In 1870 the Flour City Club received bad news: "The grounds at Jones' Park are a bequest to the citizens residing in their neighborhood, who intend after the game with the Red Stockings, to close them against ball players."

This was not simply mean-spiritedness on the part of these citizens. As cities became far more cramped, it became increasingly evident that ball clubs didn't make good neighbors. The influx of crowds brought numerous complaints about trespassing, the cutting of fences, and obscenities.

Even if crowds could somehow be persuaded to behave—no easy task—there was a far more intractable problem: the tendency of baseballs to leave the playing area and break things. When one of Detroit's first clubs began playing on the city square, the Campus Martius, in 1860, they broke so many windows in the nearby Russell Hotel that they began paying the proprietors a flat rate. Balls that flew out of the playing area often represented a double expense for clubs, since, as has been noted, the loss of the baseball itself was considerable.

In response, as early as 1860, Henry Chadwick was recommending a tract six hundred by four hundred feet for a baseball field. The requirements would expand in ensuing years to accommodate a growing number of spectators and their carriages. Even younger clubs that didn't have to worry about spectators began to find competition for the vacant lots they had once had to themselves. Joe Weiss, of Detroit's Cass Club, recalled that in the early 1870s his club shared a lot with a photographer's car, which led to predictable conflicts over broken windows.

As a result, long before the 1870s most clubs had bowed to the inevitable in selecting their home fields. Since they couldn't afford a large area of prime urban real estate, and were beginning to discover that even a locale on the outskirts offered little security, most of them were forced to carve out playing fields on land that no one else wanted. In the process, the way baseball was played was also modified.

Just getting the grounds to the point where games could be played was often a massive undertaking. When the first enclosed ballpark, a converted ice rink, was opened in Brooklyn in 1862, it required arduous work. "Notwithstanding the lowness of the ground, ample protection against water seems to have been provided, by filling up and ditching it," the *Brooklyn Times* reported. "The work of filling up the slough which was left when the pool was drained off, was a formidable undertaking, and a cart load of earth dumped down on the great field seemed to produce about the effect of a grain of sand on a billiard table. Fortunately those who had formed the project were not men to be easily disheartened and the work was persevered in until its completion, and the result is that base-ball promises to be the great feature of Williamsburgh amusements during the summer."

When two famed Eastern clubs visited St. Louis in 1868, a five-man committee was formed just to fix up the local grounds. Considering how much work was necessary to convert an ice rink or to spruce up an existing field, it can be readily imagined what an ordeal it was to hew a ball field out of a wilderness. A wide range of accounts make clear that it was taken for granted that some obstacles would remain and that accommodations would be made.

"The ground is not as well fitted up as it should be," began a description of an early ballpark that nicely conveyed this reality. "The brush is too near, and the deep gulch in the rear of home base is a great draw back. This is no fault of the club. Suitable grounds are hard to be found anywhere. But, if the ground is level, all other objections can be overcome."

And at many of the era's baseball diamonds, the playing field was anything but flat. Leveling terrain was far too massive an undertaking for early clubs even to consider, but the consequent unevenness wrought havoc on fielding.

The home field of the Dunderbergs of Peekskill, New York, for instance, was "located on the side of a hill, and it is about the poorest place for fielding purposes which can be found outside of Newburgh. The pitcher stands in a position about 8 or 10 feet above that of the catcher, and the centre fielder looks down upon the in-field from a still greater elevation. The result, of course, is that both contestants in a match have to play up-hill games. The Dunderbergs, being familiar with the ground, have an advantage over new comers and play their points accordingly."

The Irvington Club of Irvington, New Jersey, made its home on a field that was "so irregular that at times some of the outfielders would disappear into a miniature ditch." The aptly named Mountain Club of Altoona played its home games on the side of a hill so pronounced that, in addition to making fielding an ordeal, it was necessary to hire "the tallest kind of umpire to watch the movements of the out fielders as fully as should be done."

Yet when the clubs looked for flatter surfaces, they often discovered that the alternatives were even worse. Tim Murnane recollected that the Mansfields of Middletown, Connecticut, played in a "cow pasture" that was situated "close to the State Asylum, and was about the only place that the club could secure in this hilly country." As an additional disadvantage, "The ball park was located on the side of a hill close to the banks of the Connecticut River, and many a ball went bounding over the backstop to splash into the picturesque stream, when baseballs were highly prized."

Murnane also recalled that the club's fielders had another obstacle to overcome: that "the annual cutting of the grass was put off until late in July." This too was a common problem. A club in Riverton, New Jersey, for instance, made its home in an apple orchard where donations "enabled us to occasionally have the grounds cut." Naturally there were recurring complaints about the field being covered with hummocks and with dried vegetation and coarse grass reaching six inches or higher.

Clubs often played on sites that were available specifically because of poor drainage, another reality that forced all sorts of improvisations. In one 1869 game in Washington, D.C., a heavy rainfall the night before had left the grounds covered with water, but the clubs were anxious to get the game in anyway. So a "steam fire engine was employed to pump the water out, and, with the aid of a drain, succeeded in it so that only the right and centre fields were covered." Sawdust was also used freely, but the grounds were still in "a very bad condition." And most clubs lacked even these primitive means of dealing with rain, and had either to cancel games or do their best to wade through or around the puddles.

Even when it was possible to remove natural impediments, clubs often played on land that belonged to someone else and therefore had to put up with them. When a player on a University of Michigan baseball club in 1867 cleared evergreens and elms from the playing field, the team's captain had to write to the school newspaper to beg forgiveness for the actions of "some one who had more in mind the interests of ball players, center fielders in particular, than the worth of the trees or the feelings of the authorities."

Many other obstacles forced clubs to adapt. While the Union Grounds in Tremont, fourteen miles north of New York City, had the important benefit of being easily reached by railroad, unfortunately the railway embankments impinged upon the field. This necessitated a modified playing area that was "shaped like a triangular segment of a circle, fenced in on all sides with embankments, on which railroads are laid, and so small that while the catcher was obliged to play at the apex of the triangle the outfielders were compelled to stand close to the embankment at the lower part of the field and be ready to mount the bank in order to field the ball when batted over the

This illustration of an 1865 game at the Elysian Fields between the Atlantics of Brooklyn and the Mutuals of New York City makes it clear why the "old tree to the left of the home base" was so hated by local baseball players—and why they were so excited when it was finally cut down the following spring. [Collection of Tom Shieber]

railroad tracks, as very frequently happened." Such oddly shaped fields were quite common—in early baseball there were no "cookie-cutter" ball fields.

All these deterrents could have a dramatic effect on how baseball was played. Clubs, for example, were apt to station their most talented outfielder in the hilliest field. Infielders similarly checked the field for problem areas before the game and positioned themselves accordingly. As noted earlier, the Knickerbockers originally measured the distance between the bases in paces, which "was rather vague." Such imprecision would be unthinkable nowadays, but it made sense in a field strewn with obstacles. If the requisite number of paces would place a base in the middle of a puddle, it only made sense to move it to a more inviting location. At the close of the 1860s, baseball clubs began switching to dead balls, a change that was at least in part a concession to the related expenses of real estate and lost baseballs.

These various accommodations meant that the game might be played very differently—and on fields of different shapes and sizes—from town to town. As was the case with variations in the contours of bats and balls, imperfections in the playing field only added to the charm of baseball by enabling it to retain the flexibility that had long been one of its most appealing characteristics. Together these eccentricities helped baseball retain some of the innocence of a child's game, even as that status was being threatened by outside forces.

[CHAPTER 6]

Customs and Rituals

❖   As we have seen, during the early years of the game the rules
of baseball were understood to be fluid. The game was played
with the best available ball and on the best field that could be
procured, with concessions commonly being made to such practical realities. It wasn't the rules that were really important;
what mattered were the rituals and customs.

Early baseball, as I have argued throughout this book, was
more than anything else about having fun. Rules can maintain
order, but fun can only be regulated by rituals and customs,
which is why these elements of baseball became most prominent whenever there was a threat that the fun would be spoiled.
Specifically, rituals provided structure to matches between
clubs (to prevent a spirit of competitiveness from taking over),
gave everyone a role (to ensure that no one felt left out), and
stressed common bonds (to remind opposing sides that they
had much in common).

The centrality of the baseball made it the focus of the most
prominent rituals. At the close of a match game, "the opposing teams would line up facing each other, and when all were
ready the captain of the home team would step out and request of his men, 'Three cheers for the visiting nine.' These
were given with a vigorous good will, then the compliment was
returned by the visitors, and all wound up by the whole crowd
joining in with a 'tiger,' much resembling an Indian 'Pow-
wow.' This had a tendency to 'iron out' some of the rough

spots that may have developed during the progress of the games and all left the grounds with an apparently friendly feeling."

Then the losers presented a baseball to the winners while "the customary things were said on both sides." This ceremony was so important that in 1872 the National Association of Amateur Base Ball Players, an organization that tried to carry on the traditions of the defunct NABBP, issued specific instructions for "Furnishing the Ball."

Nor did the ritual end with the delivery of the ball. The recipients usually had the ball "gilded and the date and score of the game painted thereon in black letters." Initially it was common to send the ball east to be gilded, but club members soon began to assume this responsibility. The catcher of a club in Eaton Rapids, Michigan, for instance, "was very handy with the old quill and pen, and after the game the ball was cleaned thoroughly—the name of both teams, the score, place and date were printed on it in a very neat and attractive manner. After the ink dried the ball was given a coat of light-colored varnish to preserve it."

Clubs also put quite a bit of thought into the exact wording that was to be inscribed on the baseball. Once the ball had been transformed into a trophy, it was carefully preserved. Edward Clift of Bordentown, New Jersey, was typical in still proudly displaying the first baseball won by his hometown's pioneer ball club nearly four decades after the fact.

Another important ritual that followed a match game was a banquet that brought together all the players on both sides. Henry Chadwick later exclaimed: "There were base ball talkers 'in the good old days, gentlemen.'" He explained: "The clubs used to appoint committees then to attend to the varied business of a match game. There were the Committee on Nines, the Committee on Grounds, the Committee on Refreshments, and it was this latter body which bore off the palm of importance. A ball match without a supper of some kind of hospitable entertainment in those days would have been like a cricket match now a days without the inevitable 'dinner.' They used to get awful hungry toward the close of the ninth inning of a match in the good old times, and they could not get along without their grub at the end of the match. These entertainments, too, not only afforded food for the hungry players, but opportunities for speeches by the regular appointed orators of the club."

Chadwick recalled a particularly memorable speech by Harry Polhemus of the Excelsior Club of Brooklyn, who was the last member of one of New York City's oldest Dutch families. At a postgame banquet thrown by a rival Brooklyn club, "One particular dish took Harry's fancy amazingly. It was chicken pot pie. When called upon to respond to the toast given to the 'Infant of the Excelsior nine' he descanted on the merits of the pot pie in a way that delighted Mrs. Holder. Says Harry, 'There's one thing, gentlemen, in which you beat us badly today, and that is in giving us chicken pot pie.'" The quip brought down the house.

The festivities did not end when everyone had eaten their fill. Next, "the order was 'wine . . . give us of your best vintage, good innkeeper,' or words to that effect. Tom Jerome . . . called for a bucket of champagne, and drank the health of the guests in a bumper of the rosy which nearly filled a celery glass. As the novelists say, 'About two o'clock in the morning a party of jolly roysterers might have been seen issuing from the portals of the hostelry at Bedford,' etc., etc."

Lavish entertainment was sometimes part of the program. When the National Club of Washington, D.C., visited the Excelsiors of Brooklyn in 1866, "they were taken to the Mansion House in Hicks street, and here was found a feast prepared such as the gods of the olden time were wont to indulge in, every delicacy of the season contributing to make the entertainment one of the most complete on record. Not content with palatial luxuries, a perfect feast of delightful vocal and instrumental music was provided, the artists present excelling in their vocal offerings. The charming singing of Messrs. Stein, Lingard, Lockwood and Lockhart being a vocal treat of the very first order; the instrumental performance of Mr. Abbott, too, being noteworthy. For some three or four hours there was quite 'a feast of reason and a flow of soul,' speeches from the two presidents and remarks from distinguished military and civil guests present marking the occasion, one toast given by a member of the press in response to a call being by request inserted."

If the visiting team had won, the celebrations were apt to continue on the trip home. A member of the Princeton nine recalled that after a successful trip, "what a fine ride we had back, and how enthusiastical was the reception at home."

Frequently even these spontaneous celebrations were cloaked in the garb of ritual. When the Atlantic Club of Brooklyn recaptured the national championship in 1868, their return home was thus described: "In procession came three carriages, and in front of the first one was elevated a broom, the pine handle of which was ornamented with gay colored ribbons; the occupants of the carriages appeared to be enjoying a happy state of feeling. Inquiry was made, and the well-informed were heard to say that it was the Atlantic Club returning from Morrisania, after playing with the Union Club, and that the broom carried in front meant that having whipped the champions, it could now sweep everything out of its way."

When the Empire Club of St. Louis reached home after winning a tournament in Illinois, their return "was marked by an ovation hitherto unknown in the West, being in the form of a torchlight procession participated in by the following clubs: Baltic, Liberty, Atlantic, Magenta, Columbus, O. K., Resolute and Hope, all in uniform and each club accompanied by a number of its friends in citizen's clothes. It was the hour of midnight when the train conveying the Empires arrived in East St. Louis and the boys were most completely surprised at there being received with the cheers and congratulations of such an enthusiastic crowd of the base ball fraternity. Upon returning to the St. Louis side of the river (by ferry boat) the procession marched down the levee to Chestnut street, to Fourth, to Pine, to Third, to Locust, to Fourth, to Washington avenue, and then to the Empires' Hall on the West Side of Third street near St. Charles, upon arrival there forming in line in front of the old City Hotel. Facing the hall were the club's rooms, brilliantly lighted and filled with its friends and members, who deputized Mr. E. H. Tobias, Secretary of the Club, to voice their words of welcome, which he did from the balcony of the hall, 'couched in elegant and appropriate terms,' as one of the morning papers said the next day."

Like any event with ceremonial undertones, such post-match flourishes conveyed the sense that everything had built to a triumphant climax. But there were also plenty of ritual elements that occurred before and during the match.

One such custom called for the host club to meet their guests on their arrival and offer them hospitality. The Princeton Club, for example, was met at the depot by a "Committee of Reception" and escorted to their hosts' "club-room, which they placed at our disposal." When the National Club of Washington, D.C., visited Brooklyn in 1866, they were escorted to city hall by the host Excelsiors and introduced to the mayor, then taken to the monument of martyred legend Jim Creighton.

The match itself began with a ceremonial coin toss to determine first at bats. It was also "the habit of the better class of clubs [to exchange], just before each match, silk badges imprinted with the club name. The players wore these accumulated trophies pinned upon the breast, sometimes with startling color effects; and the baseball man was proud, indeed, who could pin on the outside of his deep strata of badges a ribbon from the mighty Atlantics, Mutuals, or Eckfords, attesting his worth for meeting giants, if not mastering them." This conveyed a clear message of mutual respect: you're proud of your club, and I'm proud of mine.

Another symbol of the spirit in which the game was expected to be played was that all nine innings were completed, even if the club batting last was ahead after eight and a half innings. This was another reminder that a baseball match was as much ceremony as competition.

Events during the match were more difficult to orchestrate, but every effort was made to do so. Spectators were expected to applaud good plays by either side and never to show partisanship. They were also strongly discouraged from hissing.

After the Civil War, poor sportsmanship itself was occasionally met with hisses, and this response was tolerated because it was aimed at suppressing a worse form of misconduct. But it remained unacceptable to direct such abuse toward a player who had blundered or toward an umpire. After an 1867 match the crowd was admonished: "We cannot but condemn the want of courtesy displayed by many of the spectators in hissing Mr. Urell, the umpire, on one or two occasions when his decisions did not suit the majority. Such an act is discreditable to a Washington base ball assemblage. Mr. Urell undoubtedly rendered his decisions in accordance with his judgment and his interpretation of the rules, and, if he erred, it is very unjust to manifest disapprobation in so public a manner."

Similarly, every effort was made to ensure that the players behaved themselves, with the press taking a lead role. When a Boston area player "declared himself out when the condition was such that no one but himself and his opponent knew the fact in the case," his "noble act was commented upon by all the dailies, one of which had nearly sixty lines about it." And players accordingly prided themselves on achieving a reputation that could "be held up as an example to the juniors of the fraternity to follow."

All these customs kept everyone mindful that the outcome of the match was less important than the spirit in which it was played. An equally vital task was to ensure that nonplayers still felt they were included. This was done by assigning them specific roles and then acknowledging and honoring their contributions.

The umpire, as we have seen, was initially just such a dignitary, and some clubs even included an umpire among their officers. E. H. Tobias, an early member of the Empire Club of St. Louis, remarked that the history of the era "would be incomplete were the name of Mr. John Young omitted. He was one of the first members of the Empire Club and though too advanced in years to participate in playing, he took a deep interest in the sport and was so thoroughly conversant with the rules that by general acclaim he was always in demand as umpire, which position he filled so honorably and satisfactorily that his judgment went for 'keeps' undisputed, even when his own club suffered by it."

While the umpire's role soon changed, the scorers continued to be honored. Tobias's recollections continued: "The Empire also numbered among its early members one Peter Clinton, who took the greatest pride and pleasure in his position of scorer, the labor of which was scarcely so arduous as now, only 'outs' and 'runs' being recorded in those days, but every game, even those between different nines of the club, was neatly and duly recorded in that book of Pete Clinton's." Janesville historian Frank L. Smith "was considered too small to take part in match games" during the early years "but was kindly allowed the position of official scorer."

Fans were similarly assigned a clear, well-defined role. As already noted, they were expected to refrain from hissing a mistake and to applaud both sides without partiality. A few also developed rituals to show loyalty to a favorite player. A group of young fans in Michigan regaled their favorites with the mysterious chant: "Knock, brothers, knock with care/ Knock in the presence of the compositaire." Another early devotee later recalled: "I am a base ball crank from way back. I can remember when my sole ambition in life was to rise to the glory attained by Billy Williams, who in his day was the boss pitcher. We boys used to sing a song about him with a refrain that ran: 'Billy Williams, he could split a two-inch plank.'"

Special attention was given to women spectators, who were strongly encouraged to attend matches and whose presence was invariably noted. In part this was done because the attendance of women was believed to promote better conduct, but there was more going on. Not only could women be counted on to refrain from showing partisanship, they might actually show favoritism to the visitors. "The young ladies who stood near the reporter's deck," noted an account of an 1866 tournament in Bloomington, Illinois, "were much disappointed at the result, as their brightest smiles and most energetic cheers had been, throughout the game, for the strangers."

As this account also implies, even though the standards of the era ensured that the allusions were coy, baseball matches also functioned as courtship rituals. A perfect example was a description of an Iowa nine in which the writer—after making sure to point out that eight of the players were bachelors—informs us that the players' hearts went "pit-a-pat" when they saw the "beautiful hundred ladies" who accompanied the opposing team.

In New York a handsome player named Bernard Hanigan gained a reputation as "the most popular player in the club with the belles of the village, who flock in such numbers to the Union grounds when games are in progress, the Union Club mustering a more numerous bevy of pretty girls at their matches than any other club in New York or Brooklyn." From time to time ballplayers were jocularly chastised for neglecting their duties by paying too much attention to a young woman in the stands. One, for instance, was accused of "endeavoring to make fancy catches when the ladies are on the grounds."

In some cities baseball clubs were paired with clubs of young ladies in much the way of college fraternities and sororities. In Richmond, Virginia, in 1867, for example, the Stonewall Base Ball Club staged an event for a Church Hill club of young

The dashing shortstop Bernard Hanigan of the Unions of Morrisania gained a reputation as "the most popular player in the club with the belles of the village, who flock in such numbers to the Union grounds when games are in progress, the Union Club mustering a more numerous bevy of pretty girls at their matches than any other club in New York or Brooklyn." [Collection of Tom Shieber]

ladies, who then returned the favor. When the pioneer Adirondack Club of Elizabethtown, New York, appeared in its first match game, the players sported homemade uniforms: "The lettering on the suits was of course done by Elizabethtown's fair ladies, some of whom afterwards found husbands in the ranks of those stalwart 'Adirondacks.'"

Uniforms also figured prominently in one of the most frequently recounted incidents in the annals of early St. Louis baseball. For a much-anticipated game the members of the Union Club "appeared in bright new uniforms that had been ordered from the East. One of the Union nine selected for this game, Kieselhorst, failed to put in an appearance, and Julius Smith was chosen to fill his position, but the latter's uniform had not materialized and he positively refused to go on the field without a uniform, in which resolution he was determined, more particularly so, because he had escorted his sweetheart to the grounds and naturally desired to show up to the best advantage. Jule Smith and Kieselhorst were about the same height, but the former was of much larger and more muscular development. He was finally induced to don Kieselhorst's uniform and though it was a tight fit he was so anxious to show his lady love what a fine player he was, that he put forth all his energies to outdo his fellow players . . . when his time came he hit the ball with so much force that it went sailing way down to center-field, while he himself flew like a winged Mercury to first base, where he was encouraged to continue his running by the loud shouts of his companions 'to make a home run.' At third base the shouts were more vociferous and urgent. Jule put in his best sprinting licks, and landed safe at home amid the most terrific shouts ever heard upon a ball field. When he recovered himself enough to look around it was to discover the players rolling around on the grass all convulsed with laughter and the game at a standstill." Finally, another player regained his composure enough to lead Smith "to the dressing room, where Jule was quickly brought to a realization of the fact that his pants had parted."

In Grass Lake, Michigan, the captain of the local ball club was surrounded by young women at the end of a close-fought victory. They presented him with a floral bouquet and accompanied it with this toast: "May you be as successful a husband as you are as a captain of a base ball club." Embarrassed, he stammered out a reply that paid tribute to the fairer sex ("I have always thought a great deal of the ladies, and if I was called upon to give an address, my subject would be woman. If I were to write a book, my subject would be woman") and ended with the curious promise that "if I ever marry I expect to marry a woman." The awkward speech earned him three cheers from the young ladies.

And in case anyone missed such less-than-subtle allusions to baseball games as mating rituals, matches were regularly held between married and single squads. The Empire Club of St. Louis, for instance, began each year with a game between its married and single members, with the outcome the subject of much good-natured joshing for the balance of the year.

It was also important to ensure that the many club members whose generosity paid the club's bills continued to feel included. An early Hartford ballplayer explained: "there was considerable expense connected with running the club, and as there was no admittance fee to witness the games, quite a number of lovers of the game and friends of the members became honorary members by paying $5 annually, and it was all needed. Traveling expense, entertaining out of town clubs, uniforms and equipments, amounted to a good deal annually." These honorary members also paid one dollar apiece to purchase a souvenir of the club in the form of "a piece made of a silver quarter dollar, one side of which had engraved a tree, resembling the old Charter Oak, with the letters underside, B.B.C. [Base Ball Club]."

Clubs might also give well-to-do patrons a sense of belonging by electing them to the presidency or to another executive office. These positions usually carried few responsibilities but entitled these members to a central role in any ceremonies that took place. As a result, though the Knickerbockers' game was more exclusive than its predecessors, there remained many ways for nonplayers—whether too young, too old, belonging to the wrong sex, or just not talented enough—to feel included.

Finally, no opportunity was lost to remind everyone of the common bonds and values that united them. Patriotism was foremost among them, with baseball, as noted earlier, being proudly billed as the "National Game" before it was extensively played outside New York City.

Toward this end the game was quick to establish itself as a mainstay of Fourth of July celebrations. An early Hartford ballplayer recollected that "the great game—the game which added much to the reputation of the 'Charter Oaks'—was that with Harvard, July 4, 1866. There was a great celebration on that day, a parade, balloon ascension by E. U. Bassett, the ball game, and fireworks in the evening. The largest crowd ever seen on the park up to that time gathered to see the great baseball game between the Charter Oak and Harvard University clubs. It was estimated that not less than 10,000 people were present, making it quite difficult to play the game, especially back of third base. The game was closely contested, and at the last half of the ninth inning, with the score 16 to 14 in favor of Harvard, and the Charter Oaks at the bat, with a player on second and third and two men out, H. L. Bunce rapped a two-bagger into the right field, which seemed good for two runs, but by a brilliant play by the Harvard fielder the ball was caught and the game ended with a victory for Harvard."

Another symbol of the bonds that unified the baseball community was the development of a common language. While additions to the game's distinctive jargon usually originated with the ballplayers, they were quickly picked up by the spectators, whose use of these phrases stamped them as members of a select community. One writer claimed: "The technicalities of the game, and much of its slang got somehow curiously mixed up in business talk, with a result perplexing to the uninitiated. A medical gentleman, writing out a prescription for a patient, was very much astonished at the latter's surprise. It was all explained, however, when he saw that he had recommended a 'long hit to centre field' and a 'home run,' for an obstinate case of indigestion. Not so bad advice, after all. A legal individual, who had gone out to see the Nationals play with the Forest City nine on Thursday, was heard to speak of the opinion of a Judge in one of the courts as a 'muffin decision,' and a book-keeper in a large wholesale house in town, who had always prided himself on the accuracy of his accounts, so far shared the general excitement in witnessing the game of the Cream City and Atlantic nines, that he spoiled a ponderous ledger on Friday by inserting in his account of sales several boxes of 'foul flys' and 'muffed balls.'" Presumably some of these examples were tongue-in-cheek, but the intrusion of baseball jargon into everyday speech was real.

Differences were also emphasized in some rituals, but they were done in a humorous way so as to point out that they could be overcome on the ball field. The message was unmistakable: you have pride in your club and I have pride in mine, and while our respective allegiances are important to us, by meeting on the baseball diamond in a spirit of mutual respect we recognize that if the circumstances of our lives had been different, we might be comrades instead of adversaries.

Thus it was common for members of a club or community to align themselves for nonmatch games on the basis of specific attributes. In addition to married-versus-single games, contests were held between fat and thin ballplayers, between members of specific professions, between Civil War veterans and noncombatants, and between clubs chosen on the basis of almost every conceivable distinguishing trait.

One especially prominent means of emphasizing the theme that surface differences hid underlying bonds was the frequent allusion to distinctions between rural and urban ballplayers. Stereotypes abound in these references, and it is clear that much has been exaggerated for effect. Instances of rustic dress and appearance were often remarked upon. Clarence Deming recalled, "There were few uniforms in the rural nine and such as they were they were not uniform. The country player rose to quite a peak of dignity if he could 'sport' the old-fashioned baseball cap with its huge visor, or a belt in place of the more useful than ornate 'galluses.' Baseball shoes, for such as had them, were of the homespun pattern, with spikes made by the village blacksmith and set in the soles of ordinary shoes by the local cobbler." A Detroit pioneer reminisced about playing "a rural club composed of men with long, flowing beards. I don't think one in that club weighed less than 200 pounds."

Folksy or backwoods conduct attracted even more attention. Clarence Deming wrote, "Not far away from the truth was the country captain who described his team as 'men who can't bat much, or field much, but first-rate talkers.' To dispute the umpire on every close decision was orthodox duty . . . and it made the rural ball game forensic as well as spectacular." Likewise an early Cleveland ballplayer named Bill Doubleday was recalled as "an eccentric character, a brawny six-footer in stature and a regular cyclone at the bat. It was a common thing for him to clean the bases with a home run when he was right, but 'Bill,' like [turn-of-the-century eccentric] Rube Waddell, liked to go fishing, and was frequently not to be relied upon."

And every rustic stereotype ever invented was shoehorned into a description of the early ballplayer Adoniram "Gat" Stires, who became known "as the 'terrible hayseed.' Stires was the phenomenon of those days. He knew nothing of headwork, but he had the strength of a giant. The places under the arms where the shoulders join the body are usually hollow. In Stires' case they were filled with muscles. The man could run like a deer, and had hands like hams covered with hide. No fly passed him, and his field record was generally errorless save in the matter of throwing. When he returned the ball to the diamond it was always at lightning speed, and no one could tell whether the sphere would reach the catcher or go over the fair ground fence. But it was at the bat that Stires won his name as the 'terrible hayseed.' He was not like [Cap] Anson or [Ross] Barnes a sure base hitter, but when his club and the ball did meet the result was nearly always a home run."

But no early club could match one from Pecatonica, Illinois, for engendering rural stereotypes. In 1866 this club naively entered the top division of a major tournament in Rockford, Illinois, and was thrashed 49-1 in its first and only game. For suffering the most lopsided loss, the Pecatonica club was awarded a tin horn on which was "inscribed the suggestive word 'Practice.'" By rights that should have ended the story, but instead the club's legend only grew in the years to come, with the contrast between the rural nine and their big-city rivals always emphasized.

In 1878 the *New York World* published a lengthy account in which a Pecatonica farmer had wagered three loads of hay and a yearling calf on the outcome of the game. He sat down to watch the game with the intention of using a knife and a couple of sticks to keep track of the score. After his initial high hopes had given way to a mixture of surprise and resignation, an explanation finally occurred to him and he exclaimed, "Why the goldarned fools are after the horn!" As the years went by, the story of the original game was "improved" with new details and an increasingly lopsided score. The *New York Times* published a version in 1896 in which the Pecatonicas lost 121-0 to the Red Stockings of Cincinnati, with the field including the greatest Eastern teams and such backwoods entries as the Rustlers of Cherry Valley and the Plowboys of Stillman Valley. In a 1914 story by Finley Peter Dunne, an old-timer reminisced in an exaggeratedly rural dialect about having watched legendary players Harry Wright, Cap Anson, Jim White, and "th' Forest Citys bate th' Pecatonica Blues be a scoor iv two hundhred an' eight to nawthin'." (Needless to say, none of these players actually competed in the tournament.)

Yet while stereotypes abound in such accounts, they are not mean-spirited. This is because the descriptions send a clear message that, even though the country ballplayers are old-fashioned in their ways, they are playing baseball both as it used to be played and as it ought to be played. They try to hit the ball out of sight, they enjoy themselves and don't take the game too seriously, and they are willing to take on all comers, no matter how overmatched they may be. If the humor is at anyone's expense, it is at the expense of the big-city ballplayers who have abandoned the spirit in which the game is supposed to be played.

Indeed, a number of these anecdotes convey the sense that the rustics were not only in on the joke but were slyly using the stereotypes to their advantage. A New Jersey club challenged the mighty Atlantics of Brooklyn to play them but claimed to be "a mere country club." When the Atlantics complacently sent a squad that featured several members of their "second nine," they were upset by the Jersey upstarts.

The most notable example of a club that took advantage of an overconfident group of city slickers was one that hailed from in and around Troy, New York. Although properly known as the Union Club of Lansingburgh, the club gained the informal nickname of the Haymakers of Troy because of their reputation as rural hayseeds.

Their image was cemented when they traveled to New York City to play the mighty Mutuals, a game that was later described as follows: "The Haymakers were nine grotesque country lads, who played ball without uniforms, socks or shoes. They came off the farms lying between Troy and Lansingburgh, and while they were not known outside the swamps and bottoms, where they whiled away the bright summer afternoons of eighteen years ago they had many admirers among the staid old farmers who 'lowed that the boys were pretty cute with the ball if their hands were horny and their feet bare. . . . After considerable correspondence a game was arranged between the Haymakers and the Mutuals. The match was played in New York city. When the country boys came on the field, with 'Cherokee' [Fisher] at their head, they were greeted with shouts of derision from the great crowd of spectators. They were a sun-burned, seedy-looking lot, but they were neither frightened nor depressed. Before game was called the betting was $100 to $5 in favor of the Mutuals. Fisher and [William] Craver were the Haymakers' battery, and the way they worked together that day will ever remain a part of the base ball history of the country. The Mutuals could do nothing with 'Cherokee's' delivery, and when the game ended in an overwhelming victory for the Haymakers a groan went up that could have been heard over in Jersey. 'Cherokee' and the rest of the boys were given a princely re-

The Union Club of Lansingburgh, New York, became better known as the Haymakers of Troy because of their reputation as country bumpkins who "wore blue jean pants and shirts. The pants were rolled up to the knees and the bare legs and feet looked tough as leather. On their heads they wore big straw hats, and in their hands they carried hay rakes." Another contemporary recalled, "The Haymakers were nine grotesque country lads, who played ball without uniforms, socks or shoes. They came off the farms lying between Troy and Lansingburgh, and while they were not known outside the swamps and bottoms, where they whiled away the bright summer afternoons of eighteen years ago, they had many admirers among the staid old farmers." In fact this image was more public relations than reality. [National Baseball Hall of Fame Library]

ception when they returned to Troy. A few days later the Mutuals, who were smarting under the ridicule which was being heaped upon them by press and public, went to the collar and cuff city for revenge. They were beaten a second time, however, and from that moment 'Cherokee' Fisher and the Haymakers' nine were in the mouths of sports from one end of the country to the other."

A later article made the contrast between the Haymakers and their big-city opponents even more dramatic: "an old-fashioned hayrick was driven up to the players' gate, and ten men got out and came through that gate. When they got on the ground the crowd laughed till it cried. The team was composed of nine six-footers, who wore blue jean pants and shirts. The pants were rolled up to the knees and the bare legs and feet looked tough as leather. On their heads they wore big straw hats, and in their hands they carried hay rakes. Oh! How that crowd did laugh. Ladies had hysterics and strong men cried, laughing at the ludicrous sight. The visitors took it all in good part, and paid attention to business. The game was called and the Haymakers piled up their rakes and picked out a bundle of small hickory saplings they had brought from home, each man had a stout bat." Then the Troy players proceeded to thrash their overconfident opponents.

Obviously these accounts present greatly exaggerated descriptions of the contrast between the two clubs. Fisher and Craver, the star battery of the Haymakers, in fact were both Irish Americans and, respectively, a fireman originally from Philadelphia and a Civil War veteran from Troy who eventually became a policeman. And while other club members did hail from the countryside, it defies belief that they were more familiar with hay rakes and hickory saplings than with shoes. So what's going on?

There are two plausible explanations. One is that almost all these details were added later for comic effect as stories of the Haymakers' prowess were being told and retold. The other is that the Haymakers made a conscious effort to present themselves as country bumpkins. Most likely there is some truth in both explanations, but it probably doesn't matter all that much. What's important is that the country-versus-city motif was a wildly popular one no matter which side got its comeuppance.

As it turned out, even the Pecatonica Club got the last laugh. A year after the Rockford tournament, the best club in

Chicago was humiliated by the Nationals of Washington by the score of 49-4. Shortly thereafter the big-city club received a package from Pecatonica that included the now-famous tin horn and a note of congratulations for having "fairly taken from us our hard-earned laurels."

It would be nice to be able to report that racial differences were also incorporated into these rituals, but that wasn't the case. In fairness, the African-American population was slow to move to the Northern regions where baseball first thrived, and there were in fact notable instances of racial harmony. For instance, Brian Turner and John S. Bowman demonstrated that one of the starters for the Eagles of Florence, Massachusetts, in 1865 and 1866 was of African-American descent and that his race was a nonissue.

Yet more often race remained too troubling and unsettling a question for it to be incorporated into the game's rituals and customs. When an African-American club from Philadelphia applied for membership in the Pennsylvania Association of Amateur Base Ball Players in 1867, the applicants were politely advised "to withdraw [rather] than to have it on record that they were blackballed." The club next applied for membership in the National Association of Base Ball Players, but an unfavorable report from that body's nominating committee again led to withdrawal of the nomination. A journalist explained that the nominating committee wanted "to keep out of the Convention the discussion of any subject having a political bearing, as this undoubtedly had."

The wording of these accounts tells us much about the limitations of baseball's use of rituals. The game had successfully incorporated potentially divisive issues into its customs by stressing the common bonds that were deeper than the apparent differences. But race remained too disturbing and perplexing to many Americans for them to recognize those common ties, with the result that even "the discussion of [the] subject" was painstakingly avoided.

Despite this unfortunate exception, rituals and customs played an important part in early baseball by addressing a number of important needs. They provided checks on overt competitiveness, made sure that as many people as possible remained involved in an increasingly exclusive activity, and offered frequent reminders of common bonds. In this way rituals and customs ensured that baseball remained a game. As they passed out of the sport, the era's end grew inevitable.

In reading these accounts it is easy to get the mistaken impression that the players didn't care about winning and losing. Nothing could be farther from the truth. As we have already seen, the very rituals that helped control competitiveness assigned specific roles to the victors and the vanquished, with the winners often engaging in uproarious celebrations. The outcome was even mentioned when, out of compassion for the defeated club, it could have been avoided. For example, Dr. Joseph Jones, president of the Excelsiors of Brooklyn, used the postmatch banquets "to eloquently explain the why wherefore of defeats and victories. An old Excelsior supper without a speech from the Doctor was like leaving the turkey out of a Thanksgiving dinner."

But while winning and losing unquestionably mattered, great care was taken to ensure that the importance of the outcome was kept in context. The players accepted the now clichéd maxim that it mattered most not whether you won or lost, but how you played the game. Two factors appear to have been especially important in achieving and maintaining this consensus.

First, ball sports were still very rare in the 1860s, with the result that our current mind-set that the individual skills of great athletes may enable them to dominate such activities was not yet in place. Aspiring new clubs instead consoled themselves with what I have called the "patience of hope"—an abiding faith that success on the baseball diamond would come to any club that practiced with enough diligence and learned to play with teamwork. The result was that the members of a club that lost 106-10 still believed that with a little more work they would have every chance to win, and this underlying faith enabled them to participate in the rituals of a match with sincerity. It also prompted several clubs whose work schedules precluded afternoon workouts to rise at 5 A.M. or earlier to squeeze in practice time.

Second, as we shall see in the next chapter, the rituals reminded early ballplayers of the great pride they felt in their allegiance to their club. While winning was assuredly better than losing, losing with honor was infinitely better than behaving in a way that discredited one's club.

CHAPTER 7

Club Life: The Common Threads That Bound the Players Together, and the Activities They Shared

❖ Rituals mattered to early ballplayers because they symbolized something still deeper: the sense of belonging to a club and, in many cases, a community. Now we think of a baseball club as an entity that exists to play baseball, but until the mid-1860s baseball clubs were social clubs that happened to include baseball among their activities. Their essence was the fraternal spirit they engendered, which gave members the all-important sense of belonging to something bigger than themselves. Simply put, they brought the countryside's sense of community to cities and towns.

Pride in belonging to these clubs mattered so much to their members that they strove to do their best whenever they played a baseball match. Henry Chadwick recalled of the late 1850s: "the sport then was earnest work. They went in to do their level best to win, not to fill the pockets of club stockholders or of pool buyers, but solely for the honor of victory. . . . Club matches in these days were meetings which the members gave their whole minds to for the time being. They were important affairs, something that had to be attended to as if the reputation of the club was at stake every time they met in the field."

It is easy to read these comments as refuting one of the main premises of this book by justifying the tendency to depict early baseball as a very earnest activity. Yet when read carefully, there is no contradiction. Players strove to win "solely for the honor of victory" that would accrue to their club, and played "as if the reputation of the club was at stake every time they met in the field." This led them to keep the spirit of competition within strict bounds—as already noted, early players very much wanted to win, but only if they could do so without in any way compromising the overriding concern of the club's reputation.

The club meant something precious to its members—a sense of belonging not easy to put into words but perhaps best compared to what a patriot feels about his or her country, what a believer feels about his or her religion, or what all of us feel about our closest friends and family members. It was a deep bond, and letting something as trivial as the result of a baseball game interfere with it would have been unthinkable. Clubs of the 1850s and 1860s might play baseball, and might put considerable energy into doing so, but their existence was far more profound and would not be remotely threatened if the club abandoned baseball.

The point was tellingly illustrated by a feud that occurred within a young Chicago baseball club in 1876, after the end of the era when baseball clubs were first and foremost fraternal organizations. When members of the Lake View Brown Stockings had a quarrel, one faction broke off and formed a new ball club. Then a curious thing happened: "the honor of Lake View was at stake, and the mothers and fathers of those boys, who were almost as much interested in the team as the boys themselves, decided they must go back together." But the dissension continued, "so the boys decided to play a game to decide which team should have the name 'Lake View Brown Stockings.'" After one faction won the name, however, the others had a change of heart and "came back to play on the real team."

The obvious conclusion to be drawn from this account is that by 1876 baseball was being played by youngsters who no longer felt unswerving allegiance to their club. Yet it is just as clear that this sense of belonging, even when diluted, was still powerful. And descriptions of earlier clubs leave no doubt about the magnitude of that allegiance.

Baseball clubs, like other fraternal organizations, were based upon a recognition of common traits. In addition to living in the same city or town, members were likely to have similar ages, heritages, and backgrounds. One of Chicago's most heated rivalries, for example, featured two clubs, "one representing the silk stocking district, and the other composed of Irish lads from the west side."

Of all unifying characteristics, the most common one in the building of ball clubs was occupation, a trait that was especially closely tied to a man's identity in the days when the artisan tradition was still powerful. Early baseball clubs in the New York City area, for example, included those made up of policemen, barkeepers, milkmen, schoolteachers, and physicians. As the game spread, so too did this custom, with Philadelphia boasting a club of clergymen, Chicago having one made up of the employees of the McCormick Harvester works, and Brooklyn possessing one that was informally known as "oul man Rogers and Sam Storer's fish chowder nine."

Many of these clubs took names that honored the professions of their members. One of the most successful was the Eckford Club of Brooklyn, named in tribute to the pioneer shipbuilder Henry Eckford because it consisted mostly of "young shipbuilders who were employed on the New York dry docks and in Williamsburgh and Greenpoint."

Clubs of firemen were especially prominent, since the grave threat that fire posed to the era's cities made fire companies potent symbols of civic pride. Baseball clubs wisely aligned themselves to these brave and civic-minded men. When baseball first caught on in Fort Wayne, "a tournament of baseball teams and firemen drew a large crowd to the city." Early baseball uniforms often featured bibs modeled on the ones worn by firefighters, representing that for many youngsters "the base

The Atlantics of Brooklyn were one of the dominant clubs of the pioneer era and were recognized as national champions in 1859, 1860, 1861, 1864, and 1865. They had a fiercely loyal following in Brooklyn since, as the *Brooklyn Eagle* explained, "One chief reason, why the people of Brooklyn have been so much interested in the Atlantics is that it was purely a local nine, its members all residing in Brooklyn." But the Atlantics, like so many other clubs, had a difficult transition to the professional era. One of their stars, Pete O'Brien, wrote wistfully in 1868, "they don't play ball nowadays as they used to." [Library of Congress, Baseball and Jackie Robinson Collection]

ball and fire engine were . . . the symbols of the highest earthly happiness."

While common traits brought men together, it was common feeling that made them so attached to their clubs. Concepts like brotherhood, camaraderie, and friendship are difficult to express in words without sounding mawkish, but this doesn't make the emotions they evoke any less profound.

The retirement of one well-respected player, for example, was reported as follows: "That esteemed member of the Atlantic

Club, [Peter] O'Brien, has voluntarily resigned from active service as a playing member of the club. . . . The career of Mr. O'Brien as a ball-player has been one that should be held up as an example to the juniors of the fraternity to follow. As a manly, conscientious player, one incapable of taking an unfair advantage, or of committing a single action on a ball-field in a match not consistent with the most honorable and fair play . . . his reward is a popularity in the fraternity such as any man ought to be proud of. No man who plays ball commands more of the general respect and regard of the members of the metropolitan clubs, and, in fact, of all others who have known him, than this now retired and honored veteran."

Such an effusion of sentiment cannot help but make some of us a bit uncomfortable and perhaps even suspicious of its authenticity. Even though the respect for O'Brien was unquestionably genuine, we are all too aware that such praise may be mere "lip service." Few of us spend much time making speeches about our loved ones—at least while they're alive—and while nineteenth-century Americans were more prone to paying such tributes, they too understood that they were not always sincere.

As a result, the spirit of camaraderie that unified ball clubs was usually conveyed in less direct ways. One of these was the frequent references to the "base ball fraternity," but this too carries the possibility of being mere sanctimony. Two more reliable gauges of the strength of these bonds were the pride that club members took in symbols of mutual respect and the pleasure they derived from shared activities.

A ball club's uniform was one of its most identifiable symbols. During the 1850s and 1860s uniforms were still simple affairs. Monogramming was too expensive for most clubs, so uniform tops typically identified the club only by a single letter or not at all. Instead most players wore accessories that bore the insignia or name of their club. Belts and armbands were the most common, but badges were also popular enough that the New

The Athletics of Philadelphia (top) and the Atlantics of Brooklyn (bottom) showed off their spiffy uniforms in 1866. The bibs on both clubs' uniform tops were modeled on the ones worn by firefighters; for youngsters of that generation, "the base ball and fire engine were . . . the symbols of the highest earthly happiness." [Collection of Tom Shieber]

York Badge Company advertised their availability in one of the sporting presses.

But the relatively spartan appearance of early uniforms by no stretch of the imagination prevented them from being potent symbols. Clubs took great pride in the attractiveness, cleanliness, and design of their uniforms. Frank L. Smith summed this up nicely in describing the first game played by the Bower City Club of Janesville, Wisconsin (a club that, appropriately enough, took its name from the nickname associated with its hometown). "You should have seen the Bower city nine when they made their appearance on the field," recalled Smith fondly, "attired in black trousers, white dress shirts, cuffs and collars, black necktie, glossy black tarpaulin hats (generally worn at that time in rainy weather and warranted to draw the sun's rays or no sale) and boots shined to order. What a pity there were no kodaks in those days!" It was small wonder that sportswriter Henry Chadwick recognized that "one of the last things a club should find occasion to do is to change the colors or form of its uniform." Some clubs even took pride in wearing their uniforms off the ball field, such as a club in Burlington, Wisconsin, that strutted around town in their uniforms for several days after a big win.

The other prominent symbol of identity for early ball clubs was their clubhouse or club room. While the furnishings might be luxurious or simple, depending on the club's means, however humble they were also the subjects of great pride.

Symbolic of the ability of a club's reach to far exceed its success on the ball field, the rooms of the Eckford Club of Brooklyn remained a prominent gathering place more than two decades after the club faded from the baseball scene. An 1896 description of the "cozy" rooms, located at 98 Broadway, highlighted "a large steel engraving of what was known as the Eckford base ball nine in the year 1858. In these days, the club contained many champion base ball players, and the luster of its early devotees seems to hang over them. The picture has been hung in the hallway on the first floor, where its position at once attracts the attention of visitors."

Also featured were the 168 baseballs that the club had won in match play between 1854 and 1868: "These have been built pyramid-like in a glass case in the parlor. It is customary for a stranger to the club to have them shown and their value explained to him, and while a pleasant hour is thus spent a good deal of knowledge in regard to the past history of the club is obtained in a very interesting form. At the close of every game which the club won the ball used was gilded. The names of both competing nines, the scores, and the date of the playing of the game has been painted on each ball. The leading trophy in the stand is a silver ball won by the Eckford club from the Atlantic club, September 18, 1862, and it denotes the winners of the championship for that year. The members believe that there are few collections of the kind in the country to compare with it.

None of the other old base ball clubs seem to have preserved trophies of the kind."

While the Eckford Club's great rivals, the Atlantics of Brooklyn, did not maintain a permanent club room, the club showed a similar attachment to the trophies won during its glory days. In 1905 early member Jack Chapman expressed great concern about the disposition of the trophy case that held the many baseballs won by the Atlantics. Chapman believed the case ought to go to the Brooklyn Institute or some such place where the public could see it. Apparently he got his wish at least in part, as the Spalding Collection of the New York Public Library includes a photograph of the trophy case.

Nor were such headquarters restricted to clubs that were prominent on the national scene. An early St. Louis club used a hall that "was neatly furnished and adorned with flags and pictures as well as trophies won by the club or some of its players." Chicago's leading club of the late 1860s filled its club rooms with trophies and other hard-won mementos.

And in Washington a local player attempted to provide such a base of operations for all the city's ball clubs. He purchased a cigar store in 1866 and unveiled plans to make it "the headquarters for the ball fraternity of this city. Next season he will keep a bulletin of the latest ball news. He will also keep a register of all base-ball clubs of the city, address of secretaries, etc., besides all the implements pertaining to the game. The remarkable success of the national game in this city makes such an establishment necessary."

Uniforms and clubhouses were early clubs' most prominent symbols of their identity, but they were far from the only ones. Many clubs had team songs they sang as they walked to the ballpark. At the close of the breakthrough season of 1854, the Knickerbocker, Gotham, and Eagle clubs held a celebratory dinner at Fijux's restaurant during which they all joined in a song called "Ball Days." This song was subsequently printed, as was the sheet music for a piece called "The Base

Ball Polka" which had been composed by a member of a Buffalo club.

Yet another symbol that a ball club's scope was far greater than those of the nine men who represented it in match play was the fact that most of them included second nines, third nines, and even "muffin" nines, so named because the players generally muffed the ball. Many further extended the sense of community or family by fielding junior nines (typically made up of players eighteen and under) or by affiliating themselves with a junior club.

In addition to these potent symbols of belonging to something much larger than a baseball team, the members of early ball clubs also increased their sense of camaraderie by participating in many outside activities. Most of these, naturally, occurred during the winter months.

Many clubs sponsored balls during the off-season, sometimes to raise much-needed funds but often just for the enjoyment of renewing friendships. The Empire Club of St. Louis held a ball after the 1865 season to commemorate its sixth anniversary; it "proved a success in every respect and thereafter for several years the Empire balls were recognized as one of the social functions of prominence." The Atlantic Club of Brooklyn also sponsored an annual off-season ball, to which all the local baseball clubs were invited.

Other clubs chose different types of socializing during the winter months. The Kekionga Club of Fort Wayne, for example, "continued as a debating and singing society." Some even tried to keep playing baseball, arranging matches on ice that were usually long on merriment and short on skillful play. And it is safe to assume that countless other early ball clubs sponsored less formal get-togethers during the winter.

Clubs were also bound together by membership rules and organizational meetings. At first glance the formality of these proceedings seems to belie the supposition that fun was uppermost. New members, for example, were sent formal notifications of their nomination and election.

Yet a contrary interpretation seems more plausible: that the members were so intent on having fun that rules were necessary just to get anything accomplished. This seems to be implied by this description of the activities of an early club in Grand Rapids, Michigan: "The meetings were occasionally noisy, but good order was general, for stringent rules were adopted."

Even though members had to rein themselves in at such meetings, it seems a safe assumption that these clubs spent great deals of time in good-natured fellowship. The examples of socializing cited here undoubtedly constitute just the tip of the iceberg, since it is in the nature of such activities that they are not recorded for posterity. Yet their importance is considerable, as they provided a link to the loose, unstructured bat-and-ball games of yore while also increasing the sheer pleasure of belonging to a baseball club.

Because the baseball club of this era was so much more than the nine men who represented it in baseball matches, many of these clubs put very little stock in winning or losing. To be sure, this spirit was not an absolute. As noted in the preceding chapter, clubs unquestionably cared about the outcome of the matches they played, but they kept their concern so strictly in context that a defeat seemed little more than a momentary annoyance. This spirit was neatly summarized by the early ballplayer who later recalled that his club "played ball merely to work off the effects of rich dinners the night before. We were the Seventh Regiment, I might say, of the base ball fraternity. We simply traveled on our shape, not the shape of the wee hours of the morn."

This attitude was especially well exemplified by a Brooklyn club aptly known as the Pastimes. The Pastimes played a dozen or so match games in 1859 and 1860 with decidedly mediocre results, then disbanded for good when the Civil War began. They

produced no great players, had no signal victories, and were responsible for no known innovations. Their legacy was that, as
one member recalled, "we had a good time while the organization was going."

In later years no one saw fit to chronicle the results of the
match games played by the Pastimes. Instead there are reminiscences about the club's "base ball suppers," which became
known as the "social events of the season." When a match was
recalled, it was not the game itself that mattered. "The old Pastime Club used to do things up in style," observed a typical one.
"Money was of no account where the reputations of the Club
was concerned. On one occasion they went to Hoboken to play
the Eagles. Now the latter were in the habit of seeing their opponents come on their field by parties, two or three dropping in
early, while two or three would invariably be a little late. The
Eagles were on their field practicing on the occasion in question, waiting for the Pastimes to turn up, when what should
they see coming up the roadway from the westward but a line of
carriages. Sam Yates thought it was a small funeral procession
which had lost their way; but it turned out to be the high toned
Pastimes, all in carriages. There were Frank Quevedo, Bill
Barre and the regular Pastime crowd. It turned out to be a funeral procession after all, as the Eagles whipped the carriage
customers badly."

The Pastimes were a club that played baseball among their
other activities, not a club that existed to play baseball. For a
couple of years in the late 1850s "the furor for base ball" made
that sport the focus of the club's activities, but at other times
cricket and harness racing were the recreations of choice.
What game club members were playing doesn't seem to have
mattered; what they cared about was "healthy, enjoyable exercise" and the resulting "natural, happy feeling among kindred spirits."

And they did have great times together, whether they were
getting their exercise from baseball, cricket, or harness racing

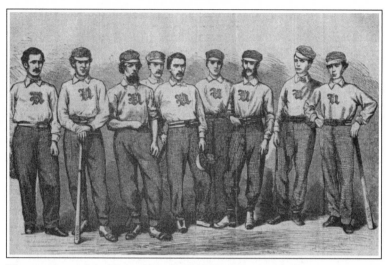

The members of the Union Base Ball Club of Morrisania posed for this picture after being crowned champions of the 1867 campaign. Like all of the era's clubs, the U on their natty uniform tops was a conspicuous symbol of team pride. Notice that the Unions even displayed the team name on their bats. [Collection of Tom Shieber]

or just enjoying the company of close friends. As explained earlier, "It was for just such enjoyment on the ball field that the old Pastime Club of 1858 was organized." Another member summed the club up with an apt rhetorical question: "But didn't we have fun though on our practice days?"

In one respect the Pastimes are an anomaly. That we know anything about them is the result of several historical accidents. The club's members were prominent in civic affairs at the time—one member recalled that they were often referred to as "the City Hall Club"—and most of them went on to still greater renown in Brooklyn social and political life. In addition they were on very friendly terms with sportswriter Henry Chadwick, who wrote many of the later articles about their activities for the *Eagle*. And the fact that the *Eagle* is now available online in an easily searchable format has made it possible to retrieve these reminiscences.

Yet in all likelihood the only thing that makes the Pastimes atypical is the fact that descriptions of their activities happen to survive. There is every reason to assume that many other clubs likewise played for fun and good-natured exercise without seeing any reason to leave a record of their activities. One likely candidate, for example, is the Eckford Club of Brooklyn, which, as alluded to earlier, reorganized as a social club at the end of the 1865 season and scarcely missed a beat as "the base ball section of the club dropped away." We have little record of this club's subsequent doings, but little should be read into that fact. It is important to bear in mind that it was the Knicker-bockers' practice of carefully recording and preserving accounts of their doings that was unusual.

Some early baseball clubs consisted of little more than the nine men on their first nine, and the commonness of such clubs increased throughout the 1860s, as did their seriousness of purpose. But more representative were the many clubs that "played ball merely to work off the effects of rich dinners the night before." For such clubs, wins and losses on the baseball diamond paled in importance to the pleasure of being part of a community.

CHAPTER 8

Intercity Competition and Civic Pride

❖ The great pride that early ballplayers felt in their clubs, and their spirit of mutual respect, most prominently manifested themselves at the showdowns that became the focus of baseball enthusiasm for many years. These were the spirited rivalries between neighboring cities in which the competitors' allegiance to their clubs was seamlessly translated into civic pride. Today this loyalty remains a basic feature of professional baseball despite the many changes that have occurred in the game.

Before the Civil War, intercity baseball competition remained uncommon because of the primitive modes of transportation then available. When such matches did occur, the visiting club was almost always an ambassador from a region where baseball was well established. The club had left home to provide instruction to less experienced clubs.

The gentlemanly Excelsior Club of Brooklyn became best known for acting as ambassadors. In 1860 the club embarked on a twelve-day, one-thousand-mile tour of the state that saw them play matches in Albany, Troy, Buffalo, Rochester, and Newburgh-on-the-Hudson. No one expected the games to be competitive, and they weren't; the purpose of the excursion was to give pointers to the upstate clubs and allow spectators outside the New York City area to see baseball played with a new degree of skill and finesse. One account noted: "no such ball playing was ever before witnessed in Buffalo. The manner in which the Excelsiors handled the ball, the ease with which they caught it, under all circumstances, the precision with which they threw it to the bases, and the tremendous hits they gave into the long field made the optics of the Buffalo players glisten with admiration and protrude."

Later that summer the Excelsiors accepted an invitation from a namesake club in Baltimore to travel to Maryland for a game. The emphasis was again on ceremony rather than competition: "It was not thought that the Baltimore Club had the least show to win, it was to be a game of instructions."

Naturally on such occasions the visitors were treated as honored guests and were showered with hospitalities by their hosts. Even so, the expenses of traveling were considerable and would have been beyond the means of most ball clubs. We do not know whether the Excelsiors' players paid for the trip themselves or whether the costs were borne by some of the club's generous "honorary members." Either way, some members of the Excelsiors were considerably out of pocket as a result of the club's assuming the role of ambassadors for baseball. The significant time the ballplayers spent on their tours and away from their jobs was another factor that kept such tours from becoming common.

The Athletics of Philadelphia, for instance, played a similar role for several years and earned praise for having "done more to advance the popularity of the game, by visits to towns and villages where base ball was previously unknown, than almost any other Club in the United States." But after the 1866 season the club was warned by a local paper about the "evil" of "gadding around the country, in answer to everybody's beck and call. This is well enough in its way—say one excursion during the season—but making these excursions is ofttimes a sacrifice, as [Athletics players Nate] Berkenstock and Dan Kleinfelder can testify."

New railroad lines continued to be built during the Civil War, making intercity competition affordable and convenient, even for workingmen. It suddenly became feasible to take a day

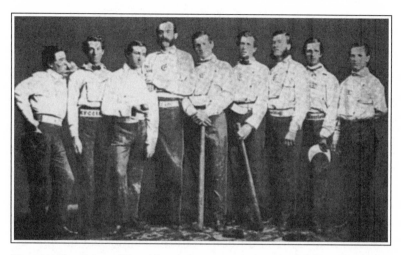

The 1860 Excelsiors of Brooklyn, left to right, Tommy Reynolds, John Whiting, Jim Creighton, Harry Polhemus, Aleck Pearsall, Ed Russell, Joe Leggett, Asa Brainard, and George Flanley. The Excelsiors were gentlemanly ambassadors for the new game of baseball, going on an unprecedented twelve-day, one-thousand-mile tour of New York State in 1860 to show how the new game was played. But they also played a major role in introducing professionalism by inducing Creighton—the game's first superstar—to desert his original club. [Courtesy of Mark Rucker]

trip to a neighboring city for so frivolous a pursuit as a game of baseball. Several clubs took advantage, and these sojourns resulted in buoyant accounts that nicely captured the sense of luxury and indulgence.

"Off we started," wrote a Princeton ballplayer of his club's seventeen-mile trip to New Brunswick. "Though the sky was overcast, it was our expectation that in a short time the sun of victory would arise and witness a triumph over the Stars. What a gay old time we passed on the route! Songs, shouts, visions of a jolly day, a glorious return, etc., filled up the time. Soon the old locomotive stopped, and the train was relieved of the impatient ball-players."

A similar note of exultation infused a description of an excursion taken by a Michigan club: "On Tuesday last, the

Kalamazoo National Ball Club paid a visit to the pretty little village of Dowagiac to meet a club of the latter place in a friendly match for superiority, according to arrangements previously made by Capt. Brown of Kalamazoo, and Capt. Palmer of Dowagiac. Besides the Kalamazoo nine, some thirty other of our citizens went along to see the sport and to participate [sic] the fate of our boys whether 'twere victory or defeat. The train that bore them was the 12:12 lightning express, and after a delightful and exhilarating trip through verdant valleys, o'er the flowered plains, by still waters, lovely meadows, and through the green palisade of forest trees, forty miles of summer scenery were left behind us, and we had reached our destination. Here we were met by a deputation from the Dowagiac Club and escorted to the hotel, where we soon found a host of friends and a kind reception."

After the Civil War the segments of railway line that had joined neighboring towns began to coalesce into a national network. This prompted the National Club of Washington in 1867 to do the previously unthinkable by becoming the first Eastern team to venture west of the Alleghenies. During their three-thousand-mile journey, the Nationals made stops in Columbus, Cincinnati, Louisville, Indianapolis, St. Louis, and Chicago.

Their tour stirred up excitement about baseball west of the Alleghenies in much the way the Excelsiors had done in the then-isolated regions they had visited. In St. Louis, for example, there was "joy when it became known that the National Club of Washington would include St. Louis in a tour to the West. . . . The Nationals' reputation and the fact of it being the first of the great clubs of the East to 'Westward Ho!' created great interest among the steadily increasing admirers of the game and when the gates of the new park were opened to the public on July 22 at fifty cents a head, there was no kick coming from the thousands who flocked there to see the Union boys throw themselves against the famed Nationals."

The players on the Nationals similarly viewed themselves as ambassadors. Four decades later Harry C. McLean, who by then had risen to the distinguished position of deputy health officer for the District of Columbia, recalled: "It was a trip that proved of incalculable value to the youth of the great agricultural districts of the west and south. A dearth of healthy means of recreation had led as a natural sequence to the adoption of sport neither physically nor morally elevating. After the labors of the day it was customary for the young farmers and mechanics to seek recreation and imagined pleasure at the village tavern, where cards and other games of chance were played; then waiting and wasting for the excitement of the race track, and between times seeking relief from the tedium of their daily occupations, which the dissipations of a city life offer. . . . Youths with vicious tendencies were transformed into beings with manly characters. . . . We entered every contest with kindly feeling, gentlemanly conduct and skilful in every position on the field, no fault-finding for accidental errors, no murdering of umpires, no attributing motives to victorious opponents, no boasting exultation when triumphant; only happy, exultantly happy, giving vent thereto singing this our anthem to the tune of 'Benny Havens, Oh.'" McLean then recited the words of the lengthy song, which climaxed with the chorus: "We're going westward ho, we're going westward ho/ Success to all who toss the ball, we're going westward ho."

The Nationals' historic tour was a great boon to the spread of enthusiasm for the game, though the results were probably not as life-altering for the hosts as McLean's recollections suggest. And such a tour was not one that most clubs could imitate.

The considerable expenses of the Nationals' tour were made possible by generous sponsors and, as we shall see, by the indulgence of the Treasury Department. What's more, getting from one city to the next in a timely manner was still very difficult. One contemporary later recalled that a history of clubs like the

Nationals "would fill volumes if the mishaps, accidents and various plans made and successfully carried through to make connections in order to keep engagements were recorded. There were no prearranged schedules, every team had its own private arrangements and went ahead and made dates without taking into consideration any other team, hence 'jolts' sometimes took place that at the last minute had to be changed, trips revised and schemes worked out to reach the points where the next games were dated. The pioneer trip of the Nationals in 1867, which was arranged by Mr. 'Jimmy' Patterson, was carried through admirably, because the advent of the Nationals into the west was a novelty and a day's delay made no great difference. Still the players had trouble on the western roads that if experienced today would send the modern gladiator over to the home on the hill beyond Anacostia."

As this account makes clear, besides all the inconveniences of traveling there was enough uncertainty that it was difficult if not impossible to stick to a schedule. The chronicler went on to describe how this affected a tour he went on with another Washington club: "I was one of the hardy patriots that went along on the trip of the Olympics in 1869, the longest of its kind up to that time, as the club visited more cities and played more games than did the famous Red Stockings, who had previously made a tour the same year and defeated every team they met.

"We had trouble everywhere, even in such small jumps as from Cincinnati to Mansfield, Ohio, nothing went properly but our worst time came when turning our faces eastward for the return trip, we ran up against a snag of huge dimensions at Cincinnati.

"On that trip the Olympics played the Red Stockings four games. In the last one they defeated us 10 to 7, the game being delayed by a rain storm. Our boys were anxious to play it out, as they imagined they had a chance of defeating the unbeatables. Well, the game was played out, but the train we were expected to take for Philadelphia was at that time many miles to the east, and there was no other train out that night for us to take in order to reach Philadelphia in time for our next game. But right here came the 'do or die' spirit of the Olympic management, Secretaries N. E. Young and Fred Schmidt in particular.

"A freight was due to leave Cincinnati at 1 A.M. and after many consultations with the agent of the railway company it was decided to add a 'box car' for the players. Say, you haven't any idea what a box car of those days was, nor can you imagine what a trip of 700 miles meant over a rough mountain road, for such was the Baltimore & Ohio in those days. It was the days before the use of air brakes, but rough as the ride, and tedious as the trip proved to be, the band never wailed, the only desire being to reach Philadelphia in time to keep their word with the Keystones of that place.

"They arrived in Philadelphia one hour ahead of the time set for the game, but every one of the players took a portion of that hour for a bath in the waters of the Schuylkill river. But they presented a sorry sight when they appeared on the field to play the Keystones, then the best team in the city of Philadelphia. Though fatigued, they played a wonderful game against their opponents, that is for that period of ball playing.

"Now I wonder how many of our up-to-date high salaried players have undergone all of the discomforts of such a long trip on hot August nights, just to keep engagements for the honor of the club and nothing else. How many?"

As these examples vividly illustrate, lengthy tours had become possible but by no means convenient. Trains brought tremendous potential to get places faster than ever before, yet there remained a lot of unpredictability. There was no assurance that clubs would arrive or leave when expected (especially since standard time zones were still in the future), or that they would reach their destination at all. Naturally, undependable methods of transportation also wrought havoc with arrangements for lodgings.

These realities had some important consequences. For one thing, they meant that traveling ball clubs continued to be treated like visiting dignitaries. The Excelsiors of Brooklyn resumed their tours after the Civil War, and on a visit to Washington in 1866 "a large delegation received them at the depot, and took them in carriages and stages to Willard's Hotel . . . where choice rooms were provided for them. After breakfast, the entire party entered carriages and were taken by their guests to the Little Falls of the Potomac, and thence in the packet Minnesota to the Great Falls, where they were sumptuously feasted at the Pavilion Hotel."

The next day the players "were conveyed in carriages to the steamer Wawset for an excursion to Mount Vernon, the Lower Potomac, Indian Head, and Fort Washington. A select and fashionable assemblage of ladies accompanied them; also the Marine Band, led by Prof. Scala; a dirge was played by the band at the tomb of Washington, and at Fort Washington the commandant received them with military honors. Early in the evening they returned, and next they proceeded to Stagg's fine rooms, which were inaugurated on this occasion, and an elegant entertainment was provided for them."

The custom of making such trips and treating them as momentous occasions also spread to new regions. In 1865 the Empire Club of St. Louis, "having successfully demonstrated that it was cock of the home walk became seized with a desire to spread its wings and let the outside world know how good a game it could put up, and in looking around for 'foemen worthy of their steel' the club managers came into correspondence with the Empire Club of Freeport, Ill., which eventuated in a match being made for the approaching Fourth of July at Freeport. As this was an event of no ordinary magnitude, the club went into extra training, more particularly as the opposing club sustained a fine reputation and on July 2, the selected players to the number of twelve accompanied by about an equal number of nonplaying members started on their journey of conquest."

After a journey marred by "a mis-connection of trains" and four players becoming ill from the water they drank on the railroad, the travelers arrived safely in Freeport and were welcomed with a lavish reception. With the game scheduled for the next day, however, the players could not fully enjoy the banquet prepared for them: "it was soon apparent that wine would flow pretty freely and at sight of the first bottle, [club captain Jeremiah] Fruin passed an order that no player should partake of it, promising that after the game they could have all they wanted. This order was obeyed strictly, not a man wishing to hazard his share of the honors and glory of playing in this the first fly ball match west of the Alleghenies, for such this proved to be."

While long-distance travel remained fraught with hazards, competition between neighboring towns became progressively more feasible. If a train didn't arrive at a convenient time, there were other options. A member of the first club in Binghamton, New York, went through quite an ordeal to get to a game in Sherburne: "I missed the train . . . but got another going that way, then got a horse and rode twenty-six miles across country. It cost me $6, but we won and the team paid the bill for me." A ballplayer from Stoneham, Massachusetts, recollected that after defeating a rival from nearby Marlboro, "there was no barge to be found to carry the victors to South Framingham; nothing daunted, the walk of twelve miles was covered and enjoyed, as the game had been won."

As trips became shorter, hospitality suffered a corresponding decline. A contemporary explained: "A dinner after the game, usually contributed by the friends of the home nine, was for a number of years conventional, and salved many wounds of temper in the actual play. This hospitality was possible when the matches of a season were few, but as games multiplied it was dropped on the ground of expense. Now and then the country teams played for a dinner as the stake of a match."

As a result, an early player from Kalamazoo recalled: "When we went to an outside town to play we paid our own expenses.

There was no admission fee charged. I remember the first game we played with Jackson. We played for the supper and we also paid for the supper. But it was a good one, I tell you. They had to play hard to win and they deserved a good meal."

Having to pay the expense of a trip and then foot the bill for supper was no small imposition. But as this account suggests, for most young men it seemed a small price to pay for the thrill of matching skills with the best players from a neighboring town. So in the years immediately following the Civil War "a frenzy for the game swept the land. Each little village and hamlet boasted its nine, and in the larger towns of the eastern states the clubs were enumerated by the score." One reporter marveled in 1866 that "The whole country seems lately to have become a vast ball-jungle."

Contests for local bragging rights generated considerable enthusiasm, but it was matches between the representatives of neighboring towns that best embodied this outbreak of "base ball fever." These rivalries seemed to embody a country pluckily bouncing back from a long, dispiriting civil war. Both the arduous treks to get to the matches and the setting aside of valuable land for such a purpose were powerful symbols of the nation's conquest of its vast and intimidating natural surroundings. And the pitched but friendly rivalries on the baseball diamond conveyed (Northern) optimism that the country was on the road toward being unified once more.

A member of a club in Stoughton, Massachusetts, gave a typical account: "We had got friendly with the Tri Mountains [of Boston] through Halsey Boardman, who was their president. . . . Well, we had beaten them once and they had one on us, and we were the two best teams in the state. We had played them once on the Boston Common, but this deciding game was to be played in Medford.

"Well, a few days before the deciding game they got a pitcher, Del Linfield, away from us and we asked for a little more time so as to get a pitcher ready for the game, but they answered and said the game was scheduled for a certain day and they should expect us there on time. We were there all right, but it was raining some and then for some reason they wanted us to wait and said that the grounds would be all wet, but Dick See-ley had been to sea some and he said that we would play if we had to get a boat or swim for the ball.

"They wouldn't postpone for us, and we wouldn't postpone for them, so we went ahead. Linfield was the best pitcher in the league, but besides him they had a professional player named O'Brien, from New York, who was supposed to be a wonder. Well, we went in and batted O'Brien out of the box and then they put in Linfield and we batted him just as bad as we did O'Brien. We had taken Capen Brown, the pitcher on our second team and he proved to be a star and they couldn't do a thing with him. We won the game, but did not get the silver ball. I don't know just why it was, but we were the champions just the same."

The camaraderie created by the game could make even the grueling trips to play such matches seem enjoyable. "The day was wet and disagreeable," when a Fort Dodge, Iowa, nine set out in 1866 to travel thirty miles by horse-drawn coach for a match in Boone, but "the boys managed to drive dull care away with songs, stories, anecdotes, sells, and yarns, reminding us more of a gay wedding excursion than a matched nine who were to contend for the championship of North Western Iowa. . . . [We arrived] in Boonsboro about dark; singing as we passed through to Boone, every thing known to vocalists, from 'One Hundred' to 'Babble, babble, little brook.' The inhabitants stared at us; children looked amazed; dogs barked."

The success of these matches between neighboring towns led to the staging of tournaments that were open to all the base-ball clubs in a region or state. One of the first was held at the 1865 Michigan State Fair, and such events came to be regular features of state fairs and agricultural fairs. At their best, tour-naments extended the sense of ceremony associated with matches to a broader community.

At one in Fenton, Michigan, for instance, observers recalled that the town buzzed with excitement. Each night the halls and streets overflowed with baseball enthusiasts, culminating with a ball for the players and spectators that featured three fiddlers and a caller and lasted into the wee hours. At the tournament in Rockford, Illinois, that would become best known for the performance of the Pecatonicas, the participants were described thus: "ten noble bands of young men that would do honor to any letter [?] represent the best blood of their respective cities; the very essence of athletic manhood." Yet far too often tournaments were plagued by problems—no-shows, ill-suited formats, competitive imbalances, inclement weather, time constraints, and the like—that undercut the sense of ceremony.

The postwar years also brought signs that matches between neighboring cities were succumbing to similar influences. More and more of them were followed by disputes over rules or umpiring, the eligibility of players, the hospitality offered by the home club, and assorted issues. Even when civility was preserved during the match and the visit, the newspapers of the respective towns often sniped at each other afterward. A significant number of ballplayers who had enjoyed such matches when they were played in a spirit of mutual respect became disenchanted by such petty bickering and gave up the game.

While these were ominous signs, in the years immediately after the war such portents seemed isolated in nature. Most clubs still tried to adhere to the spirit of sportsmanship, even if they sometimes questioned the sincerity of their adversaries. And most losers continued to be sustained by the "patience of hope," believing that practice would enable them to win next time. As a result, matches between neighboring towns remained major events in a community's calendar. Just as important, they were still plenty of fun.

The intense interest that surrounded a big match could bring out the worst in the players, but it also led to moments of hilarity that were recounted for years afterward. A match between Brooklyn archrivals the Atlantics and the Eckfords featured an event that still amused one eyewitness almost four decades later. In addition to his uniform, Eckford pitcher Frank Pidgeon "had on a sweater and an undershirt. At the end of the third inning he removed the sweater. The Atlantics were getting on to his delivery and he tore off the sleeve of his pitching arm. Trying to put an extra twist on the ball he ripped the undershirt up the back. When the game ended Pigeon [sic] had only the wrist band of one sleeve left. Notwithstanding this sacrifice of dry goods the Atlantics won the day."

In another match, early player Matty O'Brien was acting as umpire "when a point of play occurred on the putting out of a base runner at home base. Matty watched the play closely, and as the runner was touched he turned round to the place where the umpire should have been and called out 'Judgment?'"—the cry that players used to request a ruling from the umpire. This naturally brought the house down and became a much-recounted tale since O'Brien had forgotten that he himself was the umpire.

And of course the fever pitch of competition could also produce moments of glory for a player and a town. An early Kalamazoo player recalled a match in which his hometown trailed rival Grand Rapids by three runs in the ninth inning but managed to load the bases. The drama even got to Judge Ezra White, who played for the Kalamazoo nine: "Then there was some excitement. Judge White was almost wild. He got up on the bench and swung his arms and yelled at the top of his voice, 'I will give $50 for my next strike.' The judge was one of the surest hitters we had, but it was Jim [sic] McCord's turn at bat and John was another sure hitter and he stepped up to bat and the first ball that came through he hit it an awful whack and broke his bat square in two, but the ball went way out beyond the fielder and John brought in the three men and made a home run himself. Maybe we didn't go wild at that time.'"

The intense emotions produced by these matches between neighboring towns had the important effect of translating the pride of belonging to a club into civic pride. A town's ball club came not only to represent it on the ball field but to embody the hopes and dreams of the entire community.

While civic pride remains an important concept to this day, it no longer carries the sense of urgency that it did in the mid-nineteenth century. The survival of cities during these years was by no means guaranteed, and the attachment citizens felt for their hometown could play a significant role in its fortunes. Cities could be devastated or destroyed by fires, epidemics, or natural disasters, so the most conspicuous form of civic pride lay in precautions such as insurance and fire engines. A great many early clubs underscored this by choosing names that reflected one or both of these collective bodies (for example, Mutual, Aetna, Liberty).

Just as important to whether a city flourished or withered was its ability to convince outsiders—and locals—that it was a great place to live. Conveying this message was the foremost priority of local newspapers, especially in small towns. Today's concept of journalistic detachment simply didn't apply to the creators of these newspapers, which instead saw themselves as performing the crucial task of putting their hometown's best foot forward. (Many newspapers took active roles in forming baseball clubs to represent the town. The *Ionia* (Michigan) *Sentinel*, for example, announced plans to start a ball club in its inaugural issue in 1867, and news of the club was featured prominently in later issues.)

Moreover neighboring cities were often direct competitors, particularly when it came to laying railroad lines. The choice of where to situate a new line could—literally—put one town on the map and wipe another off it. Small wonder, then, that newspapers were regularly boosting their hometown and often taking subtle jabs at neighboring towns. Competition between baseball clubs could make this rivalry overt, since the large number of visitors on hand made it a golden opportunity to show off a town's charms.

It soon became clear that a proficient baseball club could, by its skill alone, help put its hometown on the map. Frank L. Smith neatly captured this reality in his account of baseball in Janesville, Wisconsin: "in the late fall of 1870, a ball club at Elkhorn had the temerity to challenge the conquerors of all Wisconsin [the Mutuals of Janesville]. Elkhorn, a town that had been scarcely heard of at that time, being known only as a place where Whitewater did its 'courting,' and where cases were sometimes taken from other courts on a change of venue, it appears to me that the ball club had quite a start on the Walworth county fair in making that town famous. Anyway, after locating the place on the map we drove across the country and were effectually done up to the tune of 36 to 21."

This appeal to civic pride was a potent force for ball clubs, but it also created a troubling problem. In 1868 the *Brooklyn Eagle* explained that "One chief reason, why the people of Brooklyn have been so much interested in the Atlantics is that it was purely a local nine, its members all residing in Brooklyn." By then, however, this state of affairs was not one that could be taken for granted, as an increasing number of clubs were "importing" ballplayers from other towns. The *Eagle*'s article, for instance, came in response to the Atlantics' loss to a rival, the Mutuals of New York City—yet, as the Brooklyn journal proudly pointed out, the "sting of the defeat of the boys, has been mitigated in the fact" that the club that beat them comprised three residents apiece from New York City, New Jersey, and Brooklyn.

Clubs in the New York City area were, as usual, well ahead of the rest of the country in their use of such imports. Clubs in other regions did suddenly add outsiders from time to time under circumstances which suggested that baseball considerations might have prompted the ballplayers to move. But the mobility of nineteenth-century Americans made this often a nice point—many American cities were so new or expanding so rapidly that everyone was more or less a recent arrival.

Thus in addition to pride in being the cradle of ballplayers, a city's residents could also feel proud of attracting a steady flow of new arrivals. This was a subtle enough distinction that clubs accused of using imports could maintain that they were "composed of only home talent; notwithstanding the ungenerous assertion of our wise neighbors to the contrary." While neighboring towns might protest, such a city was likely to be tolerant of newcomers as long as they acted like citizens rather than visitors.

Yet even locals remained mindful of the distinction between men who had come to town to pursue their careers and those who had been lured merely to play baseball. As we shall see, acceptance of recent arrivals was conditional—increasingly so as it became clear that many of these ballplayers had no intention of putting down roots. This wariness of the local citizenry was implied by an early ballplayer who later recalled: "What gave great interest to the games in those days was the fact that the players *lived* in the towns of the clubs to which they belonged."

As the role played by civic pride grew more prominent, clubs found many ways to stimulate and capitalize on it. Local businesses were invited to support the ball club and were repaid by good publicity in a variety of forms. City officials were given ceremonial roles to play, which gave spectators another reason to view the local club as a surrogate for the hopes and dreams of their community.

A perfect example occurred in St. Louis, where the secretary of one local club noticed that General William T. Sherman was a regular at local ball games. The secretary "caused the General's election as an honorary member of that club and received from the General a characteristic letter of thanks for the honor thus conferred." The election of Sherman paid additional dividends when the general's guests at these games included two other prominent residents, Colonel A. R. Easton and millionaire foundry owner Gerald B. Allen.

The attendance of such dignitaries deepened the sense that the ball club was an extension of the community, and Allen's attendance proved especially fortuitous. Before ever witnessing a match, Allen had taken a great dislike to baseball (presumably because it led to absenteeism among his employees). But after attending games with Sherman and Easton, Allen became "not only a convert but one of the most enthusiastic of all the regular attendants. From a railer at those connected with him by family or business ties, who were devotees of the game, he became such a warm supporter as to be one of the main advocates of the early closing movement for business houses on Saturday afternoons, a custom that has been upheld now for many years, thus affording employees in mercantile pursuits a half-holiday."

Obviously the implied endorsement of baseball by a man of distinction like Sherman could yield benefits both tangible and intangible. Clubs in other towns recognized the potential for such benefits and made similar efforts to encourage leading citizens to attend their games. Prominent local officials, clergymen, and business owners were inducted as honorary members and given special treatment in hopes of similarly promoting civic pride—and increased attendance.

Being thus rooted in the community enabled home games to become important civic events. And when a club went on a tour, they left as ambassadors who carried with them the good name and high hopes of the city they represented. A member of the first Fort Wayne club to go on a tour recalled: "We left Fort Wayne, full of enthusiasm for a series of contests with the teams of the east. It was a memorable trip. Everywhere they joshed us as small-town Hoosiers, and made fun of the name 'Kekionga' [the club's nickname], but we stood the jokes all right and carried off enough honors to make us feel good."

Civic pride was thus one of the foundations of the pioneer era of baseball. That this emotion still exerts so powerful an influence today, even though there is no longer even the pretense that a city is being represented by its native sons, gives us some idea of the hold it had during baseball's early days.

CHAPTER 9

The Civil War:
The End of an Era, Part One

❖ The end of baseball's pioneer era cannot be dated with great precision because it died not one death but thousands. Every time a player walked away from the game he once loved, this era of baseball died a small death, and whenever a club faded out of existence, the game was dealt another blow. More subtly, the pioneer era suffered each time a player or club turned toward commercialism or competitiveness and away from the spirit that had once ruled the game.

Pinpointing the end of this era is further complicated by the fact that replacements usually stepped in whenever players and clubs turned their backs on the game. One youngster later described the eagerness of his generation to follow in the footsteps of the "hero[es] of our boyhood days": "we youngsters used to hear with bated breath of the prowess of the Lakes and Minerals, two noted clubs made up of the leading men of our village and of some of the big boys of the school house." The result has been a phoenixlike characteristic to baseball enthusiasm (one that is still evident as fathers pass a love of the game on to their sons, and in the process often reignite their own enthusiasm). This cyclical tendency led to hopes that the initial spirit of baseball could be continued indefinitely, with each new generation reinvigorating and restoring the original spirit.

In turn this meant that the pioneer era of baseball was not brought to an end by any single event, nor did it die on a specific date. Rather it died a slow death during the 1860s as the steady accumulation of new developments made its demise increasingly inevitable.

As noted throughout this book, this decline was most readily apparent in a series of challenges to the core elements of the era's philosophical underpinnings. In Chapter Four we saw how the increased roles of the pitcher and the umpire threatened the presumption that sportsmanship would limit the need for rules. In Chapter Five we noted that the introduction of new equipment and new playing fields exposed other problems that the Knickerbockers could not have foreseen. We saw the importance of the game's rituals and customs in Chapter Six, but also remarked that some of them were succumbing to an increasing spirit of competitiveness. And in Chapters Seven and Eight we observed that the equally potent forces of club life and civic pride were similarly vulnerable.

While the triumph of new elements may seem inevitable in retrospect, that outcome was not conceded at the time. Even those who may have sensed that the old way of playing ball could not continue forever could scarcely have anticipated that an era that seemed so vibrant in 1867 would be all but over within three years. It thus took a series of significant events to draw the curtain on the pioneer era of baseball. The first of these was one that actually predated the boom years: the Civil War.

In many summaries of early baseball, the Civil War is assigned a large role in the spread of the game. The gist is usually that soldiers learned the Knickerbockers' version and brought it back home with them, spurring the great boom of 1866 and 1867. This is an appealing notion, and there is some limited anecdotal support for it. Yet as with so many of the oft-repeated generalizations about early baseball, this is at best a half-truth.

There are far more accounts of clubs that disbanded at the outset of the war and either never reorganized or were never the same again. Meanwhile many of the clubs involved in the base-ball-frenzied years of 1866 and 1867 were made up of younger players who had not seen combat duty. So this suggests an alternative version of events: that the war stopped the game's momentum, and that the postwar boom was stimulated by a younger generation in no way indebted to the war.

There is some truth in both perspectives. During the postwar boom years, baseball was being played in hundreds of communities; no single version of the spread of the game can apply to all of them. Even when the same pattern recurred, the sequence of events varied from one region to another. Having said that, the evidence seems clearly to indicate that the alternative version of events was a far more common pattern than the one that has been traditionally accepted.

One of the more notable examples of a player who was introduced to baseball by the Civil War was Al Pratt. Pratt enlisted in Pennsylvania's 193rd Infantry Regiment in 1864, and after a brief tour of duty reenlisted in the 61st Infantry Regiment, which gained renown as one of the state's most famous fighting units. Stationed near the pivotal city of Petersburg, Virginia, the 61st engaged in several skirmishes before participating in the final assault on Petersburg on April 2, 1865, and then pursuing Robert E. Lee's fleeing columns. Somehow during his war service, Pratt also learned the game of baseball.

The early star Jim "Deacon" White was another example. Growing up on a farm near Corning, New York, he was unfamiliar with the new way of playing the game until a returning soldier brought it back home with him. Pratt and White were teammates in the late 1860s and early 1870s, and White was later a teammate of A. G. Spalding—coincidences that probably had a lot to do with the notion that the Civil War spread the game. For Spalding, after a long career as player, club owner, and sporting goods magnate, wrote a book in 1911 that used a great deal of rhetoric and very few facts to attribute the game's spread to the war.

Had Spalding made a genuine attempt to examine the question, he would have found many counterexamples. In virtually every region of the country the onset of the war eradicated thriving clubs. Cincinnati's two prewar baseball clubs were just getting established when the war "absorbed every other interest during the summer, and the two Clubs disbanded, many—indeed, most of the players going into the army." The Daybreak Club of Jackson, Michigan, lost seventeen of its thirty-four members to enlistment. Fort Wayne's first club abruptly disbanded when many of its members "enlisted in their country's cause, and some died on the Southern fields of carnage." In Philadelphia, "In the spring of 1861, just as preparation was being made for an active season, the war drew most of the Equity Club to a different field, and, as a natural consequence, the organization of the club was for the time suspended."

The only place where baseball activity carried on to any significant extent was New York City, which boasted such an abundance of clubs that many of them were able to consolidate or recruit new members to replace enlistees. But even New York City was far from untouched. Many clubs disbanded for good, and the number of match games dropped notably. Before a game in Brooklyn in 1862, three cheers were offered for the many local ballplayers who were off fighting in the South.

More typical was St. Louis, where five clubs were thriving when the hostilities began. But the Cyclone Club disbanded due to enlistments, and so too did the Commercial Club when its president took a commission as an army captain. The Morning Star also went out of existence when most of its members enlisted on the Union side while the club's pitcher joined the Confederates and lost his life. None of these clubs re-formed after the war. A fourth club, the Union Club, was forced to disband in 1861 and did not reorganize until 1865. This left only the Empire Club, which managed to keep going, but of necessity played games only among its own members.

One of those games was not completed. Shortly after the installation of the Home Guards throughout the city, the Empires were playing their traditional anniversary game between married and single members. The Empires, "as usual had erected their tent at a convenient spot for the safe keeping and change of clothing, ice water and other refreshments. From the tent pole was suspended a blue and gilt banner that originally had been presented by Col. John McNeil to one of the old volunteer fire companies, from whom it was inherited by the Empire Club. About the middle of the game, when the large attendance, composed mostly of ladies and children, was getting at fever heat interest, it was suddenly discovered that the grounds were almost completely surrounded by detachments of Home Guards, a squad of whom marched straight to the middle of the field surprising the players and causing such consternation among the audience that it quickly dispersed amid the shrieks and cries of the terrorized women and children, and to the deep indignation of the members of the club, some few of whom giving way to their anger, seized on bats, bases, (they were movable in those days) and anything with which they could make a fight."

Despite the color of the banner and the intervention of an officer of the Home Guards who was watching the game, the intruders' commanding officer was adamant that he had seen "a secession flag and [that] the gathering was one of rebels. It was impossible to make the officer understand the truth of the situation." He took several of the players prisoners and marched them back to his headquarters, along with the banner. There he presented his captives and the emblem to his superior— the same Colonel John McNeil who had originally owned the banner!

As the example of the Empire Club suggests, even clubs that persisted during the Civil War did so in greatly curtailed fashion. Almost all had lost at least a few members to military service or to war-related duties, and the clubs that still had enough players to make up a nine were hard-pressed to find opponents. As a result, in towns such as Detroit and Grand Rapids where the Knickerbockers' game was established before the onset of war, there are accounts of the more flexible games of bygone days reemerging.

A similar trend is apparent in accounts of the postwar spread of the game. While there are surviving descriptions of how baseball arrived in many towns, relatively few of them mention veterans. Instead the usual pattern was for postwar clubs first to emerge in the larger towns where they had already been established before the war, and then to spread to neighboring towns. When a veteran is credited, his influence generally occurred in an isolated region such as the farming community in which Jim White grew up, or in the South, where the Knickerbockers' version was largely unknown before the war. Far more often students introduced baseball to towns and regions, suggesting that they deserve much of the credit that has previously been given to soldiers.

Equally important, few of the men at the forefront of the postwar baseball boom were Civil War veterans. This is only natural, since many veterans who saw combat duty returned home maimed while others were brought back in coffins. Even the more fortunate often were in no shape to play baseball; typical was a ballplayer who "patriotically went to the war in '61, and was at the battle of Roanoke Island, and since his return he has not taken the position in the club that he once had, that terrible scourge to athletes and ball players, rheumatism, preventing him from being as active in body as he was wont to be in the old days of the club."

Many of the men who returned home unscathed decided to move on to other phases of their lives. The need to accept new responsibilities was the most pressing reason for their departure from the game. But it was undoubtedly complemented by the difficulty of returning to an innocent game after going through the horrors of war.

The Civil War thus marked the voluntary and involuntary endings of the ball-playing careers of a great many of the first generation of men to play the Knickerbockers' game. For these players the war marked the end of an era—from their vantage point, the game was never again played with quite the same spirit. An element of nostalgia may be found in this viewpoint, since baseball not only persisted after the war but thrived, and often was played in the same spirit as before. Yet there is also considerable validity in this perspective.

Not only had the war led to the demise of many clubs, but those that exited the scene were precisely the ones that had set the standards for conduct. In the New York City area the gentlemanly Knickerbockers, Excelsiors, and Pastimes all ceased to schedule match games. The same process played out elsewhere; Michigan's pioneer club, the Franklins of Detroit, "succumbed to the war, a large portion of its members going into the service," and never reorganized.

Baseball also lost some of its most respected leaders. The future U.S. senator John S. Newberry, for example, belonged to two prewar Detroit clubs and was enthusiastic about the game. But during the war he received a lucrative military contract to build railway cars, and he never again took an active interest in baseball. Fred Benteen was a member of the Cyclones of St. Louis before the war, and after joining the Union army he formed a club by the same name in his regiment. When the war ended, Benteen remained in the military and rose to the rank of brigadier general, heading one of the battalions that split from General George Custer's ill-fated regiment on the morning of Little Big Horn.

Without the clubs that had set an example of how baseball should be played, and the players whose leadership could have ensured compliance, the stage was set for a reexamination of the game's customs and practices.

There are also signs that the war's divisiveness had a lingering effect on the spirit of postwar baseball. This was especially true in regions where loyalties had been divided during the hostilities.

In Richmond, Virginia, for instance, the Union Club challenged the Richmond Base Ball Club in 1866 and received this acid reply: "We are not or [sic] do we expect to be members of the National Baseball Convention. Our reason: we are Southerners."

A bitter postwar rivalry developed in St. Louis between another club called the Unions and one known as the Jeffersons: "Just why this special hostility existed no one knew, but these two never met without a great display of feeling on the part of spectators and players. It was hinted that the real cause of the enmity lay in the fact that many of the members of the Jefferson outfit clung to the feelings of the south, while the Unions were all former Union soldiers with well-gained knowledge of the war just over."

Even farther north, such factionalism could surface. One of the reasons why the Excelsiors of Brooklyn gave up match play may have been that the club's first baseman had enlisted in the Confederate army during the war and been expelled. In how many other clubs was the prewar fraternal spirit poisoned by such animosities?

Thus while the pioneer era of baseball survived the Civil War, and even appeared for a couple of years to be stronger than ever, the game's innocence had been lost.

CHAPTER 10

Competitiveness and Professionalism, and What They Wrought: The End of an Era, Part Two

❖ By the close of the Civil War, the elements that would lead to the end of the pioneer era were in place. In 1866 and 1867 the game seemed more vibrant than ever. But when doubts about the old standards began to arise, devotees turned to the traditional leaders and found that most of them had departed the scene. This led to a period of reexamination that moved baseball away from its childlike innocence and into the professional era.

In the process, attitudes underwent subtle alterations that produced profound changes in how baseball was played. The game's prevailing spirit of forthright honesty gave way to competitiveness, and this in turn revealed that other elements of the game's spirit were fragile. The "patience of hope" that sustained clubs after a convincing loss began to be replaced by demoralization. An unquestioning adherence to playing by the rules yielded to efforts to find loopholes in them. Unswerving allegiance to one's club was succeeded by a more mercenary approach.

Naturally such changes do not happen overnight. Competitiveness and professionalism did not batter down baseball's fortress on January 1, 1868, and pillage it. But it is fair to say that these powerful forces of change had been gathering strength throughout the decade, and that 1868 was a watershed year. It brought ominous signs that the traditional way of playing baseball could not endure.

Many still hoped at that point that the usurpers could be driven out of baseball. But in retrospect it is clear that the incursions of competitiveness and professionalism were too great to allow any going back. Henceforth baseball would be played with the object of winning and the top players would receive money for doing so (eventually being called a "competitor" or a "professional" would become a compliment). What made this inevitable was that both of these elements entered baseball quite openly and in ways that seemed unpreventable.

Competitiveness had long been actively discouraged by means of customs and rituals. Yet the need for these constraints obviously implies that competitiveness was there all along, waiting to emerge. By no means was this simply a postwar problem. Henry Chadwick admitted that even the fun-loving Pastime club had been done in by competitiveness. "Until the club became ambitious of winning matches and began to sacrifice the original objects of the organization to the desire to strengthen their nine for match playing everything went swimmingly and the members had lots of enjoyment on the field," he wrote. "But after their desire to excel in contests with rival clubs had been aroused, then things changed, and finally the spirit of the club, having been dampened by repeated defeats at the hands of stronger nines, gave out and the Pastimes went out of existence."

But it was after the Civil War that competitiveness came out in the open to such an extent as to doom the gentlemanly way of playing. A number of factors accelerated this process.

One of the main ones was that younger players were taking over the game. An extreme example occurred in St. Louis at the start of the 1869 campaign, when the first nine of the state champion Union Club was twice beaten by the club's junior nine. This unexpected result forced the members of the first nine "to bear no small amount of guying [kidding]," as did similarly disquieting upsets of well-established clubs by much younger ones in other parts of the country. Such surprising developments drove still more of the few remaining veterans out of the game, leaving it more rudderless than ever. Still more important, these outcomes exposed a serious flaw in the game's reliance on the "patience of hope." How could players retain faith that practice would allow them to steadily improve when grown men were being surpassed by raw youths?

At the same time a vicious cycle was occurring as a result of the increased prominence that had been forced upon the umpire. The more the umpire made rulings, the less the players felt responsible for upholding the standards of fair play. Even if a baseman knew he had not tagged a base runner, why not appeal to the umpire for judgment and hope that his vision was obstructed? This in turn forced the lone umpire to rule on every play. Slowly but surely, baseball games changed from ceremony to competition.

The tours of Eastern clubs, which began as ways of promoting the game itself, sometimes also served to spread tactics that were emblematic of a more competitive approach to playing the game. When the Nationals' historic 1867 tour brought the club to Louisville, one of the visiting players pulled the "trapped ball" play—deliberately allowing a fly ball to drop and forcing the base runners to try to advance. Once again it was the umpire who was put on the spot. By rule he was forced to call the confused runners out, but the decision outraged the crowd's sense of justice, and the arbiter had a "hot time of it."

The incursion of money into baseball was equally subtle and equally ominous. Money had always been part of baseball, but initially it had been in the form of players paying membership dues to purchase the necessities of the game. As one early club member explained, "in those days, membership in a club instead

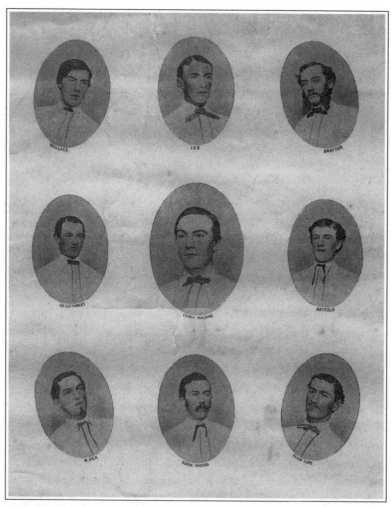

Philadelphia's Keystone Base Ball Club was a sad example of how money transformed baseball. The Keystones were an up-and-coming young club when this composite portrait was made in 1865. That ended when their star Fergy Malone left for greener pastures and eventually joined the crosstown Athletics. Malone's departure led to the defection of several other players, and the Keystones were never the same. [National Baseball Hall of Fame Library]

of being a source of income was one of no considerable expense. Uniforms would wear out, monthly dues had to be paid the club treasurer, fines were imposed for non-attendance, rude or unbecoming conduct, use of profane or vulgar language on the field and disputing the umpire entailed personal disgrace if not financial bankruptcy."

This was an unavoidable reality, but it created a troubling issue. As one early player later recalled: "The great national game is indebted to these old veterans in more ways than one. In the first place there was no salary; on the contrary, there was an initiation fee and all had to pay their dues and furnish their own uniforms, and pay their own traveling expenses. The consequence was the different businesses they followed were neglected, and, with few exceptions, they accumulated little of this world's goods." Was baseball to become an avocation that only the rich could afford?

For most clubs there was a ready solution at hand. An early member of the Niagaras of Buffalo recalled that the club made ends meet by having "350 members who each paid five dollars annually toward the support of the club." One of the pioneers of the Empire Club of St. Louis confirmed that a considerable number of club members "never participated in the game but they were regular and interested spectators and cheerfully joined the active members in sustaining the expenses of the club."

Yet this was an imperfect solution, since not all clubs were able to rely upon the generosity of such members. Moreover many nonplaying members began to resent having to foot the expenses that were incurred by only nine club members. This division of club members into those who played and those who paid was a grave threat to club unity.

So clubs began to seek other solutions. Some of them looked to local businesses for sponsorship. In the years immediately after the war, Cleveland railroad officials sponsored a club made up of railroad employees and "furnished the players with uniforms and generally stood good for their expenses." Others solicited donations from the community as a whole. A Kalamazoo newspaper gave readers this little nudge in 1866: "the ballplayers of this place have never received assistance or encouragement from the citizens, in the way of defraying expenses on match days or providing them an [sic] uniform, as almost every town is doing or has done."

Yet neither method proved to be a dependable source of revenue, and both inched the game down the treacherous road to commercialism. In addition, such fund-raising tactics did nothing to address the inequity between rich and poor clubs, and if anything widened those disparities.

So clubs increasingly turned to charging admission fees for spectators at match games. This had been done as early as 1858 for an all-star game between nines representing Brooklyn and New York City. But by and large collecting an admission charge was not practical as long as clubs played their matches on open fields.

Thus the game reached a quandary. Should clubs risk looking cheap by continuing to scrounge for funds to support them while playing on open and often very unsatisfying fields because those were the best sites they could afford? Or should they risk looking mercenary by building enclosed structures and charging admission fees?

What made the dilemma so difficult was that the latter course could not be taken tentatively. There was no question of the game dipping its toes in the murky waters of professionalism; the heavy expenses involved in building an enclosed ballpark would demand a plunge. And once the plunge had been taken, a return to the safety of shore would be equally impractical.

The dilemma was neatly laid out in an insightful article that appeared in 1862 when the first enclosed ballpark was built in Brooklyn. The article explained that there were only two ways to cover the expenses of building and maintaining the field—either by charging the ball clubs rent or by charging the public

Brooklyn's Union Grounds, the historic first enclosed baseball field, was the site of this 1865 game between the Resolutes of Brooklyn and the Athletics of Philadelphia. The distinction of having the first enclosed baseball fields made Brooklyn the center of the baseball world at this time and enabled one native son to boast: "Virginia was the mother of presidents, Brooklyn of ball players." The pagoda in center field was a place where club directors could host their guests—in effect, baseball's earliest luxury box. [Collection of Tom Shieber]

admission. It quickly dismissed the former option, observing that "the grounds, extensive as they will be, could not accommodate more than three clubs, with two practice days a week each, and the great expense of preparing them is such that it would make the quota of each club too great an amount for any ball club to pay. For instance, the estimated expense is at least $1,200, and this would make each club's share $400. Therefore, this first plan is out of the question. The second plan is the only one that can be adopted, viz., to allow the three clubs occupying the grounds free use of the same for practice, reserving the right to charge an admission fee on the occasion of every match that is played upon the grounds."

The article went on to note that "some objection is made by the fraternity to having anything to do with enclosed grounds where an admission fee is charged." But it argued that admission charges were a practical necessity rather than a moral issue: "This objection holds good as far as ball clubs themselves are concerned, but in regards to grounds laid out by outside parties, for pecuniary profit, the matter assumes an entirely different aspect. . . . The clubs do not profit from the amount

By contrast, Philadelphia's lack of an enclosed field put that city's clubs at a great disadvantage because they could not collect admission fees. As is clear from this illustration of an 1865 game in which the Athletics hosted the Atlantics of Brooklyn, there was no shortage of Philadelphians who wanted to watch baseball. [Collection of Tom Shieber]

thus received, and consequently the admission fee business loses its objectionable features."

It is safe to assume that not everyone accepted the conclusion that admission fees were unobjectionable. But the practical reality that clubs could not afford to pay the large rent charges left no alternative but to try charging admissions. Spectators initially showed reluctance about paying to watch baseball games, but they "gradually became used to the idea." Baseball had taken the fateful plunge; there would be no turning back.

As the idea of enclosed ballparks and admission fees spread to other cities, it continued to encounter resistance. When it arrived in Philadelphia in 1864, the players on the Athletic club "generally had an aversion to making the game a matter of money, and thought that the policy was a mistake," while spectators "laughed a little uneasily at the attempts to speculate in the public interest in baseball." Yet by now the practice had acquired an unstoppable momentum. As more cities built enclosed ballparks, those that didn't began to seem behind the times and even cheap.

By 1867 the cautious and generally conservative Henry Chadwick suggested that Boston consider an enclosed ground:

"It would be a good investment in any city, and certainly in Boston." Returning to the subject a few weeks later, he extended his recommendation more generally: "it is always better for a club to have its own ground, leaving the public enclosed fields for neutral matches and outside games; for then their receipts at the gate are of necessity a legitimate means of offsetting the outlay consequent upon their being obliged to secure a permanent field, and any profit accruing therefrom is merely a fair dividend from a good investment of club capital."

Chadwick also addressed another pressing concern: "It does not follow, as a matter of course, that because a club makes an arrangement for the use of an enclosed ground, looking to receipts at the gate, that their sole object is playing base ball for money, and thereby placing themselves in the category of 'professional' ball players."

This reasoning is unimpeachable: collecting admission fees did not guarantee that the players were mercenaries. But by then it was equally difficult to dispute that enclosed grounds and admission fees certainly suggested this direction.

The paying of baseball players dates back to the late 1850s. While the practice was officially prohibited by the National Association of Base Ball Players until the 1869 season, the ban served only to obscure its history since the association was powerless to prevent under-the-table arrangements. The most likely candidate to have been the first paid player was Jim Creighton, who jumped to the Excelsiors in 1859.

The Excelsiors of Brooklyn were one of the more affluent and gentlemanly clubs, and at first glance it may seem surprising that this club would initiate professionalism. Yet their status naturally meant that they would be more likely to have wealthy patrons who could afford to pay ballplayers to join the club. And the fact that the Excelsiors paid Creighton to join them appears to have raised few concerns. Some presumably felt it was in the game's best interests to have such a club at the forefront, and they were willing to look the other way at the hiring of a key player. Moreover, as long as clubs had to rely on wealthy patrons to foot the bill, it could safely be assumed that such payments would remain rare.

That changed dramatically with the introduction of enclosed grounds and admission fees. One early ballplayer recalled that once the players became aware that the owners were reaping profits by charging admission fees, they demanded, "Give us part of the gate receipts or we won't play!" An agreement was reached, but the players soon decided they had underestimated their worth and requested a greater share, "again threatening a strike." Before long the ballplayers were receiving a substantial portion of the gate receipts and dividing the money among themselves.

This new development elicited vociferous protests. To many the concept of athletes "speculat[ing] in the public interest in baseball" was an abomination. The most heartfelt dissatisfaction was voiced by members of the generation of ballplayers who had paid their own expenses, placed their careers on hold, and in consequence "accumulated little of this world's goods," only to be pushed aside by younger players. Their chorus was joined by the honorary members who year after year had paid to support their beloved club and now felt their donations were ending up in the pockets of mercenary ballplayers.

Yet the situation was not that simple. Now that ball clubs were collecting revenues, they were also assuming additional expenses, which made it far more difficult to determine when the division of gate receipts was income and when it was merely a reimbursement of expenses. Clubs that tried to abide by the principle of reimbursement were soon divided over whether players were entitled to recoup lost wages, an issue that in turn created divisions along class lines. Baseball had started down a very slippery slope, which would only grow more treacherous.

Applying moral absolutes to the situation was problematic. Younger ballplayers saw no reason that because early ballplayers had paid their own expenses, they should now make similar

sacrifices. Angry debates erupted about whether specific players were amateurs or professionals, but each side's perspective is
understandable. Even the best clubs were not drawing salaries
until around 1866, leaving plenty of room for hairsplitting
about whether the division of gate receipts constituted professionalism.

Cleveland's leading club, for example, maintained in 1869:
"we are charged with having secured professional players in our
nine, which assertion is positively untrue. We have strengthened our nine *somewhat* by the acquisition of [Al] Pratt, [Jack]
Ward and [Art] Allison, but neither [sic] of these players is a
professional, all being in business in this city, and making base
ball a secondary matter to business requirements. Our club is
strictly an amateur organization." The club and players may
well have believed themselves to be amateurs while outsiders
may have assumed that their sudden business opportunities
were linked to their ball-playing skills. There were so many gra-
dations that it became impossible to define most ballplayers as
being either strictly amateur or strictly professional.

The NABBP tried to prevent players from accepting do-
nothing jobs by decreeing that men could not accept "place or
emolument," but this was far too vague. For example, Henry
Burroughs of New Jersey joined the Detroit Base Ball Club in
1865 and simultaneously began working as a "professor" at the
Detroit Gymnasium, where he taught courses in gymnastics.
This was hardly a do-nothing job, but it had a chilling effect on
competitive balance in the state, leading the University of
Michigan student newspaper to complain: "We don't blame Detroit for thus holding out inducements to good players: she
must do it to keep pace with her sister cities. But it is somewhat
difficult for us to distinguish between these men and 'professional players,' or those who play for 'place or emolument.'"

The civic pride that resulted from having a good ball club
soon led to the dubious practice of filling government positions
with imported ballplayers. By the end of the decade, "The Mu-

tuals of New York City were under control of the coroners of that city, the players being carried on the payrolls of those officers. The Atlantics of Brooklyn, Athletics of Philadelphia, Unions of Morrisania, Nationals of Washington, all derived their support from politics." Even those exemplars of rustic life, the Haymakers of Troy, claimed the article, "were under the patronage of a large manufacturing establishment, whose head [John Morrissey] was prominent in politics, both State and National."

The worst offender was the U.S. Treasury Department, which employed most of the Nationals' players who absented themselves from their jobs for several weeks in 1867 to embark on the first tour west of the Alleghenies. Their employment and the extended leaves were facilitated by club president and future U.S. senator Arthur Pue Gorman, who held a powerful position within the department that enabled him to build a baseball juggernaut. Gorman later recalled that during a match against a club from Georgetown University (then Georgetown College), he was impressed with one of the collegians: "Upon inquiry we ascertained that the heavy batter was George Fox, and that he had just graduated and was preparing to go to live in New York. He was questioned, and urged to remain in Washington, one of the inducements offered him being a position in a Government department, for in those days there was no such thing as civil-service reform, and the majority of our members were men who held official positions and wielded a great deal of influence. Our arguments proved too potent for Fox, and he consented to remain with us."

Because the Nationals earned a reputation for gentlemanly conduct and being ambassadors for the sport, few of their contemporaries questioned their methods of player acquisition. But such practices created huge inequities between cities, and these disparities had a corrosive effect on the game.

This was most obvious in Baltimore, which was forced into Washington's shadow as a baseball town. One observer noted in 1867: "It is a singular fact that the business men of Baltimore are decidedly opposed to base ball; and when it is remembered that a majority of base ball players are employed in stores where their presence is required till sunset, instead of in the public service, as are a majority of Washington players, who are at liberty at an early afternoon, the difficulties with which a Baltimorean ballist has to contend may be appreciated. A member of one of the prominent clubs of this city recently sought a situation there, and upon giving his name was at once asked whether he was connected with the ——— club. He replied in the affirmative, whereupon the merchant instantly informed him that he would give employment to no base ball player, however capable to transact business." And this account does not even mention the most unfair element of all: the fact that many of the players on the Nationals had been recruited from New York.

Professionalism thus crept into baseball in a variety of subtle ways that were difficult to protest and even harder to prevent. Clubs in neighboring cities might sense that their rival's new pitcher had accepted his new job because of his pitching skills, but how were they to know how many hours that player put in at his place of work? Pinpointing the blame for professionalism was just as difficult. The game's woes could certainly not be placed on the shoulders of a gentlemanly young man who had moved from New Jersey to Detroit to teach gymnastics, or a Georgetown graduate who had accepted a position in the Treasury Department. It was still more impractical to suggest turning back the clock to the days before the enclosed ballparks that had become inextricably linked to professional play.

As a result, while many voiced their opposition to the game's growing professionalism in 1867 and 1868, their protestations were generally long on high-minded principles and short on practical solutions. And they came to be uttered with growing resignation.

But however vague and unfocused, these complaints were heartfelt. They conveyed the older generation's deep concern that money was tarnishing a game they loved deeply. They might not have any solutions, but nothing could stop older ballplayers from lamenting, as one did in 1868, "they don't play ball nowadays as they used to."

Many members of the younger generation, too, found mercenary behavior troubling. They had come to perceive the local ball club as the embodiment of their communities' hopes and dreams and saw the act of selling one's services to a rival as traitorous. The famed attorney Clarence Darrow conveyed this sense of betrayal and disillusionment in describing his youthful days on the baseball diamonds of Kinsman, Ohio: "When we heard of the professional game in which men cared nothing whatever for patriotism but only for money—games in which rival towns would hire the best players from a natural enemy—we could scarcely believe the tale was true. No Kinsman boy would any more give aid and comfort to a rival town than would a loyal soldier open a gate in the wall to let an enemy march in."

No one felt the distress more acutely than the players who were replaced by a hired gun. Thirty-five years after the fact, Frank L. Smith struggled to control his emotions while writing about a single game in which he was replaced on the Janesville club, as is shown by this poignant account: ". . . Extra provisions were made to guard against a scarcity of players for this occasion, so much so that we had a surplus on hand, and the night before the game I was asked by some of the directors to abdicate in favor of players to whom we had to offer liberal inducements when short handed, as they might be offended if dropped from the list—and of course 'I didn't care.' So the next day found me at the game a prospective spectator, but having arranged the game by correspondence, was called from my buggy to settle a dispute before the contest started. About that time Mr. Bird, upon whose pitching great dependence was placed for the hoped for victory, broke his thumb while catching a torn covered ball out in the field. Nice place for a pitcher under those circumstances; nice ball to bat for any one. Then it was the directors to me again and after a few minutes of conflicting emotions I took to the field, 'Sans' uniform, not to please them, but because I, above all others on the grounds, was anxious for victory, which I had the satisfaction of being called upon to save in the pitcher's box at the end of the seventh inning. Am partially justified in referring to this personal matter by being worked up over a recollection of the affair."

The personal hurt experienced by men like Smith was deeper because it was accompanied by symptoms, both tangible and intangible, that convinced many that money was tainting the game and making it unfit for gentlemen. One journalist complained, "The idea of making money out of base ball play is damaging to the game, and this benefit, show business system is reducing it altogether to too low a standard to please its gentlemen patrons." The enclosed ball fields themselves suggested unsavory associations with public spectacles—most notably the increased prominence of gamblers at ball games, which had already led to a few instances of fixed games and to many more accusations of shady behavior.

The futility of trying to combat this perceived evil was epitomized by the failure of the few efforts to find a compromise that would stave off open professionalism. Some clubs tried to become "semi-professionals" by paying a few players and using amateurs in the other positions, but this proved a disaster. Having paid and unpaid players competing together naturally caused internal dissension. Worse, these clubs still weren't competitive against the professionals and stirred up resentment among the local press and public instead of generating civic pride.

Some clubs attempted another middle course, substituting rewards such as trophies and jewelry for money. This compromise initially worked well in some areas. For instance, the silver ball that John Lowell offered to the champion team of New England in 1864 became the focus of baseball interest in the region for several years. Fittingly, bands were often hired to play the "Silver Ball March" during matches for the coveted ball.

But such initiatives were also doomed; by the end of the decade the competition had become so intense that the original ball was melted down to make smaller balls that were presented to several aspirants.

This was a telling symbol of the futility of trying to stave off the inevitable. By 1868 the game had proceeded too far along its new course for there to be any question of going back. Regardless of who was right and who was wrong, or indeed whether anyone was to blame, competitiveness and money had combined to fatally weaken all the key components of the pioneer era of baseball.

Club allegiance was one of the first components to be undermined. By the end of the Civil War, baseball clubs were beginning to show signs of putting baseball ahead of the club. Before the 1864 season a typical club voted "to abolish the committee on nines, substituting the conferring of arbitrary power on the captains of the nines, whereby he can dismiss from the nine any unruly or rebellious player." The change was described as "a good rule, providing the captain is not one likely to play the tyrant." It is easy to see this as an improvement if the primary aim of a baseball club is to win games. But if a club's underlying duty is to ensure that every member feels a sense of belonging, it becomes much less clear that such a change is for the better.

This was a fairly subtle threat to club allegiance, but the postwar trend toward competitiveness and professionalism brought much more direct challenges. Ballplayers began to "revolve" from club to club without regard to feelings of kinship. But the clubs themselves were equally guilty, accepting and even soliciting men for their ball-playing talents instead of for the traits that had traditionally mattered. By 1868 a player could be commended for what had once been taken for granted: "his fidelity to his club, a characteristic of ball players far too rare in the community."

The prevalence of "revolving" created plenty of ill will, especially among the jilted clubs and club members. A perfect example was the Railway Unions, a Cleveland club made up of workers in the local railroad shops and offices. A defection stirred up trouble: "There was considerable feeling because 'Pikey' Smith, himself a railroad man, preferred to cast his lot with the Forest Citys instead of with the Unions. He was a crack player and both teams coveted his services. It was said that the offer of the captaincy was the weight in the balance that finally settled the question in favor of the Forest Citys."

These developments had a particularly devastating effect on discipline and sportsmanship. Formerly the existence of a club rule was enough to ensure compliance because club membership was so greatly treasured that a member wouldn't dare risk expulsion. But once players began flitting from club to club, such threats lost their power.

The idea that a baseball club was a club made up of men with common bonds had been fractured. And once this pillar of the pioneer era of baseball came tumbling down, the rest of the edifice soon followed.

Naturally, once clubs were no longer unified by a common bond they ceased to act as ambassadors and began acting more like mercenaries. In 1868 the Atlantics of Brooklyn announced plans for an ambitious Southern tour that would include stops in New Orleans, Mobile, and Savannah. But the tour was eventually canceled due to cold weather and what was tactfully described as an inability to "come to terms as to the share of receipts."

Civic pride was an equally important casualty. Cities still felt proud of a local club *if they won*. If they didn't, the local fans and press were quick to turn on the club, asking what right these men had to represent their city. Remember the team that set out from Fort Wayne in the late 1860s with the aim of setting straight those who "joshed us as small-town Hoosiers, and made fun of the name 'Kekionga'"? Just a few years later the representatives of the Kekionga name were a group of professionals who "made the name of the club (hard as it is to speak) a by-word and reproach wherever they stopped by their wanton behavior." What must the original players have thought of this development?

The resulting disillusionment was especially evident if the club included imported players, which occurred more often even when the club was made up entirely of locals. The few surviving remnants of the "patience of hope" soon vanished, and baseball clubs began to be formed and to operate on the tacit assumption that losing would not be acceptable. Instead of taking pride in the best efforts of the leading local club, cities began to be represented by all-star squads.

The city of Jackson, Michigan, chose to be represented at a major 1867 tournament in Detroit by such a team, which was aptly dubbed the Unknowns. When the Unknowns unexpectedly won the tournament, considerable controversy ensued. The Detroit organizers felt that the Jackson "club" had violated the spirit of the event while the men from Jackson found that viewpoint hypocritical coming from the city that had brought to Michigan the practice of importing ballplayers. Clearly the landscape of baseball had changed for good.

This reality had manifested itself in some of the big Eastern cities before 1868. A perfect example was the Athletics of Philadelphia, a club with a short but tumultuous history.

The Athletic Club was one of the first to be formed when baseball reached Philadelphia in 1860, but its first couple of years were marked by struggles to maintain enough interest to survive. Then the addition of several local cricket players—Philadelphia had long been America's primary cricket hotbed—catapulted the club into national prominence. From 1864 to 1868 the Athletics were perennial contenders for the national title.

The New York clubs, however, were able to take advantage of the championship system by scheduling games so that the title never left the New York City area. Just as ominously, while the Athletic Club had closed the talent gap on the New York teams with remarkable speed, it was fighting a competitive disadvantage that continued to widen. For Brooklyn boasted two enclosed ball fields by the end of the Civil War while Philadelphia did not yet possess a single one.

Athletics president Colonel Thomas Fitzgerald nonetheless made an effort to collect admission fees at one important match by posting his sons all around the field. The results were disappointing: "The receipts of the afternoon were $14. This was not a heavy return, considering especially that the crowd was greater than had ever up to that time attended a match in that city. But the entrance charge was considered more or less as a joke by nearly everybody."

Meanwhile the pressure to remain competitive was forcing the club to bend or break the NABBP's rules on professionalism. Star pitcher Dick McBride "was put into the City Treasurer's office, with a $1200 salary and nothing to do." Then the club began to recruit players from New York. It "captured Al Reach from the Eckford, of Brooklyn, and set him up in a cigar store on the south side of Chestnut street, above Fourth."

Reach took the business opportunity seriously, making connections that eventually enabled him to found the sporting goods firm that made him a wealthy man. But he was followed to Philadelphia by other New York players who expected their jobs to be jobs in name only; Patsy Dockney, in particular, "used to play ball every afternoon and fight and drink every night." And the arrival of these men naturally led the local ballplayers to request similar treatment. Before long "the nine was composed of players for cash, although an attempt was made to keep it from the public."

These financial inducements were made possible by "subscriptions from the members and extra donations by particular and particularly able friends." But the generosity of these "able friends" was not unlimited. Before long, trying to compete with the New York clubs for players without having a similar source of revenue began to catch up with the Athletics.

As was explained in an 1879 account: "In those good old times there was considerable visiting among the clubs of Philadelphia, Brooklyn, New York, etc., but the bills of the visitors were always scrupulously paid by the resident club. Things are slightly different now, when not only no receptionary spread awaits the visitors, but when they very often see nothing of the opposing nine until they reach the ground ready for play. . . . Philadelphia had been to New York last, and had its board-bills paid and been treated to divers cold collations, and had been brought to the ball-ground in almost regal state in a six-horse omnibus, and it was now the Athletics' turn to reciprocate. But the Athletics' will was stronger than their ability. The chancellor of the exchequer said that, if balls and shoes were selling at $5 per hundred pairs, the club couldn't buy a shoe-string, it was so poor."

Eventually the club got its enclosed playing field, but rising expenses offset the new revenues and the club's financial situation remained precarious. The club also faced a mounting local backlash against its reliance on imported professionals and the disregard that players like Dockney showed for pursuing the jobs that had been lined up for them. Finally the Athletics announced plans "to confine their nine to Philadelphians in the future, Reach being the only exception; and he has made Philadelphia his home, having a host of friends there and a good business."

This temporarily soothed the wounded civic pride of Philadelphians, but the next season brought new affronts. Before the ball-playing campaign even started, a local journalist warned: "We wish to draw attention to another matter which should receive the earnest attention of ball players. We refer now to clubs engaging in two or three games a week during portions of the season. This necessitates players neglecting business, and, as it frequently happens, at times when their services can illy be spared. It induces others not players to resort to various devices whereby they can witness the sport at the cost sometimes of a situation. We were informed by the Secretary of the Irvington Club, who was in the city last week, that the invariable question put to young men applying for situations in New York is whether they are members of ball clubs. If they answer in the affirmative they are told their services will not be needed. The same exists here, and we know of a player belonging to one of our crack clubs who was unable to get a situation from the notoriety he had acquired as a ball expert. He wisely gave up playing. There are higher aims in life than ball playing. It may and doubtless does suit those who live by blackmailing to encourage such a disregard of the duties of life, but it is purchased at a fearful cost."

The advice was ignored, and the new season saw the club bring in several "revolvers" and show ingratitude to many longtime supporters. By July the Athletics' longtime president, Colonel Fitzgerald, denounced its new course in an open and very candid letter: "Gentlemen of the Athletic Club: I write this hurriedly. I am very busy. You have discovered to your mortification and sorrow that all my predictions have been verified. You were strong. You have become weak. Your reputation was wide-spread and most respectable. What is it at this moment? And the tone of the organization, has it not fallen very low? I left you with an overflowing treasury—over $1,000. How much money have you now? Your exchequer is empty, and you are deeply in debt. . . . You hired players, but you had not a dollar for the old and well tried servants of the club. Who took you out of the depths of poverty? Who advanced the money to hire your ground? Who fenced the ground and benched it, and showed you how to make money? Who carried you through five years of struggles, and finally left you in the highest state of prosperity?"

Fitzgerald then enumerated the club's specific missteps and chided: "Your once strong and proud organization is falling to pieces. Several of your players are under pay. I will not stoop to personalities or I would point out the mercenaries in your 'hired men,' as they are designated by an observant and critical public. Have you no head? Are you deaf, dumb and blind? Can you not arrange a few matches which will bring in some money? You cannot. You are in a fog and would like to get out."

He concluded by counseling, "The past—the bitter past—may be retrieved, by a course of honorable conduct. All is not lost yet. Shake off bad influences. Endeavor to recover your lost tone. Do right. Be true to principle. Frown on blackguards, gamblers, roughs. Discourage profanity. Do all in your power to make Base Ball a game for gentlemen, and believe me your friend."

But the torrent of change was making it impossible to retrieve the past. By 1868 the effects of competitiveness and professionalism were no longer restricted to the large Eastern cities and were having dramatic consequences in areas that had never striven for national acclaim. While there is always some imprecision about dating the end of a vague concept like "baseball's pioneer era," there is no doubt that 1868 was a pivotal year.

A perfect example occurred in St. Louis, a city where the leading ball clubs had "kept clear from such innovations [as professionalism], satisfied with its two leading clubs and a long list of ambitious younger amateur organizations. The Empire and Union clubs kept on in their own original way of playing ball for the sport there was in it, but neither declined to cross bats with even the highest salaried aggregations that pranced along the road to St. Louis and, in general, they gave a good account of themselves, especially when it is borne in mind, as it should be, that the majority of players in these two clubs were not sole arbiters of their own time, but were closely tied down to either business pursuits or, as was the case with several of the Union Club, restricted by their studies at college."

But that changed in a single season: "It was early developed in 1868 that the year would mark an era in local base ball." The impetus was the opening of the city's first enclosed ballpark in May, which made it possible to charge admissions for the first time. As a club member later explained, the logic behind this move was impeccable: "The leading spirit of the [Union] club, Asa W. Smith, had devised plans to advance his club to the foremost and to maintain that position being animated mainly by that true spirit of sportsman and athlete, love of the game for its own intrinsic merit. At no time were either the Union or Empire Clubs actuated by a desire to make money and when they adopted the plan of placing a price upon admission to the games, it was because necessity forced them into it. The increased and still increasing interest of the general public demanded better accommodations and surroundings and Asa Smith, recognizing this fact, set afoot plans that he deemed best calculated to promote the National game by catering to the desires of the public. . . . That the game had reached that stage when it was one of the most popular of entertainments was attested by the experience of the previous year when charging admission was inaugurated with success. In order to gratify this public taste it was necessary to incur large expenses, particularly so whenever it was desired to secure the presence of any of the great clubs of the East or West and these demanded one-half of the gate receipts, the home club bearing all expenses with the other half."

Yet the fact that this step was unavoidable and that it was planned with care scarcely mattered. The excesses and abuses that already characterized Eastern baseball almost immediately began to surface in St. Louis. Before the opening of the new ballpark, baseball in St. Louis had still been "what the originators of the game intended it should be, a means of recreation for themselves and entertainment for others." By the end of that watershed season, the attitude had irrevocably changed.

The long-standing friendly rivalry between the Union and Empire clubs for local supremacy was one of the most obvious casualties. When the Empire Club lost the first match between the two sides, it appealed to a five-man judiciary committee "on the ground that the umpire in the eighth inning after having declared one of the Empire players 'not out' reversed himself at the suggestion of the Union captain and decided him out, and for a second reason cited fact that the umpire failed to sign the score." A new legalistic spirit had taken over.

It became equally apparent that the city's ball fans were no longer "satisfied with its two leading clubs and . . . their own original way of playing ball for the sport." When the best Eastern clubs took advantage of the new ballpark to pay visits to St. Louis, the lopsided results were "very disgusting to the base ball public." The new ball field had created new expectations; a decisive defeat of the Union Club was "a great disappointment to the public and provoked sharp criticisms upon the players of the Union Club and also upon its management for lacking of judgment in selecting the players and their dispositions upon the field, and while according the club no lack of material complained that it was not properly handled." By the end of the pivotal 1868 season, the longtime Empire captain Jeremiah Fruin had stepped down, and many other veterans followed suit, leaving St. Louis baseball rudderless as it entered a new era.

Similar developments occurred in many other cities that had been on the fringes of the baseball world. These cities felt emboldened to make tentative dips into professionalism but soon came to regret having done so. In Mansfield, Ohio, for instance, interest in the game had been steadily rising until in 1868 the city's leading club added two New Yorkers to its regular nine. More locals were replaced with imported players from Philadelphia in 1869, but the club disbanded before the end of that season and it was five years before Mansfield again had a notable club. Similarly dramatic changes gripped the ball clubs of Michigan and West Virginia in 1868.

As the historian William Ryczek observed, "by 1868 . . . no one was bearing any defeats gracefully." An era had ended.

CHAPTER 11

The Cincinnati Base Ball Club and the Red Stockings

❖ No club better embodied the bittersweet ending of the pioneer era than the best-known club in baseball. But just as accounts of early baseball that emphasize the game's seriousness tell only half the story, so too the Cincinnati Base Ball Club's history is a twofold one, and only one part of it has been told.

The typical version of events goes something like this. In 1869 the Red Stockings of Cincinnati formed the first professional team, made up mostly of Eastern players and led by captain Harry Wright. They surprised the country by ending the Eastern domination of the sport with an undefeated season. More impressively, they crisscrossed the nation to take on all comers, even making an unprecedented foray to California. Along the way they impressed everyone with their gentlemanly conduct and thereby paved the way for acceptance of the professional era. The people of Cincinnati embraced the club because it brought the city great acclaim. But midway through the 1870 season the Red Stockings' long unbeaten string finally ended. The first defeat was followed by several more, along with some well-publicized instances of bad behavior. At season's end the club's president decided to end the experiment with professionalism. The professional players continued their careers in Eastern cities, with many of them joining Harry Wright in Boston and forming a new version of the Red Stockings.

By and large this is a factually accurate account. The common description of the Red Stockings as the first professional team (or as the first openly professional team) is not true to the facts, however; as we have seen, a significant number of clubs were professional before 1869. But in that year the National Association of Base Ball Players permitted professionalism for the first time, and about a dozen clubs chose that option, making the Red Stockings *one* of the first openly professional clubs, though certainly not the only one. Some historians have tried to suggest that the club was the first all-salaried one, but even this is debatable.

Nevertheless the Red Stockings' role in ushering in the professional era was enormous. The necessarily covert nature of professional play before 1869 had created unsavory associations in the public's mind, and suspicions had grown as gamblers became more prominent at ballparks. As a result, the fact that the dominant club in the first year of open professionalism exhibited model conduct was a vital development. So while the nature of the Red Stockings' contribution to baseball needs to be restated, it is difficult to overstate the importance of what they accomplished at a crucial juncture for professional baseball and for the game itself.

Nor is the common version of events grossly biased or unbalanced. To many contemporary observers, the above summary is essentially what happened. One of the Cincinnati newspapers that closely covered the Red Stockings supported that perspective. And a modern historian, after sifting through all the evidence, could reasonably arrive at that conclusion.

Yet this generally accepted version of events is told primarily from the perspective of Harry Wright and his players. Less attention has been paid to the views of the men who had belonged to the Cincinnati Base Ball Club before that club became synonymous with the professional Red Stockings. And those men, as I shall try to explain, had legitimate reasons for their misgivings about the professionalization of the club.

[*185*]

As noted earlier, Cincinnati took to baseball belatedly. Town ball was still the game of choice until shortly before the Civil War, and even it was pursued halfheartedly: "We really had no athletic sport that commanded general attention from the rising Porkopolitans [a nickname reflecting the city's status as the country's chief hog packing center]. Marbles, shinny, foot ball and the kite were each taken up for a time, but down as quickly thrown, neither of them seeming to possess a lasting charm for our lively young men. . . . Loafing had more attraction for the great mass of our boys than any active exercise."

And while other communities showed great enthusiasm when the Knickerbockers' game did arrive, the residents of Cincinnati had to be all but shamed into forming a club. A baseball club had been formed in the small neighboring town of Dayton, Kentucky, and it "published a challenge, in 1859, to any club within a hundred miles. This note of defiance aroused [Cincinnati's] few importations from the East who had played base ball in their old homes, and efforts looking to organization were begun."

The result was a club called the Buckeyes, but Cincinnati's first baseball club was not accorded a warm reception: "This club managed to live through the year; the principal reason of their being tolerated was to be found in the fact that they selected the Pest-house Commons for their play ground." The Pest-house in question was a hospital for patients with infectious diseases, and this unusual home base precluded opposition: "the enemies of the game let them practice, entertaining a suspicion that the end of it and its lovers would soon come."

Instead it was the Civil War that brought an end to the Buckeye Club, and throughout the war years and even during 1865 there was no organized baseball activity in Cincinnati. The game was finally reestablished in 1866 with the revival of the Buckeyes, under the new name of the Live Oaks, and the debut of several new clubs. But interest remained tepid, with the ball-playing season not beginning in earnest until July.

One of the new clubs was comprised mostly of local lawyers, and the members apparently initially called themselves the Resolutes. Unlike some of its predecessors, the club lived up to its name: "The players were prompt in attendance and earnest at practice. The cholera was prevalent in the city at that time, but the players had taken good medical advice, and after the great exertion of each inning took a taste of the preventive."

Yet there was nothing to suggest a bright future for this club. Despite their diligence, the only skill the players are reported to have shown was "in the use of strong words." As shocked as the members of the Knickerbocker club would have been if someone had suggested during their early years that their game would become the national pastime, these Cincinnati lawyers would have been still more dumbfounded had anyone forecast that within three years their club would ascend to the top of the baseball universe and become forever linked with the dawn of professional baseball.

Instead, like the early Knickerbockers, the Resolutes were too concerned with simply surviving to entertain grandiose dreams. Finding suitable grounds was especially difficult. Initially the club shared with the Live Oaks a modest field known as Mill Creek Bottom, located at the foot of Eighth Street. The players used a clubhouse that was just as unprepossessing; it "consisted of a room in Blymyer's foundry, where bats, balls and bases were stored."

Problems soon began to plague this location. The first was the need to mow the grass and, with the Live Oaks pleading poverty, the Resolutes had to dip into their treasury to cover the not inconsiderable charge of ten dollars. In less than a month, however, "the mud proved too formidable an obstacle," and the club began searching for a new headquarters.

The club's initial choice of this modest field and clubhouse had befitted their aspirations. "Holmes Hoge was chosen as Captain," explained an 1870 account, "and being thought to have a wonderfully superior knowledge of the game, he was invested with full powers in the selection of his players. The club, through its President, positively enjoined him from promising to pay any of them money, as they only had three or four dollars in the treasury, and were not certain of any addition to that fund soon. This injunction was the outgrowth of modesty, which generally is found in mutual admiration societies, and resulted in each attaining his darling wish, viz., a place in the first Nine." In other words, the members wanted to play on the baseball club they had founded. Given the choice between winning with a team made up of hired outsiders or losing with a club of friends, they preferred the latter option.

Captain Hoge, however, believed that a berth on the first nine was a privilege earned by demonstrating baseball skills rather than a right derived from membership. And it had taken less than a month of practice to reveal glaring deficiencies in several aspiring ballplayers. Shortstop Drausin Wulsin, for example, "was found to be short in several important particulars; his judgment of flys [sic] was not good, and then when they fell into his hands they would not stay there." Charles E. Scanlan "hid the enormity of his terrible muffs by his promptly spoken pleasantries, which bit of strategy saved him from retirement for at least two weeks." Henry A. Glassford tried admirably to excel as a second baseman, but the position proved too onerous for the bespectacled forty-year-old Civil War veteran. And of the efforts of another player, the unknown author of these candid commentaries could only bring himself to say: "Fry tried to play first."

The shortcomings of these players and the dire need for a playing field led the club to a fateful decision. The Resolutes formed an alliance with the local Union Cricket Club, which allowed them joint tenancy of the Union Cricket Grounds, situated at the foot of Richmond Street. At the same time the club adopted a name suggesting more ambitious aims: the Cincinnati Base Ball Club.

Soon four members of the Resolutes had lost their coveted spots on the first nine, replaced by members of the cricket club.

The chronicler who had dissected their fielding weaknesses naturally considered this to be no great loss: "Scanlan, Fry, Wulsin and Glassford were lost forever from base ball clubs as players, and they are known no more, fortunately." While there is no reason to doubt his judgment, the ousted ballplayers understandably didn't see it that way. Wulsin came to believe that "justice was not dealt to him, and a rising ballist was ruined by Captain Hoge's tyrannical rule." From Glassford's perspective, "some lack of appreciation by Captain Hoge made his career at second very brief." And Scanlan joined the others in believing "that he awarded too much confidence to Captain Hoge at the outset."

Despite the signs of greater seriousness of purpose, there is no reason to think the members of the Cincinnati Base Ball Club entertained dreams of national prominence. Nor was the club likely to have attained much stature except for a stroke of good fortune: one of the new additions from the Union Cricket Club was a man named Harry Wright, who soon replaced Hoge as captain of the baseball club.

Harry Wright was the son of a British professional cricket player who had immigrated to the New York City area to further his career. Sam Wright's four sons grew up playing cricket but also learning the new game of baseball; Harry had been a member of both the Knickerbockers and the Gothams. Given his father's profession, Harry naturally saw nothing wrong with earning a living by playing ball. But he disliked the hypocrisy of baseball's under-the-table payments, so in 1866 he had accepted a paid position as the cricket pro in Cincinnati.

The conviction with which he held these views, coupled with Wright's scrupulous integrity, enabled the new captain of the Cincinnati Base Ball Club to successfully steer the club through uncharted waters. Over the next three years his astute eye for talent and his disciplined leadership brought the club to the pinnacle of the baseball world. Still more impressive is that he accomplished this feat without losing the support of the members of the Cincinnati Base Ball Club who surrendered their positions to imported professionals. Yet while Harry Wright's skillful captaincy enabled the ball club to avoid the perils that capsized so many other clubs, his Red Stockings did not escape unscathed.

Wright's course was made smoother by the success the club experienced under his leadership. In 1866, after initial struggles, the Cincinnati Base Ball Club captured a season-ending tournament. The club's sophomore season saw it lose only once, and that to the mighty touring Nationals of Washington.

These triumphs made it easier for local fans to accept the reality that outsiders were continuing to replace the original players. The growing tendency toward professionalism was similarly made more palatable by the club's commitment to spending its earnings in ways designed to enhance civic pride. In 1867 the club moved to spacious new grounds. At some point during this period the club also assumed a distinctive look: a "unique uniform . . . [that] consisted of a white cap, white shirt, with knee breeches and red stockings, and taken in contrast to the green turf presented a very pretty appearance." Because of the new outfits, the ball club became unofficially but universally known as the Red Stockings (though, as we shall see, credit for this innovation would be disputed).

Perhaps the most important ingredient was Harry Wright's felicity for communications and public relations. In other cities, as we've seen, locals viewed professional players as civic employees and resented them if they failed to show due gratitude. By contrast, Wright used innovations like the new grounds and uniforms to show that the ballplayers took similar pride in the community—yet he also introduced them gradually so that locals would have time to get used to them.

Despite Wright's sensitivity to the need for diplomacy, it was still essential to win. It had become clear that 1868 would be a pivotal year for baseball in Cincinnati, just as it proved to be in St. Louis, Detroit, and many other Western cities. While

Gentlemanly Harry Wright began playing baseball on Hoboken's Elysian Fields with two strictly amateur clubs, the Gothams and the Knickerbockers. His father, however, was a professional cricketer, and Harry inherited a deep conviction that there was nothing wrong with being paid to play baseball. As captain of the trailblazing "Red Stockings" of Cincinnati, he showed the world that professional baseball could be played with class and dignity. [National Baseball Hall of Fame Library]

the 1867 loss to the Nationals had been expected, the lopsided 53-10 score produced what one observer aptly described as "a feeling of goneness that the brilliant record of later seasons has not driven entirely away." He added that the "Waterloo defeat . . . showed to the officers that unless the club was strengthened, Cincinnati would never reap honors in first-class ball contests, and being without money the prospect was gloomy."

So it was clear that the time had come for the Red Stockings to either rein in their aspirations or make an all-out commitment to professionalism. And if the latter course were pursued, it would take all of Harry Wright's considerable skills to do so without alienating the locals.

He received help from an unexpected quarter: a local rival known as the Buckeyes (not the same club as the prewar team of that name). The Buckeyes plunged aggressively into professionalism from the start of the season, importing Easterners Andrew Leonard, Charles Sweasy, and Patsy Dockney, the last named being the same ballplayer who had caused so much dissatisfaction in Philadelphia by spending his evenings fighting and drinking. When the Red Stockings responded by hiring two professionals, the Buckeyes went out and signed four more.

This forced the Red Stockings' hand and made it a fairly easy decision for the club's directors to continue their pursuit of imports. The very people who would find such practices objectionable were also eager not to let the Buckeyes gain supremacy, since the latter club's "adherents were of the rougher elements, while the Cincinnatis had the sympathy of the better class of citizens." So the Red Stockings' directors knew that the Buckeyes would be blamed for having started things and that their club could follow the same course and escape criticism— *as long as they won.*

Thus the 1868 season saw the Red Stockings became far more brazen in their pursuit of players than ever before. New Yorker John Hatfield "was secured after a great amount of correspondence, at a salary of $1,500 per annum, and furnished with a situation (?) in the Boatmen's Fire and Marine Insurance Company as recording clerk." Asa Brainard and Fred Waterman, "like Hatfield, were provided with nominal situations at a remuneration of $1,400 each, the former's services being secured by the law firm of Tilden, Moulton & Tilden, and the latter by a Water street commission house as shipping clerk. It has been asserted that while there Fred never shipped a pound of freight, and that on any fine afternoon before the practicing season opened he could be found outside the door seated on a barrel of sauer kraut, arguing base ball to any who would listen."

Next came the all-important matter of demonstrating that bringing in such players would produce a winner. The revamped Red Stockings beat the Buckeyes in the year's first match between the two rivals. They followed by splitting two games against the former national champions, the Unions of Morrisania, and posting a respectable 20-13 loss to the mighty Athletics of Philadelphia.

Yet for most onlookers the true test would be a late-season showdown against the Buckeyes. The match was scheduled for the Red Stockings' home park on September 2, and as that date approached it "created more excitement than has probably ever before or since attended to a game played in Cincinnati. It was to be a desperate struggle for supremacy. Both Clubs recognized the fact that but one of them could exist next year, and this was, therefore, to be life to one and death to the other. . . . Excitement over this game ran so high that many people did not go to bed the night before the great contest."

Anticipation was further enhanced when the Buckeyes brought in two more professionals from the Nationals of Washington just for the game. Meanwhile the city buzzed with gossip about the Red Stockings. According to one local paper: "Since Saturday there has been a great many rumors in regard to the different Clubs. On Tuesday morning it was reported that one of the prominent members of the Cincinnati Club had deserted his companions in their time of need, and had joined the Buckeyes."

While this tale proved false, another had a little more basis in fact: "Tuesday night the excitement at the hotels and on the streets was intense, and the great game of the following day was the chief topic of conversation, but the rumors flew thicker and faster, and among them there was pretty plain talk about the drugging of one of the Cincinnati members, and that another of his companions was very weak, caused by drinking whisky which had been given them by enemies of the Club. As soon as these rumors had reached a proper shape, the friends of the Buckeye Club immediately commenced offering large sums of money upon the result of the game, and Cincinnati stock began falling at an alarming rate. The appearance of Messrs. [Harry] Berthrong and Shields (who were lately members of crack Eastern clubs), increased the excitement and the betting upon the game was large. Thousands of dollars were staked upon the game. One gentleman who resides at Chicago won $2,210 upon the game. The two players referred to were Brainard and Hatfield. The Directors of the Club held a meeting the night before the game occurred, and brought the two accused before them. They confessed that they had been 'approached' by the Buckeye ring. Both begged off, and pronounced fidelity. Brainard was allowed to play under assurance that his actions would be closely watched, and if any laxity in his play should be discovered he would be promptly removed in the midst of the play. Hatfield they concluded not to trust, and Mose Grant was put into his place. . . . Brainard was not trusted in the pitcher's position for this game [he instead played second base], and Harry Wright took that honor upon himself."

The game took place in front of a frenzied crowd estimated at six thousand, and lived up to its billing. The lead seesawed back and forth until the Red Stockings scored six runs in the eighth to secure a 20-12 win.

Just as important, the match solidified the Red Stockings' image as the good guys. While eight of the nine Buckeyes were imports, including the two who had just arrived, the Red

Stockings featured five native sons plus Harry Wright. The decisions to bench Hatfield and to let Wright do the pitching also sent a powerful message: that the Red Stockings were still at heart the Cincinnati Base Ball Club.

On the heels of this signal triumph, the Red Stockings embarked on a brief tour that proved successful enough to encourage off-season planning for bigger and better things in 1869. That winter the NABBP finally conceded the inevitable and sanctioned open professionalism. This presented the ideal opportunity for Harry Wright to act on his long-standing conviction that it was not professional ball-playing that was sordid, only the hypocrisy of having to disguise the payment of money.

He impressed upon the club's directors the benefits of hiring an openly all-salaried nine for 1869. Of course, with his typical diplomacy he was careful to do this in a way that ruffled as few feathers as possible. The directors were consulted and involved in all the decision-making, and original members of the club, such as the attorney Aaron Champion, were allowed to act as the club's public face. And, we can be sure, Wright stressed that as captain he would ensure that the Red Stockings comported themselves as ambassadors for the city of Cincinnati.

The sense that the Red Stockings still embodied the Cincinnati Base Ball Club was reflected in the way the club severed its ties with John Hatfield. Rather than simply not inviting him back, the club solicited testimony about his actions from numerous eyewitnesses. They then staged a formal hearing at which they voted to expel him, and even printed a transcript of the proceedings. The replacement of one player clearly did not warrant such thoroughness, but the document proclaimed something much more important: the intention to continue to function as a club (and a club of lawyers, at that).

Having reassured the directors, Harry Wright was given approval to assemble a club of paid professionals. He had one enormous advantage, as his younger brother George had emerged as one of the game's greatest stars and was easily persuaded to enlist. Soon Wright had signed a nine that he believed could give Cincinnati winning baseball and would never embarrass the city.

He delivered more than anyone had a right to expect during the glorious 1869 season. His eye for talent and ability to develop young players proved outstanding, with unproven youngsters such as Cal McVey and Doug Allison emerging as stars. Meanwhile Asa Brainard, best known as a second baseman before arriving in Cincinnati, blossomed into one of the game's best pitchers. The club took on all comers and never lost a game.

Still more important was the club's gentlemanly conduct as it compiled that record. Several of Harry Wright's choices for players had raised eyebrows; Brainard and Waterman had been retained despite the doubts aroused by their conduct, and a few of the newcomers had come over from the Buckeyes. Yet Wright believed these men would respond to his leadership and discipline, and his faith was rewarded. Some observers attributed the club's success to teetotaling, and while there is no reason to believe that all the players were abstainers, they did complete the season with no documented incidents of misconduct.

A whirlwind of publicity followed—for baseball, for Cincinnati and for the Red Stockings, all of it positive. From coast to coast, observers who had been disillusioned by the discord that had plagued the 1868 season became interested in baseball once more. And many who had seen 1868 as the end of an era were forced to reconsider their cynicism toward professional baseball. Was it really possible for the spirit of the pioneer era of baseball to survive the transition to professionalism?

Of course the city of Cincinnati and the members of the Cincinnati Base Ball Club were even more delighted. One local citizen typified the exultant response when he marveled, "They've done something to add to the glory of our city!" At the end of such an astonishing season, it would have seemed churlish not to share this elation.

The famed "Red Stockings" of Cincinnati during their extraordinary unde-feated season of 1869. The Red Stockings popularized knickers and dead balls, among other things, but their most important contribution was to show Americans that professional baseball could be played in a gentlemanly fash-ion. Yet, just a year after bringing glory and acclaim to Cincinnati, their stay in the city ended abruptly when they were told they were no longer welcome to represent the Cincinnati Base Ball Club. [Collection of Tom Shieber]

Yet the fact remained that the Red Stockings and the Cincinnati Base Ball Club had diverged into two very different entities. Only one of the nine men who donned the signature knickerbockers was a native son, and even Charley Gould had started with another club and switched for a higher salary.

The ballplayers did their best to show their allegiance by singing the club song on their way to matches, but the lyrics of-fered ironic reminders of the displacement of longtime stal-warts. Its verses proclaimed that "Johnny How/ As a player is first rate" and "you shan't catch 'Moses Grant'/ A napping in right field"—yet neither of these players could show their skills because they had been replaced by newcomers. Especially ironic was the verse that described J. William Johnson as "all that's 'left'/ Of the 'riginal first nine." By 1869 Johnson too had been supplanted, meaning that all the men who had formed the Resolutes three years earlier now had to settle for vicarious pleasures.

This underlying problem surfaced in 1870. The Red Stockings' extraordinary winning streak ended with an extra-inning loss in Brooklyn in June. After so many consecutive wins, the club had acquired an aura of invincibility that made the defeat seem shocking. It really shouldn't have been; other clubs had upgraded their talent, and it was inevitable that the streak would end at some point. In cabling the result back to Cincinnati, Aaron Champion closed with these significant words: "Though beaten not disgraced."

The message was clearly a reminder that Harry Wright's implicit promise had not been broken. Wright had undertaken to provide high-quality baseball and a well-behaved club and had delivered on both. A loss or even a handful of losses might be disappointing, but no one had ever guaranteed that the club would be unbeatable.

But this initial loss was followed not only by several more losses but also by the first chinks in the club's chivalric armor. The most notable came when second baseman Charley Sweasy walked into a tavern wearing his Red Stockings uniform. Now the club was, in the eyes of some members, not only beaten but disgraced.

The season nonetheless ended with the Red Stockings boasting a sterling record. Then came more shocking news. The Cincinnati Base Ball Club announced that it would not field a professional squad in 1871, instead reverting to pure amateurism.

This dramatic decision prompted vigorous debate. The *Cincinnati Chronicle* quite unfairly termed Harry Wright a "fraud." Meanwhile the rival *Commercial* sprang to Wright's defense, maintaining that "the facts prove that he has not been well treated." It reasoned that the club's about-face "seems to be in some degree spiteful toward professional players—and

The 1870 match in Brooklyn in which the Atlantics finally ended the Red Stockings' unbeaten streak. By this time some baseball fields had a bench for the players—but only one, and obviously not large enough for all the players. [Collection of Tom Shieber]

every player *must* be a professional who can devote sufficient time to practice and keep himself in the best condition." The *Commercial* also published a revealing interview with Wright, who expressed disappointment but characteristically avoided vindictiveness.

One of the *Commercial*'s writers was not nearly as inclined to mince words, writing caustically: "The biggest 'Irish dividend' we ever heard of is that just declared by the Executive Board of the Cincinnati Club. They have fine grounds and no debts. Hence no players will be hired. Matches are in order between the Fats and Leans, the Puffers and the Rheumatics, the slim legged second juniors and the sedate first juniors. In a word, we are to get enthusiastic over gratuitous amateurs, who, if they turn out handsomely, will remove to some other city and get salaries."

The *Commercial*'s assessment has, by and large, been the judgment of history as well, and it is not without validity. Its proponents have drawn support from the subsequent histories of the two parties. Harry Wright took the Red Stockings name and many of the players to Boston and established another dynasty (which is why this club's legacy is acknowledged in the nicknames of both the Cincinnati Reds and the Boston Red Sox). By contrast, the Cincinnati Base Ball Club produced no notable victories after reverting to amateur play.

Yet surely the later records of the two sides are beside the point. No one doubted that the players brought in by Harry Wright were far superior to the locals they supplanted. Nor did anyone expect that the amateurs who would now represent the Cincinnati Base Ball Club would become world-beaters.

Instead the longtime members of the Cincinnati Base Ball Club chose to end their relationship with the Red Stockings not for financial reasons but because they wanted a return to their old, familiar game. From their perspective, the club had been theirs initially, and they had allowed the newcomers to join them. Not stopping there, they had graciously stepped aside and let these outsiders take their places. All they had asked was that the newcomers behave in a manner that upheld the club's name and traditions. When embarrassing incidents multiplied, they decided it was time to take back their club.

One director maintained that the situation was "very much as though some old gentleman who had been put upon slim fare by his physicians should hire a fellow of large appetite and powerful digestion to go around the country and represent him at public dinners." Meanwhile Aaron Champion echoed the complaints that had emanated from Baltimore two years earlier, contending that Cincinnati could not compete with clubs from Washington, where players "are paid by the government of the United States to play baseball."

A self-described "old member" of the club even questioned whether Harry Wright was entitled to take the name Red Stockings to Boston with him. He maintained that in an 1866 game against the Buckeyes, "Mr. George B. Ellard, now a resident of this city, wore the uniform, then white shirt, white pants and red cap, and added to and appeared in 'red stockings,' in the manner of the present costume of the Club, and in three or four games played that year he alone wore the red stockings. Harry Wright played in the above mentioned game, but appeared in ordinary citizen's clothes. From this it will be seen that the assertion that he was the originator of or introducer of the Red Stocking uniform, is untrue. In the season of 1867 this uniform was worn by the first Nine as a matter of choice, and in that year the Club was first called 'Red Stockings,' being so dubbed by a reporter of a city paper, in a derisive article. In the spring of 1868, the red stocking uniform was formally adopted by the Club, has been by its representatives worn ever since, and will be worn hereafter."

Therefore he contended, "Where should the uniform and name go, if it is to be taken away from Cincinnati? The public may judge. The Cincinnati Club still exists. . . . Abolition of the system of hiring players is not a destruction of the Club. It still lives, and is neither dead nor sleeping."

Was this "old member" right and the accepted judgment of history wrong? No. But as his comments suggest, this was not a situation where a postmortem needs to conclude that one side was right and the other wrong. Rather, the marriage of the Red Stockings and the Cincinnati Base Ball Club is best compared to a relationship that simply wasn't meant to last. From the first it had been too unstable to endure. Yet while it did, its results were spectacular.

CHAPTER 12

Looking Backward

❖ The pioneer era of baseball thus effectively ended by 1868, and while the Red Stockings briefly created hopes of a revival in 1869, these were soon dashed. As professionalism came to the forefront, the first generation of ballplayers gradually withdrew—voluntarily or involuntarily—from active participation in baseball. Once relegated to the sidelines, they responded with a wide range of emotions.

Some of them turned to other sports in hopes of finding the traits that had once drawn them to baseball. The most obvious alternative was cricket, a game with an ambience and customs that were reminiscent of the way baseball had once been played. Joe Sprague of Brooklyn and Ford Hinchman of Detroit were two players who enjoyed especially long careers as cricketers after giving up baseball. George Wright eventually retired from baseball to attend to his sporting goods store and play cricket.

Early Brooklyn ballplayer Leonard Bergen became an expert roller skater. George Wright ultimately dabbled in tennis and golf. Rowing became the sport of preference for many of West Virginia's early baseballists and, a few years later, for four ballplayers from Hillsdale, Michigan, who captured the national championship. But for most early baseball players, there was no real substitute for their first love.

Some made a seamless transition from playing the game to being involved as owners or fans. The early ballplayers J. Wayne

Neff, William Conant, and Frederick Stearns later were owners in whole or part of the National League clubs in their respective hometowns of Cincinnati, Boston, and Detroit.

Another early Detroit ballplayer, Richard Fyfe, could have afforded to buy several teams but preferred to be a fan, attending Tigers games until shortly before his death in 1931 at age ninety-two. Others shared his passion. The treasurer of the first club in Pana, Illinois, was reported in 1921 to be "as much of a fan as ever." An original member of the Kekionga Club of Fort Wayne reported in 1908: "I'm still an enthusiastic fan, as I was while a member of the original crack team of Indiana in the early seventies, but I couldn't catch a feather bed now and it's all I can do to throw a kiss."

H. Clay Sexton, the longtime captain of the Empire Club of St. Louis, was another who remained devoted to the game after his playing days ended. He could be seen at every local game, and "at critical points of a game Sexton's excitement is almost ecstatic. He fills the air with 'Dog-gone my cats,' or is speechless and breathing hard." In deference to his position as chief of the city's fire department, however, he was accompanied by his fire buggy, "and turns the horse's head toward the northern gate, which in the event of fire is swung open, and Sexton dashes away, even should there be three men on bases and Billy Gleason at the bat."

One early Wilkes-Barre ballplayer took solace in his allegiance to the game while battling the disease that ultimately claimed his life in 1887. According to a teammate, John Woodward "never lost his interest in the game. In that year when he was ill unto death he had a remarkable interest in the fight for the pennant of the National league and was anxious for Detroit to win it."

But going from playing to cheering proved a difficult adjustment for many early ballplayers. Theirs had been the first generation of Americans to play team sports with great seriousness, so there was no precedent for them becoming spectators.

For many of them, the whole point of a sport was the exercise and fun; the notion of sitting still and watching it seemed bizarre. One old-time ballplayer later chided: "The question with our young people should be to decide whether they will have enjoyable exercise in an attractive and harmless game among themselves or whether they will pay for a ticket to burn or bleach themselves in a cramped position for two or three hours on a hard seat to see two men throw and catch a ball while seven others do a great deal of standing around, the only relief being rising on their feet for a few minutes between innings, and to resume their discomfort when play begins again."

As a result, most of these men felt at least some unease about the transition from participation to vicarious involvement. One of the fun-loving Pastimes conveyed this distinction when he remarked, "When the Pastimes broke up I joined the Atlantic, only as a paying member, however." It was all very well to stay involved with the game, but it wasn't quite the same.

Others elected to turn their backs on baseball altogether. It was reported in 1894 that Charley Smith, one of the greatest stars of the 1860s, had not seen a professional game since 1872 and had no idea of the meaning of terms like bunt and sacrifice hit. While this report was probably exaggerated, it would have been apt for these new approaches to be shunned by a player from the era when it was taken for granted that batters would swing lustily.

Frank Pidgeon, the man who wrote the delightful account of the early days of the Eckford Club and became a leading pitcher of the 1850s, turned into one of the "most bitter opponents" of professional play: "Frank would have nothing to do with the Eckford club when its nine became professionals, as they did in the sixties." Pidgeon was joined in this sentiment by his close friend Pete O'Brien, the man who in 1868 had bemoaned the fact that "they don't play ball nowadays as they used to." As a result of the strong feelings of Pidgeon and many of his contemporaries, the Eckford Club was restructured: "On

The legendary talents of Charley Smith, third baseman of the Atlantics of Brooklyn in the 1860s, continued to grow after he retired from the diamond. In 1897 a contemporary wrote, "Charley is still the unassuming gentleman he was on the ball field. Would there were more Smiths and less Tebeaus on the ball field to-day. He bears with ease his 56 years. His crooked fingers testify to many a hot grounder and difficult fly. I have seen tens of thousands cheering his running catches of what seemed impossible foul flys [*sic*] over third base, and while at the bat his terrific grounders between the short stop and the bases. It was said of him that he never missed a ball nor struck out. Loving cups are presented to and benefits given for the pioneers of other vocations, but I know of no more deserving ones than the few who are left of those old veterans, who back in the fifties sacrificed their business future, disfigured themselves for life, while contributing their skill to make popular the national game of America to-day, and if I was called upon to name 'the noblest Roman of them all,' it would be that gentlemanly, unassuming one who occasionally drops into my office, one who will not thank me for bringing him into prominence again, the great third baseman of the old Atlantic Club of Brooklyn—Charley Smith." [Collection of Tom Shieber]

September 16, 1865, the Eckford was organized as a social club.
. . . As professionalism advanced the base ball section of the club
dropped away. The present [1896] membership of the club numbers about seventy."

Smith, Pidgeon, and O'Brien all starred for Brooklyn clubs,
but as the excesses that began in the East spread to other parts
of the country, so too did the disillusionment. In Grand Rapids,
Michigan, an article written in the early 1880s reported: "Among
those who display but little outward interest in base ball are some
who were the fiercest of players fifteen years ago."

Others shared these men's bitterness but were not quite
ready to turn their backs on the game. Some of them settled for
expressing a resentment that their contributions were being forgotten (as has been the case with every generation of ballplayers since). As one man put it: "Loving cups are presented to and
benefits given for the pioneers of other vocations, but I know of
no more deserving ones than the few who are left of those old
veterans, who back in the fifties sacrificed their business future,
disfigured themselves for life, while contributing their skill to
make popular the national game of America to-day."

Another course was to indulge in vehement denunciations of
the excesses that now plagued the game. The emphasis on rules
was an especially sore subject. One observer greeted the annual
set of additions and clarifications to the rules by harrumphing
what "a fine lot of rules they are. They are drawing the rules so
close and fine that the game is about as much like what it used
to be, as a jack-knife handle is like an oyster stew. Give us the
old-fashioned game when 'three tick-in-airy' put a man on the
retired list, and 'over the fence' was 'out.'"

Others saw pretty much all of baseball's changes as being for
the worse. "We used to think then that base," wrote one early
ballplayer sarcastically, "was yet a very simple matter, quite
within the comprehension of the little fellows whose school
troubles and triumphs were all yet to come. . . . We were content,
and thought, poor ignorant chaps, that we had played base, and

that our scores—kept on a tally stick, chalked on the fence, or mayhap, only scratched on a smooth piece of ground—were a sufficient record of our skill and our endurance. But it seems that we were woefully ignorant and unsophisticated. We should have had umpires and uniforms. The fellows that were out catching should have been severally designated as long-stop, short-stop, centre-fielder, and so forth; we should have had printed rules and regulations, and, above all, reporters to give an account of our games in the newspapers. For what satisfaction is there—although we used to think there was some fun— in a few lads or young men playing half-a-dozen games at baseball, if their doings cannot be recorded in print for the benefit of an admiring world?"

The most common complaint was about the incursion of money. "The game of base ball," bemoaned a typical observer in 1879, "has of late years no less deservedly acquired notoriety as a national disgrace. From the hands of amateurs the game passed largely to the control of professionals; and for very logical reasons. The professionals so conducted it as to bring it into very bad repute. When large sums of money were at stake individual players and clubs were bought up; the game was jockied and otherwise conducted with more or less 'crookedness.'"

Yet the very fact that it still seemed worthwhile to write such harsh words implies some hope that the game was not doomed. This last article went on to express optimism that such troubles were being addressed, and so too did many others. Even some of the observers who merely raged presumably felt that the situation was not quite as bleak as did those who turned their backs on baseball.

Others voiced their disenchantment more subtly, in the form of nostalgic reminiscences implying that the "good old days" were far superior to what baseball had become. These accounts credited the early players with epic prowess. Charley Smith was said to have "never missed a ball nor struck out." The college student who introduced baseball to Decatur, Illinois, became "as famous as a baseball pitcher as was Joe McGinnity in modern times. Corwin [Johns] could throw a ball further than any other man in Decatur."

Descriptions of the early players' accomplishments became the stuff of legend. A member of the first club in Pana, Illinois, "was known as the Babe Ruth of Central Illinois, and won the state championship by knocking the ball out of the state fair grounds at Decatur, Illinois, for a home run and brought in three men with him, winning the game and the silver cup."

Even their failings seemed mythic. One such oft-recounted tale involved a match in which the Athletics of Philadelphia overwhelmed a nine from Pottsville by a score of 107-2. During the Athletics' lengthy first at bats, a player named Jimmy Foran made all three outs. In the second inning he made the first two outs and at that point claimed to be sick and withdrew.

Some recollections attributed godlike qualities to an entire ball club. Of the Aquidnecks of Newport, Rhode Island, it was later said: "Even if they played after a hard day's work there seemed to be as much ginger in them as if they had done nothing previously. . . . Newport had a team made up of players who were not afraid to hustle every minute they were in the game, and of whom it could never be said that they were tired."

Most early ballplayers arrived at some way of balancing their conflicting emotions and did their best to hold their tongues about the forces that had transformed the game of baseball. As one old-timer tactfully put it, "Here's to the memory of the Olympics and Bay States, who played straight ball and never did anything to cripple a delightful game, and here's to the early clubs in the national game and the memory of pleasant and enjoyable happenings of younger days. The other things do not count."

Yet when asked to reminisce about "the good old times" of baseball, their delight was unmistakable. A Kalamazoo journalist remarked in 1906, "There are but few left who can tell of the exciting times when patch ball was the only kind of baseball that

Charles Commerford's father was one of the most influential labor organizers of the 1840s and 1850s. But Charles's most enduring memories of those tumultuous decades involved playing shortstop for the Gothams—and he never tired of reminiscing about that bygone era. [Collection of Tom Shieber]

was played in this city. To talk with one of these old timers is really amusing. They get as excited as a young boy when he sees his first circus parade. The times when all baseball men were amateurs and played the game only for the sport there was in it are the best times for them. While they take up the new game and enjoy it with the rest of the crowd still it does not quite take the place of the game they used to play when they were boys."

Others were equally exuberant in describing the early days of the Knickerbockers' game. In old age, Charley Commerford could still muster his "old flow of language, especially when baseball is the topic." When the Detroit attorney Joe Weiss was asked about the early days of the Cass Club, he dropped his legal work "with celerity and tackled his favorite topic of base ball with avidity."

And several of these old-timers were not merely enthusiastic but also eloquent.

After acknowledging that some aspects of the early game might seem crude, Clarence Deming offered this defense: "Yet may the *laudator temporis acti* [a "praiser of time past"] claim for the elder sport certain vantages. It had speed, range; breeziness, and a horizon; it made fun while not lacking intensity; nine men played it, and the battery did not focalize the match game; on the larger scale of runs and fielding the better team more often won than in the sport of to-day, where the timely base hit or untimely error wins victory or loses it, and, paradoxically, has made the game more uncertain in proportion as it is more scientific; and the term 'professional' had not then entered the baseball vocabulary. Yet, were the virtues of the old days in baseball purely legendary, the gray-headed ball player would still love them. Again with memory's eye he would mark the rough diamonds of the shaggy country land, the outgoings in the sunlight and the homecomings under the moon; hear the cheers for victory, and see the forms of the old players against so many of whom in college triennials the Great Umpire has set his final 'out' and marked his grim asterisk of death."

The same Latin phrase occurred to the editor of a newspaper in Elizabethtown, New York, who published a reminiscence written by an early ballplayer: "Upon such occasions we readily recall the lines of the poet:

Backward, turn backward, Oh, time in thy flight
Make me a child again, just for tonight

It is well that we are able occasionally to brush the cobwebs from the corners of memory and live over again that which made up careless, happy innocent childhood, boyhood, youth and early manhood. Shades of departed glory this night hover o'er us and we are in the midst of happy boyhood when base ball was constantly on the bill of fare, morning, noon and night, our day dream and our innocent nightmare! What glorious days were those, so free from care and toil and so full of highly tinted promise. But we must go slow else we be called *laudator temporis acti.*"

Henry Chadwick in 1877 poignantly captured the contrast between the erstwhile ballplayers and the successful middle-aged men they had become: "What a magician time is! Think of Registrar [William] Barre running for first base as if the world's existence depended on his success. Consider ex-Sheriff [John] McNamee, now carving out fame for himself as a sculptor in Florence, pitching or catching as though all life were a ball field and the only success worth anything that of securing a home run. Who would think that Bob Furey, up to the ears in local politics and divers contracts, at a time not yet remote chiefly gloried in his length and strength of arm. Fred. Massey, Frank Quevedo, Harry Polhemus, Dr. Jones, Commissioner Shields, Thomas Jerome, Sam Patchen, and a score of others, drop their present habiliments and take their place among the old boys who used to make the fields resound and the night merry when victory perched upon the banner of their respective clubs. It reconciles one to what are undoubtedly the excesses of youth to see that they do not necessarily stand in the way of serious work in after life. Take the old boys who used to run with the machine, who would rather have seen the city in flames than have permitted another company to get ahead of them. Consider the grave and excellent President of the Board of Education, Mr. Whitlock, jumping like a young dervish and brandishing a trumpet at some alien head, with the vigor of a trooper. In this connection, come before the mind the forms of County Clerk Delmar, of Commissioner McLaughlin, of Controller Barry, of Daniel D. Whitney, and any number of assemblymen, justices, lawyers and successful business men. And after all, how many of the old boys do not now and then look back with regret from the point of their present success to the time when the base ball and fire engine were to them the symbols of the highest earthly happiness."

Harry C. McLean, by then the deputy health officer for the District of Columbia, wrote with similar eloquence in 1907 to a former teammate on the Nationals of Washington. He expressed some displeasure over the changes that the game of baseball had witnessed. Yet those resentments paled in comparison to the pride he felt in recalling "the days of our youth, when you and I, and a host of good fellows, were the exponents in fact of the game that is still 'winging' its flight to parts unknown, and long years after we have joined those who made their last 'home run' will continue to be marching under the banner of Excelsior as the sport par excellence of the civilized globe."

He concluded: "For the remainder of my allotted days I must, however, be content with singing the praises in my humble way of the game, of which no 'fan' tireth, and hum to myself, as time speeds by:

My base ball battles are all fought,
And all my bases run,
I can but wait my turn at bat
To make my last 'home run.'
And though our flags long ceased to fly
Where I so oft did go,
I ne'er forget those jolly days
When we went westward ho!"

The words were a modified version of ones in the song that the Nationals had used as their anthem during their celebrated 1867 tour.

But while most of the earliest players were inclined to look backward in later years, some looked ahead. By doing so—in a process that parallels the Knickerbockers' largely inadvertent creation of a national pastime—they began a new tradition that has had a lasting impact on the game. Their story will be told in the final chapter.

[CHAPTER 13]

Moving Forward: "Muffin" Ballplayers Start a New Tradition

❖ As we have seen, many members of the first generation of baseball players ceased playing after the Civil War. The vast majority of the remainder, along with most of the younger players who had fueled the feverish years of 1866 and 1867, joined them on the sidelines when professional play supplanted the amateurs. A select few had the talent and desire to make the transition to professionalism, but most had neither. A few of these displaced men became club owners or die-hard fans, but most ended their involvement with professional baseball.

Yet a significant number of these men continued to play. Their stories have been almost entirely ignored by baseball historians, whose narratives have traditionally concentrated on professional leagues, pennant races, and statistics. Most of the members of the pioneer era of baseball who continued to play had not the slightest interest in such things.

These men had a hard time seeing professional baseball as the legitimate heir of the game they had played. Despite all the obvious similarities, their game had seemed flexible in all the aspects that made professional baseball appear rigid and structured. As a member of Fort Wayne's first club later put it, "I recollect that the [early] game was played on the same lines as that of the present day. . . . The rules, of course, were more flexible and the game was not played with the serious purpose that prevails today."

The game they remembered had been inclusive, but professional baseball was highly exclusive, without a place for the men who had built baseball. Or, to be more accurate, these veterans were cordially invited to fund the local ball club but were not welcome in other roles. As one observer complained: "In most of our ballclubs the brunt of the expense of maintaining them, season after season, falls upon the liberal minority, who do not hesitate to expend considerable money in their efforts to sustain the club and the game they are so much attached to. This is not fair. Every club ought to be a self-sustaining organization, and with the proprietorship of an inclosed ground would always be so. It does not follow, however, that because a prominent club finds that a ground of this kind pays that it should become a source of pecuniary profit to the few at the expense of the many."

Thus for early players, professional baseball seemed to have taken the feeling of being included, which they had treasured during their youth, and turned it on its head. One of them reflected: "It seems to me now as I look back and recall those early days that the young people enjoyed their sports and games and entered into them with far more zest than young people do at the present day. There was no feeling of envy or superiority, or the feeling that you don't belong to my set. All were on a level, and everyone was just as good as any other." Similarly, Clarence Darrow has the narrator of his autobiographical 1904 novel *Farmington* remark, "We played ball; we did not work at the trade of amusing people."

Most fundamentally, from the perspective of these men, it seemed as if no one was having fun playing baseball any longer because of the all-consuming obsession with winning. Rules that had once ensured that the fun of baseball remained within bounds were now fostering a spirit of mirthless competition. On the surface the game might appear much the same, but it had been stripped of its joy and its sense of release, and in the process had become barren.

This new attitude was most evident among the professionals, but it soon was having a corrosive effect on every level of play. A Chicago sportswriter noted with dismay in 1870: "It became customary last season to publish the scores of games played between the less known clubs of this city—clubs with barbaric, comic, stupid or overridiculous names, and whose scorers did write most villainously, and spelt at random. . . . A report of one of these games would be left at the office, stating that the Young Americas had beaten the Hopefuls by a gigantic score. The next day the Captain of the Hopefuls, aged 4 to 9, after climbing our 80 stairs with great difficulty, would appear panting, and claim that his organization had the great score, and the others, the small one. He would frequently argue for half an hour as to the vital importance of a correction, and would denounce the unscrupulous mendacity of the Young Americas. Repressing a strong inclination to give him five cents to buy marbles with, we promised to correct, and he went downstairs exultant."

While many of these displaced old-timers settled for grumbling about this overemphasis on winning and losing, some of them started a new tradition. Befitting the way they believed baseball ought to be played, theirs was not a formal movement or an organized rebellion; it was not hatched in a committee meeting or supervised by a board of governors. Rather than specifically pointing out the excesses of professional baseball, they sought to keep alive the elements of baseball they had cherished. Their play had no structure and no statistics, and resulted in the awarding of no championship flags. The participants made no effort to articulate a message and might not have been able to do so if they tried. They were too busy having fun playing what became known as "muffin games."

As noted earlier, "muffin games" had their roots in the rapid growth of baseball during the 1860s. To accommodate the swelling club membership rolls, would-be ballplayers who were unable to earn one of the coveted spots on the "first nine" were instead placed on "second nines," "third nines," and so on. At first, members of these auxiliary nines were bolstered by the "patience of hope" and believed that diligent practice would enable them to earn spots on the first nine. Some of them did improve and earn starting roles, but more learned that all the perseverance in the world could not compensate for a lack of innate ability. And the farther down the hierarchy a player was, the less realistic it was for him to believe he would ever represent the club in match play.

With discouragement already beginning to set in for many players, things grew worse when clubs began importing outsiders. Suddenly even players on the first nine were being displaced, leaving members of the other nines with no realistic hope of moving up the ladder. Worse, they felt like second-class citizens in their own clubs. The first nine often monopolized practice time on the club's grounds, meaning that other club members had still less hope of improving and might not have a chance to play at all. When Eugene Robinson, one of Detroit's pioneer ballplayers and a distinguished war hero, was inadvertently referred to by one of the city's newspapers as a "second rate man" instead of a "second nine man," it seemed sadly typical.

Baseball seemed to have no place for such men except as financial supporters, and neither did their own clubs. Then a surprising thing happened. Club members with self-deprecating senses of humor began to form "muffin" nines so they could play baseball for the simpler pleasures it afforded. Shunning any pretext that they were trying to master the game's intricacies, "muffins" stubbornly refused to feel any contrition when they muffed the ball. As a matter of fact, they took a perverse glee in their own misadventures.

Still more amazingly, in 1867 and 1868 these games suddenly became all the rage. Newspapers that were finding less and less room to devote to the results of the most talented local clubs began to fill entire columns with accounts of the games played by some singularly inept ballplayers. And a public that was growing reluctant to support the town club began to flock to watch "muffins" bumble their way through a burlesque of the national pastime.

These games spread from city to city as quickly as the Knickerbockers' game once had. No national association aided their popularity—indeed, the men who played in them had no doubt had their fill of national organizations. Instead they spread organically, propelled by the exuberance and enthusiasm they inspired.

For all the columns of newsprint prompted by the muffin games, no one tried to explain why these games were popular. There was no need. Everyone who witnessed or read about one intuitively understood that it was no coincidence they had sprung up just when professionalism and competitiveness were transforming baseball. At the most obvious level, muffin games served as a parody of the excesses that were besetting the game. But their basic message was far simpler: a reminder to Americans that baseball could still be played just for fun.

The direct relationship between baseball's uneasy transition to professionalism and the rise of muffin games was vividly illustrated in St. Louis. As we have seen, the 1868 season was a tumultuous one there, with the excesses associated with Eastern play affecting the long-standing friendly rivalry between the Empire and Union clubs. It was therefore highly significant that the season climaxed on October 17 with "one of the most noted games ever played in St. Louis. It was a 'mixed' game in that the players were chosen from the honorary members of the Empire and Union Clubs with view as to their weight, a game between 'light' and 'heavy weight' or 'Shrimps vs. Whales.'"

The game began and ended with displays that gently poked fun at the increasingly contentious tendencies of the professionals. "Considerable time was lost in opening the game," Empire Club member E. H. Tobias later recalled, "owing to the inability of the field captains to find a piece of coin suitably large for the occasion, to make a legendary 'toss up.'" And at the game's end, according to his dry account, "the umpire, Jack Stinson, was not required to swear he had received no bribe." In between there was plenty of "lofty tumbling," "agitating the dust," and out-of-shape players struggling to recover "from a too sudden encounter with the ball."

Other muffin games parodied the excesses of professional play in ways both subtle and transparent. In contrast to the exclusionary practices of the professionals, in muffin games players were urged to participate. An account of a muffin game in Connecticut began with a lengthy description of two reluctant honorary members being tricked into playing—each man was told that the other had agreed to play if he did. After years of being told that they were not good enough to be allowed to play, muffin games sent the welcome message that everyone was good enough to play.

This was underscored by descriptions that highlighted and no doubt exaggerated the ineptness of the players. At a match in South Boston, "But one fly was taken, and that was purely accidental, for which the unfortunate author was severely reprimanded—it being deemed a violation of the rules of base ball for muffins to catch flies. We noticed but one ball that was stopped, and that was by the fielder prostrating himself upon the approaching ball in genuine muffin style. The spread-eagle manner of effecting the stop was taken into account, and the play excused."

The point of such uproarious descriptions is unmistakable: *Of course you can play in a muffin game. You couldn't possibly not be good enough.*

You say you have physical shortcomings that prevent you from playing? No problem! This message was dramatically illustrated by the wildly popular "Fat versus lean" games. In a typical encounter, "the Heavies were sent blowing all over the field, after that d——d ball which would either carom off their shins or corporations, or be sent to distant parts of the field, very troublesome to reach in going after it."

One reluctant player, when approached about participating in a muffin game, protested, "I haven't played ball for ten years. I'm too fat to run." But he might as well have saved his breath. "That's the fix we're all in," he was told. "There's really only one fair player—Macpherson; and we will handicap him, so the difference won't be noticed. If you can't run, some one may run for you." Indeed an infirmity might allow a player to be paired with one with a different handicap. A muffin club from Hartford used "an agile but near-sighted muffin, who could not see a ball to hit it himself, to do the running for a corpulent muffin, who was a splendid batsman, but could not follow up his advantage by any vigorous locomotion."

Nor was it a problem if a team already had nine players. In another throwback element, muffin sides used eight, ten, or eleven players when necessary—the more the merrier. One team in Connecticut featured thirteen players to a side: two men apiece manned shortstop, left field, and right field, and there was also "a B.C. (behind the catcher)." If a club member didn't play in a muffin game it was because he had resisted all efforts to convince him. There was no such thing as exclusion, with one exception—before a muffin match in Detroit, players were warned: "all who have any knowledge of the game are to be excluded from the nines."

After years of seeing the rituals of the game trivialized, muffin games restored rituals to a central place. Players paraded onto the field in comically ostentatious displays, presented one another with badges with appropriate inscriptions, and in general focused on everything but the game itself.

Most conspicuously, the postgame banquet resumed its status as the focal point of the rituals. Sometimes the point was underscored by appropriate additions to the bill of fare, such as the "muffin soup" that was the first course following a game in Connecticut. Many of the players made it evident during the game that they could scarcely wait for the contest to end and the banquet to begin. The captain of a muffin nine in Saginaw, Michigan, for instance, was said to have had trouble positioning his fielders, "as most of them wished to be stationed near the brewery on Hamilton street."

The postgame feast in Connecticut was highlighted by the reading of a lengthy poem written by one of the participants, a divinity student. The verse aptly summed up the pleasure of once again feeling included in the beloved game, concluding:

"Hail! Order of Muffins! Your glorious mission,
Should arouse in each breast a noble ambition;
To be first 'at the front,' in this world-renowned war,
Gainst the empire of mind, which all muffins abhor,
Let us fill up the ranks—let our camp be enlarged—
Let's enlist for the war, unless sooner discharged!"

Muffin games also restored the umpire to a position of distinction. While most of the satire employed in these games was gentle, the role of the umpire was burlesqued more forcefully. After making a ruling, the umpire was sometimes surrounded by a throng of players in an amusing but unmistakable rebuke of the contentious spirit that too often prevailed at professional games.

With the professionals becoming increasingly literal-minded in interpreting the rules, muffin games also offered reminders that the spirit of the rules was what really mattered. It was common for a long list of facetious printed rules to be distributed, yet the players themselves were prone to forgetting even the most basic strictures. A batter who made a tremendous clout in the game in South Boston "would undoubtedly have secured a home home run had he not unfortunately mistook the pitcher's point for the first base."

The "home home run" referred to an early-days rule occasionally used in some regions whereby a batter could count two runs if he completed the circuit of the bases on his own hit and then made it back to first base again. This variant was never adopted or even considered by the NABBP, but it was just the sort of long-forgotten element that was likely to resurface in a muffin game.

All these elements sent the message that muffin games were throwbacks to the impromptu way of playing that had flourished thirty years earlier. The feeling was neatly captured in one 1869 account of a muffin game: "The gyrations of the players in their vain attempts to catch the flying or even rolling balls were laughable in the extreme. Having many of them retired from participation in ball sports long before base ball came into vogue, they very naturally were troubled with visions of 'Town Ball,' 'Tip Cat,' 'Socky,' 'Shinny,' 'Barn Ball,' 'War Ball,' and other of the old fashioned games that were 'all the go' when they were boys. Some of the little Eagles came near getting badly socked by the ball being hurled at them—a principle of the old games, but not of base ball."

Also parodied was the tendency for the true object of the game to get lost amidst the minutiae of record-keeping and parliamentary proceedings. Before the first game of a series between muffin nines from Hartford and Waterbury, a committee presented this report on the etymology of the term muffin: "Your committee to whom was referred the inquiry as to the origin and definition of the word 'muffin' beg leave to report: That from a careful examination I find the origin somewhat obscure, but am satisfied that it had a very early origin, from the fact that I find it compounded with the word 'rag' as far back as the Crusades, when the appellation was esteemed highly honorable, indicating valor, virtue and perseverance; indeed, virtue has often been found clothed in rags. The definition of the word is less obscure, though some lexicographers have given it a very simple definition as 'a spongy cake'; but it is evident that the error has arisen from a lack of knowledge of our illustrious order. The word Muffin is derived from the Latin *Muggins*, the French *Mufti* (high priest), and the German *Bumm*, and is a clear compound of *Muff* and *fin*. These words are then conjointly conjoined from their close proximity, indicating, among other things, comfort and grace, two conditions closely aligned to our order. There are several other words I find belonging to the same family, e.g., *puffing* and *bumming*, and into the latter of these the Muffin generally merges. The definition of the word Muffin I have given in my earlier writings, where it can be found elaborately elaborated. . . ." This report also shows the determination of muffin players to redefine their weak ball-playing skills as a source of pride.

More than anything else, muffin games served as timely reminders that as long as winning was not made the be-all and end-all, a great time could still be had playing baseball. As one muffin game participant recalled, "to use a slang expression, 'There was more fun than a barrel of monkeys.'"

This was an extremely important development because the end of the pioneer era of baseball left the game at a crossroads. The decision by the Cincinnati Base Ball Club to sever its ties with the Red Stockings at the end of the 1870 season left no doubt that baseball had entered a new era. But no one had a very clear idea of what that new era would bring, and especially whether there would be any role in it for the first generation of ballplayers.

In March 1871 baseball's amateurs and professionals underwent the same sort of messy divorce that the Cincinnati Base Ball Club and the Red Stockings had gone through a few months earlier. The game's longtime governing body split into two entities—the National Association of Professional Base Ball Players and the National Association of Amateur Base Ball Players. The clubs that opted for the latter organization had little need for a centralized body, however, with the result that the NAABBP never amounted to much. By contrast, the professionals' organization functioned as the first baseball league for the next five years and so eclipsed the amateurs' governing body that it came to be known simply as the National Association.

In 1876 the National Association gave way to the National League, but the basic challenge faced by both leagues during the 1870s was the same. Much of the public remained disenchanted or openly hostile toward the whole concept of professional baseball, and for this and a variety of reasons, both leagues were on precarious financial footing. Harry Wright's Boston version of the Red Stockings were the stalwarts of both leagues, in their play and in their conduct, but too often this club's example was overshadowed by the misdeeds of others.

Throughout the decade, amateur baseball maintained the lowest of profiles. The clubs representing a few prestigious colleges received attention, but otherwise, to the extent that the press and public thought of baseball, their attentions were drawn to the professional game. All too often, though, they weren't thinking of the game at all.

But then the 1880s saw amateur baseball begin a return to prominence. At the same time professional baseball achieved profitability, with the result that the National League was joined by a second major league, several other challengers, and the first minor leagues. While the focus remained on the professionals, the amateurs played an important complementary role. After more than a decade of seeing themselves as rivals warring for control of baseball, the two camps realized they could coexist and even benefit each other by generating enthusiasm for baseball.

Playing no small part in this important development was the popularity of muffin games during the late 1860s and throughout the 1870s. These games didn't prevent professional baseball from suffering the excesses of commercialization and competition, but they did something just as important by providing a vivid reminder that baseball didn't have to be played that way.

In doing so they kept the untainted spirit of the pioneer era alive. They also helped keep quite a few of the earliest amateur clubs going during these tumultuous years by renewing faith that all the members belonged to the same club, whether they were part of the first, second, third, or even the muffin nine. A perfect example is the Olympics of Philadelphia, the club that began playing town ball in the 1830s and switched to the Knickerbockers' game in 1860. While clubs like the Olympics ceased to draw much attention after the dawn of the professional era, they were still a vibrant amateur club in the late 1880s when an article reported, "Dr. Neil is one of the most noted players of the club. He has played for twenty years. When a game cannot be arranged, he gets a number of boys together and bats the ball to them. He never goes without his exercise."

Muffin games continued throughout the 1870s but gradually faded in the next decade. By then they were ready to be supplanted by the rebirth of a robust amateur scene. Since then, amateur and professional baseball have largely pursued different courses, but each has thrived. The sense that the two are no longer rivals has even allowed a hybrid, semiprofessional play, to emerge and also build a long-standing tradition.

Amateur and semipro play have flourished in many different formats over the years, but perhaps the most notable is one that was also a staple of the pioneer era of baseball. By the 1880s, games between the best players from neighboring cities were again attracting great attention and producing great loyalty. No longer did the participants belong to a specific club, but it didn't matter. They resided in a community and represented it, so they were—once more—sources of great civic pride. In several cities, amateur ballplayers found a most fitting way to demonstrate that pride: by parading in uniform through the center of town.

Smoky Joe Wood recalled that as a teenager living in Ness City, Kansas, in the early twentieth century, "I pitched for the town team—it was only amateur ball, you know, but that was the big thing in those days. We'd play all the surrounding Kansas towns. . . . The ball game between two rival towns was a big event then, with parades before the game and everything.

The smaller the town the more important their ball club was. Boy, if you beat a bigger town they'd practically hand you the key to the city. And if you lost a game by making an error in the ninth inning or something like that—well, the best thing to do was just pack your grip and hit the road, 'cause they'd never let you forget it."

Matches like these remained great events in towns across the country for many decades. Eventually they too declined in importance, but by then baseball's status as the national pastime was well established, and the game has made an easy transition to other modes of competition. Today one may choose to be a devotee of amateur, semipro, or professional play—or all three—and be considered simply a baseball fan. Each of the three levels of the game has in turn spawned subgroups based on age, region, and skill, a development that has renewed the sense of baseball as an inclusive game.

The renaissance of amateur play during the 1880s enabled muffin games to exit the baseball stage, but they were replaced by other types of contests that were specifically designed to provide reminders of the fun-loving side of the game. Baseball has had a kind of parallel history ever since, with the tendency to take it too seriously being offset by vivid reminders that it is still just a game at heart. Whether the celebrants are barnstormers from the House of David or the Negro Leagues, or Bloomer girls, or members of the late Eddie Feigner and his Court, or vintage base ball players recreating the pioneer era, or just the frolickers at a company picnic or a family reunion, their message is the same. They remind us that there is no reason for anyone to be left out, that almost anything might happen in the course of the game, and that the one thing we should be able to take for granted is that everyone will have a good time.

So while the pioneer era ended in the 1860s, its spirit remains alive. We see it every time the fan sitting next to us sighs about the good old days—even though he or she is likely thinking of an era a century or more later than the one described in this book. We see it when children head onto the ball field with the "patience of hope" that is perpetually renewed with each new generation. And we see it even on professional ball fields—not as often as we might hope, but far more often than the game's detractors will admit. This spirit is most frequently seen at minor league and independent league ballparks, but it also surfaces regularly at major league stadiums.

I was reminded of this again while watching a Tigers game on television in July 2006. When Detroit rookie Brent Clevlen collected his first major league hit, the ball was rolled back to the dugout, where it was scooped up by his gleeful-looking teammate Dmitri Young.

Tiger broadcaster Rod Allen summarized the ritual that would now be enacted. While the actual baseball was carefully preserved, a fake ball would be created and "all sorts of crazy things written on it." The fake ball would be presented to Clevlen after the game, and, once he had looked suitably dismayed, the real ball would be produced.

Allen's partner, Mario Impemba, took exception, saying that the gag was so old that Clevlen must know better than to be tricked. "He probably does," allowed Allen, before adding with a chuckle, "but it's still a lot of fun."

Baseball has come a very long way since the early days when only one ball was available for a match, afterward inscribed and preserved with great care. But in some ways the distance isn't really that far.

The Doubleday Myth

❖ In 1905 the early ballplayer-turned-sporting goods magnate A. G. Spalding commissioned a panel to investigate the origins of baseball. The group solicited the public's input and received a letter from an elderly man, Abner Graves, who described the contributions of a man named Abner Doubleday in Cooperstown, New York, around 1839. On this basis, and without an iota of corroborating evidence, the panel anointed Doubleday the game's inventor. Making their verdict all the more extraordinary was the fact that Graves had been about five years old when the purported events had occurred. Nonetheless the general public accepted Doubleday as the game's inventor, and many people still assume this to be the case.

In the years since, the evidence regarding Doubleday has been sifted by many historians who have concluded that there is no credible evidence he had any role in the development of baseball. Some have gone further by pointing out that Doubleday was at West Point in 1839 and could not have invented the game. In fact, as I described at some length in the appendix to my book *Baseball Fever: Early Baseball in Michigan*, this is probably irrelevant, since there were two Abner Doubledays and Graves likely confused them. So it's conceivable that Graves's recollections had some slim basis in fact.

But what Graves and either Doubleday may have done in 1839 doesn't matter in the least to the history of baseball. As I describe in these pages, many people played important roles in the game's development. Perhaps they will now be accorded some of the credit that has unjustly been bestowed upon Abner Doubleday.

The Knickerbockers'
Original (1845) Rules

1. Members must strictly observe the time agreed upon for exercise, and be punctual in their attendance.

2. When assembled for exercise, the President, or in his absence, the Vice-President, shall appoint an Umpire, who shall keep the game in a book provided for that purpose, and note all violations of the By-Laws and Rules during the time of exercise.

3. The presiding officer shall designate two members as Captains, who shall retire and make the match to be played, observing at the same time that the players opposite to each other should be as nearly equal as possible, the choice of sides to be then tossed for, and the first in hand to be decided in like manner.

4. The bases shall be from "home" to second base, forty-two paces; from first to third bases, forty-two paces, equidistant.

5. No stump match shall be played on a regular day of exercise.

6. If there should not be a sufficient number of members of the Club present at the time agreed upon to commence exercise, gentlemen not members may be chosen in to make up the match, which shall not be broken up to take in members that may afterwards appear; but in all cases, members shall have the preference, when present, at the making of a match.

7. If members appear after the game is commenced, they may be chosen if mutually agreed upon.

8. The game to consist of twenty-one counts, or aces; but at the conclusion an equal number of hands must be played.

9. The ball must be pitched, not thrown, for the bat.

10. A ball knocked out of the field, or outside the range of the first or third base, is foul.

11. Three balls being struck at and missed and the last one caught, is a hand out; if not caught is considered fair, and the striker bound to run.

12. If a ball be struck, or tipped, and caught, either flying or on the first bound, it is a hand out.

13. A player running the bases shall be out, if the ball is in the hands of an adversary on the base, or the runner is touched with it before he makes his base; it being understood, however, that in no instance is a ball to be thrown at him.

14. A player running who shall prevent an adversary from catching or getting the ball before making his base, is a hand out.

15. Three hands out, all out.

16. Players must take their strike in regular turn.

17. All disputes and differences relative to the game, to be decided by the Umpire, from which there is no appeal.

18. No ace or base can be made on a foul strike.

19. A runner cannot be put out in making one base, when a balk is made by the pitcher.

20. But one base allowed when a ball bounds out of the field when struck.

Acknowledgments

A book like this requires many lonely hours of research poring over microfilm, a reality that has enhanced my pleasure from interludes with friends. I have been blessed by many who have gone out of their way to make my life easier in one way or another. I owe Bill Anderson, Ron Haas, David MacGregor, and Rebecca Hansen a special debt of gratitude for reading drafts of this work and offering valuable critiques. The number of baseball researchers and historians who have graciously shared their insights makes it impossible for me to mention all of them. John Thorn, Richard Malatzky, Peter Mancuso, Reed Howard, Larry McCray, Joe Simenic, Bob McConnell, David Ball, Priscilla Astifan, Rick Huhn, Tom Shieber, David Block, Jane Finnan Dorward, Frank Vaccaro, Paul Hunkele, Al Smitley, and Jim Lannen have made especially valuable contributions to this work, but I am no less grateful to the many other researchers who have helped expand my understanding of the national pastime.

Every writer dreams of finding a farsighted publisher and a wise editor. I have been most fortunate to find both in Ivan Dee, who wears both hats with equal dexterity. Many thanks to him, to Maureen Ryan, and to the rest of his always helpful and accommodating staff.

My gratitude also goes out to Tom Shieber for sharing so many of the bounties from his collection of Early Baseball and

Cricket Prints. Tom is a legend in the baseball research community for both his generosity and his expertise on baseball history. I am also indebted to Pat Kelly of the National Baseball Hall of Fame and Museum, John Thorn, and Mark Rucker for their capable assistance in identifying and locating images.

I am also very grateful to the helpful and professional staffs of the Library of Michigan, the Michigan State University library and the many other libraries I visited. Thanks also to Eileen Canepari of SABR for amiably handling my many requests for microfilm.

My deepest debt is to the many friends and family members for their support, camaraderie, and love. John Beasley has been the most accommodating of bosses. I have been most blessed by the many friendships I have made through the MSU volleyball program (you haven't really experienced volleyball until you've watched a match with John Hohl and Ron Schatzle). My immediate family—Ray, Anne, Joy, Corinne, Doug, Pippa, Owen, Harmony, and Dave Morris, Richard Perkins, and my late mother Ruth—are a constant source of strength. The sad reality of living so far from them is eased by having dear friends like the Reslocks, the Roods, Kim Schram, and Dan and Mary O'Malley. I am blessed to have incurred more such debts than I can possibly acknowledge, and apologize to those I have neglected to mention.

Finally, I am grateful to Frank L. Smith, E. H. Tobias, Charles Peverelly, Henry Chadwick, Frank Pidgeon, Robert S. Pierce, John Clark, G. Smith Stanton, Clarence Deming, Jimmy Wood, and the many other early ballplayers whose story it's been my privilege to tell. We all owe them a great debt for giving us baseball, and another for leaving such fascinating accounts of the pioneer age. It is my sincere hope that this book will finally award these men some of the recognition they so richly deserve.

Notes

(Full citations of many sources will be found in the Bibliography.)

1. Before the Knickerbockers

page

12 "Cricket we have always had": *Spirit of the Times*, March 10, 1860. See George B. Kirsch, *The Creation of American Team Sports*, for a full discussion of why cricket failed as an American sport.

12 "the United States are": Peter Novick, *That Noble Dream: The 'Objectivity Question' and the American Historical Profession* (Cambridge, England, 1988), 72.

12–13 the baffling array of accounts of pre-1840 American bat-and-ball games: David Block's *Baseball Before We Knew It* and Larry McCray's Protoball website are the most important efforts to classify these games, but it is important to bear in mind that there is much we will never know.

13 "The variants of tag . . .": Alice Morse Earle, *Child Life in Colonial Days*, 344–345.

13–14 "it is not cricket by any means": "Yankees at a Yankee Game," article in the *Chadwick Scrapbooks* from August 1880, *New York Times*, August 28, 1880, and "Wicket," *Brooklyn Eagle*, August 28, 1880, 1.

14–15 "played in Cooper Lane . . .": Major Julius G. Rathbun, "Baseball Here Forty Years Ago," unidentified article circa 1907, *Chadwick Scrapbooks*.

16 "played a form of cricket": *Kalamazoo Telegraph*, December 10, 1901.

16 appearances in Brooklyn and Hawaii as well as in several New England states: Wicket appeared in Brooklyn around 1880; see "Yankees at a Yankee Game," article in the *Chadwick Scrapbooks* from August 1880; *New York Times*, August 28, 1880; "Wicket," *Brooklyn Eagle*, August 28, 1880, 1, for details. See the Protoball website for its appearance in Hawaii and other parts of New England.

16 "Massachusetts Run-Around": A letter to the Mills Commission dated November 24, 1905, from a man named T. King uses this name to describe what seems to be the same game.

16 "We used to play . . .": *Boston Globe,* June 27, 1909.

16–17 "The game of round-town is played . . .": *Chadwick Scrapbooks,* unspecified article.

18 The Olympic Ball Club: *National Police Gazette,* October 20, 1883.

19–20 The Olympics' constitution: the entire constitution is reprinted in Dean A. Sullivan, ed., *Early Innings,* 6.

20 "So great was the prejudice . . .": Charles Peverelly, *The Book of American Pastimes;* in John Freyer and Mark Rucker, ed., *Peverelly's National Game,* 98.

20 "quite a footing in St. Louis": E. H. Tobias, first of sixteen-part history of baseball in St. Louis to 1876, *Sporting News,* November 2, 1895, 5.

20 "two 'Town Ball' clubs have been formed . . .": *Davenport Daily Gazette,* May 29, 1858; reprinted in John Liepa, "Baseball Mania Strikes Iowa," *Iowa Heritage* 87:1 (Spring 2006), 3.

20 "Town ball found more favor in those days . . .": *Cincinnati Commercial,* August 21, 1870.

21 "consisted of a catcher, thrower . . .": Letter from Hiram H. Waldo, Rockford, Illinois, to the Mills Commission, July 7, 1905; reprinted on Protoball website.

21 became more common as stakes were replaced with flatter objects: Frank G. Menke, *The Encyclopedia of Sports,* 26; *Boston Journal,* February 22, 1905.

21 town ball received its name because it was played at town meetings: Letters to the Mills Commission from Hiram H. Waldo, Rockford, Illinois, April 8 and July 7, 1905, and T. King, November 24, 1905, all reprinted on the Protoball website. An alternative theory of the term's origins was proposed by Henry Chadwick in 1867: "Sometimes the name of 'town ball' was given to it, because the matches were often played by parties representing different towns" (*The Ball Player's Chronicle,* July 18, 1867).

21–22 "we played the old-fashioned game of round ball . . .": "The First Detroit Base Ball Club Formed in the Free Press Office Twenty-Seven Years Ago," *Detroit Free Press,* April 4, 1884.

22 "was played very much like pass ball is played today . . .": Jerome B. Trowbridge, quoted in "Ball Tossers of Olden Days," *Kalamazoo Gazette,* February 11, 1906.

22 "what was known as 'long ball,' 'square ball' and 'sock ball,' . . .": Robert S. Pierce, ten-part history of baseball in Cleveland in *Cleveland Press,* part 1, 1908, from the *Chadwick Scrapbooks.*

22 "ballplaying, barnball, one, two or three-old-cat . . .": Major Julius G. Rathbun, "Baseball Here Forty Years Ago," *Chadwick Scrapbooks,* circa 1907. David Block, in *Baseball Before We Knew It,* 209–210, similarly cites British author James O. Halliwell, whose 1847 *Dictionary of Archaic and Provincial Words* makes little attempt to distinguish the bat-and-ball games it lists, defining, for example, base-ball as "a country

game mentioned in Moor's Suffolk Words, p. 238," rounders as "a boy's game at balls," and tut-ball as "a sort of stobball."

22–23 "years before the formation of the Atlantic Club . . .": John Clark, "From Milan," *Brooklyn Eagle*, January 14, 1876, 2.

23 "would take our bats and balls with us . . .": quoted in A. H. Spink, *The National Game*, 54.

23 "no regular bases . . .": "How Baseball Began—A Member of the Gotham Club of Fifty Years Ago Tells About It," *San Francisco Examiner*, November 27, 1887, 14.

23 "I forget now as to many points of the game . . .": Letter from Andrew Peck, Canada Lake, New York, to the Mills Commission, September 1, 1907; reprinted on the Protoball website.

23 The historian David Block: David Block, *Baseball Before We Knew It*, especially Chapter 2.

23–24 "This pastime was merely a source of fun and frolic . . .": *Chadwick Scrapbooks*, 1886 article, apparently from the *Base Ball Gazette*.

24 At most, rounders is one of a family of games that shares that distinction: The Protoball website includes a few references to rounders being played in the United States, but it also cites several knowledgeable contemporaries who had never heard of that name. And a 1905 article observed: "It is claimed that our game of ball came from the game of Rounders, but after much search and research no book can be found which gives a description of that game or anything more than a mere mention of it" (*Boston Journal*, March 6, 1905).

24 Chadwick's own description: *Chadwick Scrapbooks*, 1886 article, apparently from the *Base Ball Gazette*. David Block, in *Baseball Before We Knew It*, cites other accounts that confirm that rounders included these and other extraneous characteristics. See, for example, his account on page 208–209 of the description in *The Every Boy's Book of Games, Sports, and Diversions*. One point that has been made in rounders' favor is that English observers who saw baseball for the first time often noted the similarities. But this reflects the fact that rounders survived in England so that such comparisons could be made, whereas early American bat-and-ball games died out after the triumph of the Knickerbockers' game. Had the American games survived, there can be little doubt that their resemblance to baseball would have been even more striking.

24 the new version as pretty much town ball (or one of the other games) without the soaking: *Spirit of the Times*, March 10, 1860, "Base ball has been a school-boy's game all over the land from immemorial time, but it was, until recently, considered undignified for men to play at it, except on rare holidays, and then they were wont to play on some out-lying common, where they would be unseen of their more staid associates." The *Detroit Free Press* confirmed in 1867 that "base ball, under various and rude shapes has of course been played in America for many years, but was never cultivated to any great extent or under regular rules and

by numerous players of skill until twenty years ago" (*Detroit Free Press*, May 2, 1867).

24–25 "Base-ball sprang entirely from the old game of town-ball . . .": *Chadwick Scrapbooks*, 1879 article from the *Cincinnati Enquirer*.

2. The Knickerbockers' Game Becomes the New York Game

27 several early members report that a predecessor had been active: Charles DeBost, quoted in Robert Henderson, *Bat, Ball and Bishop*, 150; William Wheaton, quoted in "How Baseball Began—A Member of the Gotham Club of Fifty Years Ago Tells About It," *San Francisco Examiner*, November 27, 1887, 14; Duncan Curry, quoted in A. H. Spink, *The National Game*, 54.

27 "it had been our habit to casually assemble. . . ." and "His plan met with much . . .": Duncan Curry, quoted in A. H. Spink, *The National Game*, 54.

27 "It was customary for two or three players . . .": Charles Peverelly, *The Book of American Pastimes*; in John Freyer and Mark Rucker, ed., *Peverelly's National Game*, 10.

27 no fewer than three headquarters in Manhattan: Duncan Curry, quoted in A. H. Spink, *The National Game*, 54; Charles Peverelly, *The Book of American Pastimes*; in John Freyer and Mark Rucker, ed., *Peverelly's National Game*, 10–11; Harold Peterson, *The Man Who Invented Baseball*, 69.

28 "one day upon the field proposed a regular organization": Charles Peverelly, *The Book of American Pastimes*; in John Freyer and Mark Rucker, ed., *Peverelly's National Game*, 10.

28 "it was found necessary to reduce the new rules to writing": "How Baseball Began—A Member of the Gotham Club of Fifty Years Ago Tells About It," *San Francisco Daily Examiner*, November 27, 1887, 14.

28 Two of these rules . . . were revolutionary: See Chapter 6, "How Slick Were the Knicks?" in David Block's *Baseball Before We Knew It*, for a fuller discussion of why these rules were new while others weren't.

30–31 Recalled Daniel Adams later: *Sporting News*, February 29, 1896, 3.

32 "trousers impeded their movements . . .": James Wood, as told to Frank G. Menke, "Baseball in By-Gone Days," syndicated column, *Indiana (Pa.) Evening Gazette*, August 14, 1916.

32 "Little or no attention . . .": Horace S. Fogel, two-part article, *Philadelphia Daily Evening Telegraph*, March 25–26, 1908.

33 "rather vague": *Sporting News*, February 29, 1896, 3.

33 "The same standard still exists . . .": Charles Peverelly, *The Book of American Pastimes*; in John Freyer and Mark Rucker, ed., *Peverelly's National Game*, 11.

33 "Stay-where-you-am-Wail" and "full of good-humor . . .": Charles Peverelly, *The Book of American Pastimes*; in John Freyer and Mark Rucker, ed., *Peverelly's National Game*, 10, 13.

34 "The utmost hilarity prevailed . . .": Charles Peverelly, *The Book of American Pastimes*; in John Freyer and Mark Rucker, ed., *Peverelly's National Game*, 16.

34 "played in a 'scrub' way": *Boston Journal*, February 27, 1905.

34–35 "Hamilton Square . . .": *Chadwick Scrapbooks*, circa 1878, apparently from *Spirit of the Times*.

35 "vacant fields then existing in South Brooklyn": *Brooklyn Eagle*, July 16, 1873.

36 "Base ball practically received its first start in this city": *Brooklyn Eagle*, August 10, 1890, 18.

36 "Virginia was the mother of presidents, Brooklyn of ball players": *Brooklyn Eagle*, August 5, 1897, 5, a July 28 letter from G. Smith Stanton of Great Neck, New York.

36 "Verily Brooklyn is fast earning the title . . .": *Porter's Spirit of the Times*, June 20, 1857.

36 "Along in the late '50s . . .": Major Julius G. Rathbun, "Baseball Here Forty Years Ago," article in an unidentified Hartford, Connecticut, paper, circa 1907, *Chadwick Scrapbooks*.

37 "A year ago last August . . .": *Porter's Spirit of the Times*, January 10, 1857.

37 begun to refer to baseball as the national game: see introduction to Chapter 25, Peter Morris, *A Game of Inches*, volume 2.

37–38 "the convention seems to be rather sectional . . .": *New York Clipper*, April 3, 1858.

3. The New York Game Becomes America's Game

39 the appearance of the club's rules in a national publication: The publication of the Knickerbockers' rules might appear to contradict my contention that the club members had little interest in spreading their game. But there is probably a very simple explanation: the rules were published because these two periodicals approached the Knickerbockers, and the club gave them permission. The Knickerbockers, in my view, were not opposed to the spread of their game, just not inclined to do any proselytizing.

39–40 "baseball was the first game Americans learned principally from print": Tom Melville, *Early Baseball and the Rise of the National League*, 18.

40 newspapers had become affordable, accessible, and a vital part: Paul Starr, *The Creation of the Media*, 131–135; Patricia Cline Cohen, *The Murder of Helen Jewett*, 19–33.

40–41 "There was an old fiddler here in the city . . .": "The First Detroit Base Ball Club Formed in the Free Press Office Twenty-Seven Years Ago," *Detroit Free Press*, April 4, 1884.

41 "One of our young townsmen . . .": *Chadwick Scrapbooks*, handwritten account by Albert G. Spalding.

41–42 "Cricket has its admirers . . .": *Spirit of the Times*, December 3, 1859.

42 "Base ball is quite national . . .": *Erie Observer*, September 15, 1855, 2.

42 "The 'rage' moved Westward slowly . . .": *Chadwick Scrapbooks*, 1879 article from the *Cincinnati Enquirer*.

42 "The first baseball ground laid out in Decatur . . .": *Decatur Daily Review*, June 28, 1914, quoting from an article entitled "Prehistoric Baseball in Decatur" that appeared in the *Review* "several years ago."

43 "It was in 1868 . . .": "'Bob' Fisher Talks of Old Kekiongas," *Fort Wayne News*, April 1, 1908, 7.

43 the "regulation game" arrived in Essex County, New York: *Elizabethtown Post and Gazette*, May 7, 1903.

43 High school students formed the Union Club: E. H. Tobias, first of sixteen-part history of baseball in St. Louis to 1876, *Sporting News*, November 2, 1895, 5.

43 "engaged in the game after school": early Cleveland baseball editor Robert S. Pierce, part two of ten-part history of baseball in Cleveland in *Cleveland Press*, 1908, *Chadwick Scrapbooks*.

43–44 "At school we scarcely took time to eat . . .": Clarence Darrow, *Farmington*, 210–211.

44 "the faculty of the college . . .": William A. Cochran, "The Olympians," *The Round Table*, April 22, 1898. At the Michigan Agricultural College, Professor of Botany Alfred N. Prentiss joined in the play with his students, but this proved a bit much for the students, since Prentiss "was so awkward that most of us preferred that he should play on the side of our opponents" (*M.A.C. Record* 21, no. 32 [May 23, 1916]).

44 Following the Erie Canal: Buffalo and Erie: *Spirit of the Times*, April 10, 1858, reported two clubs in Buffalo and one in Erie; Rochester: Priscilla Astifan, "Baseball in the Nineteenth Century," *Rochester History* (Summer 1990), 6–7; Syracuse: *Syracuse Journal*, March 20, 1939, said that the city's first club was the Syracuse Base Ball Club in 1858, though it played only married-single matches. This club's existence was also mentioned in *Central City Daily Courier* on March 1, 1859. The game also arrived in Cohoes, New York, in 1859 (Arthur Haynesworth Masten, *The History of Cohoes, New York* [Albany, 1877], 141); Michigan: see my *Baseball Fever* for a lengthy discussion of clubs of the late 1850s and early 1860s; Chicago: according to the *Chicago Tribune* of October 19, 1919, the first Chicago club was the Unions in 1856, and the game was established by 1859 (*Chicago Tribune*, April 15, 1859); Milwaukee: *Spirit of the Times*, January 14, 1860, reported the possible formation of a club, while the *Milwaukee Sentinel* of April 2, 1859, mentioned a married-single game; California: *Spirit of the Times*, March 27, 1858, reported the formation of the San Francisco Base Ball Clubs and on March 10, 1860, the same journal announced it would play a club from Sacramento; Baltimore: see William Ridgely Griffith, *The Early History of Amateur Base Ball in the State of Maryland*, reprinted in *Maryland Historical Magazine*, vol. 87,

no. 2, Summer 1992; Washington: *French Scrapbooks*; Richmond: *Spirit of the Times*, June 12, 1858.

45 "The old town-ball clubs merged themselves gradually . . .": *Chadwick Scrapbooks*, 1879 article from the *Cincinnati Enquirer.*

45 "after considerable urging . . .": quoted in A. H. Spink, *The National Game*, 406; E. H. Tobias, in the first of a sixteen-part history of baseball in St. Louis to 1876 that appeared in *Sporting News* on November 2, 1895, 5, confirms that these events occurred in 1859 and resulted in the formation of the Cyclone Club.

45–46 "John [McCord] used to play the old game of patch ball . . .": "Ball Tossers of Olden Days," *Kalamazoo Gazette*, February 11, 1906.

46 "It was certainly up-hill work . . .": *Janesville Daily Gazette*, February 8, 1905, 5.

46 far less resistance in Philadelphia: *French Scrapbooks*; *Chadwick Scrapbooks*; Charles Peverelly, *The Book of American Pastimes*; in John Freyer and Mark Rucker, ed., *Peverelly's National Game*, 101; John Shiffert, *Base Ball in Philadelphia*, 21–22.

46 "also to give them a set of implements": Charles Peverelly, *The Book of American Pastimes*; in John Freyer and Mark Rucker, ed., *Peverelly's National Game*, 91.

47 The trophy remained the subject of heated competition: *New England Base Ballist*, August 13, 1868 and November 5, 1868.

47 every single club that had played the Massachusetts game: *The Ball Player's Chronicle*, June 6, 1867.

47 "that period of time being long enough . . .": E. H. Tobias, third of sixteen-part history of baseball in St. Louis to 1876, *Sporting News*, November 16, 1895, 5.

47 the few remaining holdouts were eliminated: For example, Major Julius G. Rathbun stated in "Baseball Here Forty Years Ago," an article that appeared in an unidentified Hartford paper around 1907 and is reprinted in the *Chadwick Scrapbooks*: "In our own city in the years of the Civil War, baseball was occasionally played, but by no organized club. But in 1865 interest was taken to the new game, and a club was formed in Hartford under the name of 'The Charter Oak Baseball Club,' while soon after similar clubs were organized in New Haven (Yale), Waterbury, Springfield, New London, Norwich, and other towns in Connecticut, a most excellent club being formed in Collinsville." A 1909 article recalled that the new version was introduced in Stoughton, Massachusetts, "in 1866, not long after the war, when Halsey J. Boardman, who was president of the Tri-Mountains of Boston, got us interested in the present game, which we called the New York game. Boardman lived in Stoughton, and showed us boys how to play the new game and coached us right along until we organized the Chemungs and got some uniforms" (*Boston Globe*, June 27, 1909). Similarly, in predominantly rural Essex County, New York: "Old fashioned base ball was

played here, also two old cat and barn base, as long ago as the oldest resident can remember. Modern base ball was introduced here just after the close of the late civil war and its progress and development has been watched with keen interest by Elizabethtown residents" (November 16 paper presented by George L. Brown, summarized in the *Elizabethtown Post and Gazette*, November 22, 1906). Regarding the South, the editor of the *Richmond Daily Dispatch* wrote in 1866 that "the game of baseball was imported from the North since the close of the war" (*Richmond Daily Dispatch*, August 31, 1866; quoted in W. Harrison Daniel and Scott P. Mayer, *Baseball and Richmond: A History of the Professional Game, 1884–2000*, 3).

47 "an exotic . . .": *Spirit of the Times*, March 10, 1860.

48 "the scene of nearly all of the important base ball contests in this vicinity": *National Chronicle*, June 12, 1869.

48 "The left-fielder had about the hardest position to field . . .": A. H. Spink, *The National Game*, 402.

49 "Base ball has been a school-boy's game . . .": *Spirit of the Times*, March 10, 1860.

49 well-to-do backgrounds: see Melvin Adelman, *A Sporting Time*, 123–124, for a refutation of the tendency to describe them as bluebloods.

49–50 "some of the brightest young men of St. Louis . . .": E. H. Tobias, first of sixteen-part history of baseball in St. Louis to 1876, *Sporting News*, November 2, 1895, 5.

50 "were nearly all scions of the best families in Cleveland . . .": Robert S. Pierce, described as probably the first Cleveland baseball editor, in a ten-part history of baseball in Cleveland in the *Cleveland Press*, 1908, from the *Chadwick Scrapbooks*.

50 Malcolm MacLaren's success in introducing regulation baseball to Elizabethtown, New York: *Elizabethtown Post and Gazette*, May 7, 1903.

50 "there is no doubt . . .": James D'Wolf Lovett, quoted in Phil Bergen, "Lovett of the Lowells," 63.

51 "We used the 'lively' ball . . .": An unidentified article from about 1899 in the *Chadwick Scrapbooks*, based on an article in the *Luzerne Union* on August 30, 1865.

51 "The pitching, instead of swift throwing . . .": James D'Wolf Lovett, quoted in Phil Bergen, "Lovett of the Lowells," 63.

51 "who used bats four feet long . . .": *Boston Journal*, March 6, 1905.

51 "struck the longest ball yet batted on the field . . .": *Brooklyn Eagle*, July 11, 1865.

51–52 "To this day the students relate a tradition . . .": Peter Morris, *Baseball Fever*, 149. And many other examples could be cited. After the Chemungs of Stoughton, Massachusetts, switched to the New York game, one of the incidents they most enjoyed recounting in later years was a game against the Tri-Mountains on the Boston Common during which one of the Chemungs knocked the ball over a building on Tremont Street

(*Boston Globe*, June 27, 1909). The first club in Janesville, Wisconsin, featured the powerfully built Dr. J. W. St. John, and "It is said that the doctor had a willow club of his own that he used to swing when he came up to bat which weighed in the neighborhood of seven pounds and that every time he took his position at the bat the crowd were [sic] much disappointed if the doctor did not make a home run" (*Janesville Daily Gazette*, March 26, 1904).

53 a group of young Brooklyn men decided "to 'get up' a Base Ball Club . . .": Charles Peverelly, *The Book of American Pastimes*; in John Freyer and Mark Rucker, ed., *Peverelly's National Game*, 52.

53 when a reporter interviewed Henry Starkey: "The First Detroit Base Ball Club Formed in the Free Press Office Twenty-Seven Years Ago," *Detroit Free Press*, April 4, 1884. The entire interview is reprinted in my *Baseball Fever*, 22–24.

53 "Why, I suppose some might say . . .": John Clark, "From Milan," *Brooklyn Eagle*, January 14, 1876, 2.

53–54 "B. B. Clubs outnumber the debating societies . . .": *Spirit of the Times*, March 10, 1860.

54–55 "After longing for a match . . .": *Porter's Spirit of the Times*, January 10, 1857.

56 "The fact of it being the first match game . . .": E. H. Tobias, first of sixteen-part history of baseball in St. Louis to 1876, *Sporting News*, November 2, 1895, 5.

56–57 "There were a number of young men . . .": *Boston Journal*, February 27, 1905.

57 "Thirty years ago last Spring a right merry party . . .": "Old Chalk" [Henry Chadwick], "Base Ball in Its Infancy," *Brooklyn Eagle*, December 15, 1889, 4.

4. How the Game Was Played

58 "the sturdy, hard-hitting game of men . . .": *Sporting News*, November 11, 1893.

58–59 "The heavy hitter, rather than the good fielder, was the Nestor of the game": Clarence Deming, "Old Days in Baseball," *Outing*, June 1902, 358.

59 "Batting ought never to be placed . . .": *Chadwick Scrapbooks*, unidentified article, circa 1861.

59 "In those days the player's bench . . .": *Brooklyn Eagle*, August 5, 1897, 5; a July 28 letter from G. Smith Stanton of Great Neck, New York.

59 booing a misplay, or in order to show animosity toward the opponents or the umpire, was considered a serious breach of decorum: After an 1868 game, for example, a sportswriter recorded witheringly: "In one case, where a few loafers tried to hiss [umpire] McMullen for deciding on a close thing, he turned and made a slight bow toward them. This proper

rebuke was cheered by the entire body of respectable spectators, and showed the roughs how few and unimportant they were" (*Cincinnati Daily Times*, July 10, 1868).

60 "the subject of personal opinion rather than of formal rule": Clarence Deming, "Old Days in Baseball," *Outing*, June 1902, 359.

60 "The old time umpires were accorded the utmost courtesy . . .": James Wood, as told to Frank G. Menke, "Baseball in By-Gone Days," part two, syndicated column, *Marion* (Ohio) *Star*, August 15, 1916.

60 "The umpire's place was usually . . .": Clarence Deming, "Old Days in Baseball," *Outing*, June 1902, 357–358.

61 In a game in Stoughton, Massachusetts: *Boston Globe*, June 27, 1909.

61 "Mr. S. Hoyt, of the Garden City Club . . .": E. H. Tobias, second of sixteen-part history of baseball in St. Louis to 1876, *Sporting News*, November 9, 1895, 5.

61 "Mr. Henry of the Tri-Mountains . . . .": *Boston Journal*, March 6, 1905.

62 "The umpire was chosen . . .": *Brooklyn Eagle*, August 5, 1897, 5; a July 28 letter from G. Smith Stanton of Great Neck, New York.

62 "In the scrub games tricks were often resorted to for advantage . . .": *Boston Journal*, March 6, 1905.

62–63 "the feat fairly astonished the natives, who at first roared with laughter": James D'Wolf Lovett, *Old Boston Boys and the Games They Played*, 153; see also *Boston Journal*, February 20, 1905.

63 "the large crowd roared in glee . . .": *Buffalo American*, reprinted in *Daily Kennebec Journal*, December 9, 1907, describing early Washington player Seymour Studley. The *French Scrapbooks* contains an unidentified clipping of a similar account of Studley's slide, which occurred in an October 25, 1867, game between the Nationals and Irvingtons.

63 "threw himself feet first at the bag": *Sporting News*, February 2, 1933.

63 "we should like to see the abolition of sliding . . .": *Cleveland Herald*, February 21, 1884.

63 fielder's gloves and protective equipment of any sort were almost unheard of . . .: see my *A Game of Inches*, vol. 1, Chapter 9, especially entries 9.3.1 and 9.4.1, for an extended discussion of the few limited exceptions to this rule.

64 "the pitcher was of no more importance than any other man in the team": *Boston Globe*, reprinted in *Cincinnati Enquirer*, October 12, 1884. The narrator of Clarence Darrow's autobiographical 1904 novel similarly emphasized, "The contest was not between the pitcher and the catcher alone; we all played, and each player was as important as the rest" (Clarence Darrow, *Farmington*, 215).

65 "the existing code of 1850 . . .": *Sporting News*, December 31, 1904, 7.

65 "In 1859 a ball weighing ten ounces . . .": "Old Chalk" [Henry Chadwick], "Base Ball in Its Infancy," *Brooklyn Eagle*, December 15, 1889, 4.

66 presentism or Whig history: The phrase "Whig history" was coined by the British historian Herbert Butterfield in *The Whig Interpretation of*

History (1931). Edwin Jones, a student of Butterfield's, makes interesting use of its thesis in his 1998 work *The English Nation: The Great Myth.* Jones notes that Whig history soon became so entrenched that many of its leading practitioners were actually Tories (page 186). Likewise, though the phrase has most commonly been attached to the study of British history, it is perfectly applicable to the study of the history of anything, including baseball.

66 "The 'fans' of [the 1850s] were opposed to any and all changes . . .": *Sporting News,* December 31, 1904, 7.

67 as Warren Goldstein has documented: Warren Goldstein, *Playing for Keeps: A History of Early Baseball,* 48–53.

67 "One of our best ball players remarked to us . . .": *Spirit of the Times,* March 24, 1860.

67 "became ashamed of the boyish rule of the bound catch": Henry Chadwick, "Old Boys," *Brooklyn Eagle,* December 2, 1877, 1.

68 "about the same notion as is used in pitching quoits": Frank L. Smith, *Janesville Daily Gazette,* February 8, 1905, 5. Quoits are similar to horseshoes but circular.

68 "sends the ball with exceeding velocity . . .": *Porter's Spirit of the Times,* December 6, 1856; quoted by William Rankin, *Sporting News,* May 25, 1901.

69 "split heavy boards with the balls he pitched": *Portsmouth Daily Times,* June 18, 1898.

69 "arm swinging perpendicular . . .": *St. Louis Post-Dispatch,* January 2, 1884.

69 "Frank Pidgeon, Tom Van Cott, Matty O'Brien and Tom Dakin . . .": Henry Chadwick, "Old Chalk's Reminiscences: The True Story of the Old Eckford Club," *Brooklyn Eagle,* January 18, 1891, 16.

69 "Prior to [Jim] Creighton's day . . .": *Chadwick Scrapbooks,* undated article.

70 "speed was blinding": James Wood, as told to Frank G. Menke, "Baseball in By-Gone Days," part two, syndicated column, *Marion* (Ohio) *Daily Star,* August 15, 1916.

70 "above the batsman's hip . . .": *Brooklyn Eagle,* August 6, 1860.

70 "fair square pitch": *Brooklyn Eagle,* August 6, 1860.

70 Creighton was dead: He died in 1862, and legend attributed his death to a mighty home run swing, though the evidence for the claim is dubious.

70 "took a sharp twist . . .": James Wood, as told to Frank G. Menke, "Baseball in By-Gone Days," part three, syndicated column, *Indiana* (Pa.) *Evening Gazette,* August 17, 1916.

70–71 "was so long and drawn out . . .": A. H. Spink, *The National Game,* 57, 139.

71 By 1855 there were reports . . .: Writing in 1893, Henry Chadwick described the first game of the Atlantics of Brooklyn in 1855: "It will be

seen that it took the players over 2 hours to play three innings [2:45], so great was the number of balls the pitcher had to deliver to the bat before the batsman was suited" (*Sporting Life*, October 28, 1893).

71 "Those were the days that tried pitchers' bodies . . .": *Brooklyn Eagle*, August 5, 1897, 5, printing a July 28 letter from G. Smith Stanton of Great Neck, New York.

72 "Suppose you want a low ball . . .": *New York Clipper*, August 2, 1862, reprinted in James L. Terry, *Long Before the Dodgers*, 31.

72 "seized the ball, and swinging his hand behind him . . .": "B. P.," "'Nassau vs. Star'—The Trip of Our Nine," *Nassau Literary Magazine*, March 1863 [23,6], 6.

72 in one 1860 game, Jim Creighton delivered 331 pitches: William J. Ryczek, *When Johnny Came Sliding Home*, 45.

73 "Last season, McKever's . . .": *New York Clipper*, July 9, 1864; almost certainly written by Henry Chadwick.

74 "the constant cry of 'judgment on that,' 'how's that,' etc.": *The Ball Player's Chronicle*, July 11, 1867.

74 "it should be stopped at once by the Umpires . . .": *Brooklyn City News*, May 16, 1862.

75 fielders began deliberately to trap catchable balls in order to start double plays: *New York Clipper*, June 25, 1864.

75 some clubs simply ignored new rules they didn't like: In an 1865 game in Freeport, Illinois, for example, the home team and the visitors from St. Louis discussed beforehand whether to use the fly rule (E. H. Tobias, second of sixteen-part history of baseball in St. Louis to 1876, *Sporting News*, November 9, 1895, 5). A club in Battle Creek, Michigan, was still using the bound rule in 1866, as was a club across the state in Howell the following year (*Detroit Advertiser and Tribune*, July 14, 1866; Peter Morris, *Baseball Fever*, 129–130). And undoubtedly there were many such clubs.

5. Bats, Balls, Bases, and the Playing Field

76 Robert Henderson's *Bat, Ball and Bishop*: Robert Henderson, *Bat, Ball and Bishop: The Origins of Ball Games*, passim, especially Chapters 3–7.

77 "the orthodox 'white' ball . . .": Clarence Deming, "Old Days in Baseball," *Outing*, June 1902, 358.

77 "What a host of the boys . . .": quoted in Priscilla Astifan, "Baseball in the Nineteenth Century," *Rochester History* LII, no. 3 (Summer 1990), 10–11.

77 "the ball was delivered in a very manly speech . . ..": "B. P.," "'Nassau vs. Star'—The Trip of Our Nine," *Nassau Literary Magazine*, March 1863 [23,6], 6.

78 "came across a German immigrant . . .": ex-Fire Marshal John Durkee, quoted in *San Francisco Examiner*, November 19, 1888.

78 "An old rubber shoe, melted down . . .": *Chicago Tribune*, January 31, 1954.

78 "Most men of to-day remember. . . .": *Chicago Herald*, May 1, 1890.
78–79 "it was not difficult to procure . . .": *Boston Journal*, March 6, 1905.
79 "weighed over six ounces . . .": Henry Chadwick, *Sporting News*, December 31, 1904, 7.
79 In Chadwick's hometown of Brooklyn . . .: A. J. Reach, one of the first professional players and later a sporting goods magnate, reported that the first ball makers in the mid-1850s were Harvey Ross, a member of the Atlantics of Brooklyn and a sail maker by trade, and John Van Horn, a member of the Union Club of Morrisania, New York, and a manufacturer of boots and shoes (*Sporting Life*, March 13, 1909).
79 "the great hit of the day": *Mansfield News*, June 3, 1895.
79 "those good old days of the game . . .": "'Bob' Fisher Talks of Old Kekiongas," *Fort Wayne News*, April 1, 1908, 7.
79–80 "persistency of bound and roll . . .": Clarence Deming, "Old Days in Baseball," *Outing*, June 1902, 359.
80 Even Chadwick acknowledged . . .: unidentified article, *Chadwick Scrapbooks*.
80 "were put in a vessel . . .": "Base Balls," *Brooklyn Eagle*, February 3, 1884, 7.
80 "There was only one base ball in the town at the time . . .": *Bellingham Bay Mail*, no date given; reprinted in Dave Larson, *Wide Awakes, Invincibles and Smokestackers: Early Baseball in Tall Timber Country, 1869–1905*, 12.
80 "In the lake regions . . .": "Base Balls," *Brooklyn Eagle*, February 3, 1884, 7.
81 "It was understood that balls for this game . . .": *Boston Journal*, February 27, 1905.
81 "would not last through a game . . .": *Boston Journal*, March 6, 1905.
81 "We used but one ball then . . .": Al Pratt, quoted in *Sporting News*, March 23, 1895.
82 Harry Wright . . . once waded across a creek: F. X. White, *Bismarck Daily Tribune*, July 7, 1891.
82 "situated on a flat piece of ground . . .": *Elizabethtown Post and Gazette*, May 28, 1903, letter from Peter Flint of New York City.
82 the phrase "the base ball" replaced with its plural: John H. Gruber, *Sporting News*, November 11, 1915.
82 "When we played a match . . .": *Detroit Free Press*, January 13, 1889.
82 "a baseball which the young fellows of Milwaukee used to play with . . .": unspecified article from Milwaukee, *Chadwick Scrapbooks*.
83 "had no protection against a foul . . .": The first catcher to try gloves may have been Ben De la Vergne of Albany, around 1859 (*Sporting News*, June 28, 1886; *Detroit Free Press*, May 17, 1887). The reference to catchers putting slabs of India rubber in their mouths is from Major Julius G. Rathbun, "Baseball Here Forty Years Ago," unidentified article circa 1907, *Chadwick Scrapbooks*.

83 catchers being knocked cold by foul balls: Major Julius G. Rathbun, "Baseball Here Forty Years Ago," unidentified article, circa 1907, *Chadwick Scrapbooks*.

83 "work through a game with the blood dripping from his bruised hands": Stanley B. Cowing, early player for the Niagaras of Buffalo, quoted in *Kalamazoo Evening Telegraph*, March 26, 1906.

83 "crooked fingers . . .": *Brooklyn Eagle*, August 5, 1897, 5, a July 28 letter from G. Smith Stanton.

83 In Kalamazoo: *Kalamazoo Telegraph*, December 10, 1901.

84 "selected the wood and whittled their own bats . . .": John H. Gruber, *Sporting News*, November 11, 1915.

84 "logs of wood . . .": quoted in *Boston Herald*, reprinted in *Cincinnati Enquirer*, April 29, 1888.

84 Rules were gradually adopted to restrict their length and thickness: In 1857 the rules specified that a bat had to be rounded, as opposed to flat, and could not exceed two and a half inches in diameter. The diameter was changed to two and three-quarters inches in 1895 and has never changed since. In 1868 bats were limited to forty inches in length, and the next year this was modified to forty-two inches. See my *A Game of Inches*, vol. 1, pp. 409–410, for additional details.

84 "A hard wood bat was barely or never seen . . .": Clarence Deming, "Old Days in Baseball," *Outing*, June 1902, 359.

84 "they were compelled to use the handle of a shovel as a substitute for a bat at the finish": *Chadwick Scrapbooks*, 1879 article from an unspecified source.

84–85 "The striker shall be privileged . . .": John H. Gruber, *Sporting News*, January 27, 1916.

85 "no regular bases . . .": "How Baseball Began—A Member of the Gotham Club of Fifty Years Ago Tells About It," *San Francisco Examiner*, November 27, 1887, 14.

85 "Because so many players were injured . . .": Frank G. Menke, *The Encyclopedia of Sports*, 26.

85 the change from stakes to bases may well have helped the new name spread: An old-time Boston ballplayer, for example, recalled an 1855 game: "The word base was not used at that time, the infield being shown by bounds, or byes: it was probably introduced to designate the game from other games of ball and on account of the bounds being changed to a firmer base" (*Boston Journal*, February 22, 1905).

86 "much of the danger of the game . . .": *Kalamazoo Telegraph*, December 10, 1901.

86 "D. M. Ferry played with us . . .": "When D. M. Ferry Played Ball," *Detroit Free Press*, June 14, 1903.

86 "a dangerous practice": Priscilla Astifan, "Baseball in the Nineteenth Century," *Rochester History* LII, no. 3 (Summer 1990), 9.

86 "carrying the old style sand bag bases . . .": E. H. Tobias, third of six-teen-part history of baseball in St. Louis to 1876, *Sporting News*, No-vember 16, 1895, 5.

86–87 "stakes driven in the ground or bits of board": *Kalamazoo Daily Tele-graph*, June 3, 1871.

87 Base runners also began to cause controversy by cutting in front of the bases: The *Brooklyn City News* of May 16, 1862, chided a player who "ran past the first to second base without either touching the first base or go-ing within three feet of it. This practice, we notice, players are getting in the habit of, and it should be stopped at once by the Umpires. It is ab-solutely requisite that the bases should be touched in running round, un-less the player passes outside of them, and when this is not done he should be made to return to the base he left."

87 as George Kirsch has suggested: George B. Kirsch, *The Creation of Amer-ican Team Sports*, 95–96.

88 "I first played baseball in the forties . . .": *Chadwick Scrapbooks*, letter from Charles Commerford.

88 Commerford repeated this claim in another article: article in unspecified Waterbury, Connecticut, paper, *Chadwick Scrapbooks*.

88 strong evidence that the Eagle Club was organized by 1840: see David Block, *Baseball Before We Knew It*, 223.

88 "From all the information the writer has been able to gather . . .": *Chad-wick Scrapbooks*, unspecified article.

88–89 "had its headquarters and grounds . . .": article in unspecified Wa-terbury, Connecticut, paper, *Chadwick Scrapbooks*.

90 "had to employ all my rhetoric . . .": *Sporting News*, February 29, 1896, 3.

90 the site at the Elysian Fields: Cricket was played at a different location in Hoboken, as shown in several of this book's illustrations. But I have found no evidence of the cricket field being used for baseball, or vice versa, and do not believe that cricket could have been played at the base-ball field.

90 "bat most of their balls": *Brooklyn Eagle*, October 3, 1861.

90 "The old tree to the left of the home base . . . ": *New York Times*, April 23, 1866. The *Times* added that "[Elysian Fields owner John Cox] Stevens consented to the removal of the venerable relic only after the most un-tiring efforts of [Mutuals officer] Coroner [John] Wildey, who will hold an inquest this afternoon."

90 unmowed grass impeded the fielders: William J. Ryczek, *When Johnny Came Sliding Home*, 33, 65.

90–91 "There were not enough members . . .": *French Scrapbooks*, describ-ing a game of July 6, 1866, between the Nationals and Gothams at Elysian Fields.

92 The field was surrounded by railroad tracks: William Ryczek, *When Johnny Came Sliding Home*, 31, 34.

92 "vacant fields then existing in South Brooklyn": *Brooklyn Eagle*, July 16, 1873.

92 "when base ball was a bucolic pastime . . .": Richard Weddle, 1901 letter to Henry Chadwick, *Sporting News*, January 19, 1901.

92 "the days the old Atlantics used to play . . .": unspecified 1894 article, *Chadwick Scrapbooks.*

92 "the vacant ground on the block between Douglass, Degraw, Hoyt and Smith streets": "Old Chalk" [Henry Chadwick], "Base Ball Reminiscences," *Brooklyn Eagle*, June 7, 1891, 16.

92 "old York street lot, near the station house . . .": John Clark, "From Milan," *Brooklyn Eagle*, January 14, 1876, 2.

93 "to play twice a week on the Orphan Asylum lot . . .": *Chadwick Scrapbooks*, 1879 article from the *Cincinnati Enquirer.*

93 "a wide stretch of cow pasture . . .": Robert S. Pierce, ten-part history of baseball in Cleveland in *Cleveland Press*, part one, 1908, from the *Chadwick Scrapbooks.*

93 baseball's success in supplanting wicket in Hartford: Major Julius G. Rathbun, "Baseball Here Forty Years Ago," unidentified article, circa 1907, *Chadwick Scrapbooks.*

94 "go on and have a good time, boys, but don't hurt the trees!": *Kalamazoo Telegraph*, December 10, 1901.

94 "Boys! Boys! Playing ball is nice sport . . .": *Washington* (Iowa) *Press*, March 1859; quoted in John Liepa, "Baseball Mania Strikes Iowa," *Iowa Heritage* 87:1 (Spring 2006), 4. The difficulties of playing baseball in a public square are also aptly summed up by the narrator of Clarence Darrow's *Farmington*: "Our usual meeting-place was on the public square. This was not an ideal spot, but it was the best we had. The home-base was so near the hotel that the windows were in constant danger, and the dry-goods store was not far behind the second base. Squire Allen's house and a grove of trees were only a little way back of the third base, and many a precious moment was lost in hunting for the ball in the grass and weeds in his big yard. The flag-pole and the guide-post, too, stood in the most inconvenient spots that could be found. We managed to move the guide-post, but the mere suggestion of changing the flag-pole was thought to be little less than treason; for Farmington was a very patriotic town" (Clarence Darrow, *Farmington*, 212–213).

94 "the scene of nearly all of the important base ball contests in this vicinity": *National Chronicle*, June 12, 1869; *New York Clipper*, November 7, 1857.

94 running a "Red Ball" ticket of candidates: Stephen Hardy, *How Boston Played*, 85.

94–95 "the Babbit tract . . .": Edmund Redmond, "Subject of Famous Verse, 'Casey at the Bat,' Played Ball on Early Team Here," *Rochester Democrat and Chronicle*, July 24, 1927.

95 "The grounds at Jones' Park . . .": *Chadwick Scrapbooks*, article from the *Cincinnati Commercial*, June 1870.

95 numerous complaints about trespassing, the cutting of fences, and obscenities: see, for instance, Charles Brian Goslow, "Fairground Days: When Worcester Was a National League City (1880–82)," *Historic Journal of Massachusetts*, Summer 1991, 134.

95 broke so many windows: Richard Fyfe, letter to Clarence Burton, Burton Collection, Detroit Public Library.

95 Henry Chadwick was recommending a tract six hundred by four hundred feet: *Beadle's 1860 Dime Base-Ball Player*, 17.

95 Joe Weiss . . . recalled: *Detroit Free Press*, January 13, 1889.

96 "Notwithstanding the lowness of the ground . . .": *Brooklyn Times*, May 16, 1862.

96 a five-man committee: E. H. Tobias, fourth of sixteen-part history of baseball in St. Louis to 1876, *Sporting News*, November 23, 1895, 5.

96 "The ground is not as well fitted up as it should be . . .": *The Northern Star* (Snohomish, Wash.), September 22, 1877; reprinted in Dave Larson, *Wide Awakes, Invincibles and Smokestackers: Early Baseball in Tall Timber Country, 1869–1905*, 105.

97 "located on the side of a hill . . .": *Chadwick Scrapbooks*, 1870 account in an unspecified paper.

97 "so irregular that at times . . ": unidentified 1868 guide, quoted in "Quaint and Odd Things from Baseball Guides of the 60s," *Washington Post*, June 30, 1907.

97 "the tallest kind of umpire . . .": *Chadwick Scrapbooks*, 1863 account in an unspecified paper.

97 a "cow pasture" that was situated "close to the State Asylum . . .": *Boston Globe*, January 24, 1915.

97 "the annual cutting of the grass was put off until late in July": *Boston Globe*, January 24, 1915.

97 A club in Riverton, New Jersey: Louis A. Flanagan, quoted in the *New York Times*, June 4, 1895.

98 "steam fire engine was employed . . .": *French Scrapbooks*, account of an October 5, 1869, game in an unspecified newspaper, in which the Olympics of Washington hosted the Eckfords of Brooklyn.

98 "some one who had more in mind . . .": Peter Morris, *Baseball Fever*, 141.

98–99 "shaped like a triangular segment of a circle . . .": William Ryczek, *When Johnny Came Sliding Home*, 31, 34.

6. Customs and Rituals

101 "the opposing teams . . .": Harry Slye, "Early Days of Baseball in Baraboo," part two, *Baraboo* (Wisc.) *Daily News*, June 26, 1925. The

"tiger" mentioned was a "peculiar cheer" created by Princeton students (*New York World*; reprinted in *St. Louis Globe-Democrat*, March 16, 1877).

102 "the customary things were said on both sides": "B. P.," "'Nassau vs. Star'—The Trip of Our Nine," *Nassau Literary Magazine*, March 1863 [23,6], 6.

102 specific instructions for "Furnishing the Ball": *Bay City* (Mich.) *Journal*, July 30, 1872.

102 "gilded and the date and score of the game painted thereon in black letters": E. H. Tobias, first of sixteen-part history of baseball in St. Louis to 1876, *Sporting News*, November 2, 1895, 5.

102 "was very handy with the old quill and pen . . .": W. Scott Munn, *The Only Eaton Rapids on Earth* (Eaton Rapids, Mich., 1952), 250–251.

102 Clubs also put quite a bit of thought into the exact wording: see, for example, Scott S. Taylor, "Pure Passion for the Game: Albany Amateur Baseball Box Scores from 1864," *Manuscripts* LIV, no. 1 (Winter 2002), 7.

102 Edward Clift of Bordentown, New Jersey: *Trenton Times*, June 25, 1901. The earliest known inscribed baseballs date from 1858 ("Oldest Baseballs Bear Date of 1858," unidentified newspaper clipping, January 21, 1909, held in the origins of baseball file at the Giamatti Center of the Baseball Hall of Fame, cited on the Protoball website).

102 "There were base ball talkers . . .": Henry Chadwick, "Old Boys," *Brooklyn Eagle*, December 2, 1877, 1; on another occasion Chadwick recalled Polhemus's talk as "the speech of his life" ("Old Chalk" [Henry Chadwick], "Base Ball in Its Infancy," *Brooklyn Eagle*, December 15, 1889, 4).

103–104 "they were taken to the Mansion House . . .": *French Scrapbooks*, describing a match game played on July 5, 1866.

104 "what a fine ride we had back . . .": "B. P.," "'Nassau vs. Star'—The Trip of Our Nine," *Nassau Literary Magazine*, March 1863 [23,6], p. 6.

104 "In procession came three carriages . . .": *Brooklyn Eagle*, October 7, 1868.

104–105 "was marked by an ovation hitherto unknown in the West . . .": E. H. Tobias, second of sixteen-part history of baseball in St. Louis to 1876, *Sporting News*, November 9, 1895, 5.

105 "club-room, which they placed at our disposal": "B. P.," "'Nassau vs. Star'—The Trip of Our Nine," *Nassau Literary Magazine*, March 1863 [23,6], p. 6.

105 taken to the monument of martyred legend Jim Creighton: *French Scrapbooks*, describing a match game played on July 5, 1866. As noted earlier, Creighton's death was often said to have resulted from the exertions of hitting a home run, though the claim is dubious.

105 "the habit of the better class of clubs . . .": Clarence Deming, "Old Days in Baseball," *Outing*, June 1902, 359.

106 "We cannot but condemn . . .": *French Scrapbooks*, unspecified Washington paper, account of an October 25, 1867 game. The umpire in ques-

tion, Colonel Michael Emmett Urell, was a distinguished Civil War veteran, making the crowd's behavior all the more inappropriate.

106 "declared himself out . . .": *Boston Journal*, March 6, 1905.

106 "be held up as an example . . .": *French Scrapbooks*, unspecified article about the retirement of Pete O'Brien, circa 1865.

107 "would be incomplete . . .": E. H. Tobias, second of sixteen-part history of baseball in St. Louis to 1876, *Sporting News*, November 9, 1895, 5.

107 "was considered too small . . .": *Janesville Daily Gazette*, February 8, 1905, 5.

107 "Knock, brothers, knock with care . . .": *Adrian Daily Times and Expositor*, May 1, 1876.

107–108 "I am a base ball crank from way back . . .": *Boston Globe*, May 30, 1886, article by "Jack Plane."

108 "The young ladies who stood near the reporter's deck . . .": *Chicago Times*, September 14, 1866.

108 the players' hearts went "pit-a-pat": *Iowa North West* [Fort Dodge], exact date not given, approximately September 26, 1866; quoted in John Liepa, "Baseball Mania Strikes Iowa," *Iowa Heritage* 87:1 (Spring 2006), 6.

108 "the most popular player in the club . . .": *Chadwick Scrapbooks*, unspecified article about Bernard J. Hanigan, shortstop of the Union of Morrisania.

108 "endeavoring to make fancy catches when the ladies are on the grounds": Peter Morris, *A Game of Inches*, vol. 2, pp. 121–122.

108–109 In Richmond, Virginia: W. Harrison Daniel and Scott P. Mayer, *Baseball and Richmond: A History of the Professional Game, 1884–2000*, 7.

109 "The lettering on the suits . . .": *Elizabethtown Post and Gazette*, May 7, 1903.

109–110 "appeared in bright new uniforms . . .": E. H. Tobias, fifth of sixteen-part history of baseball in St. Louis to 1876, *Sporting News*, November 30, 1895, 5.

110 In Grass Lake, Michigan: *Jackson Daily Citizen*, August 21, 1872, describing William Allen, captain of the Stars of Grass Lake.

111 The Empire Club of St. Louis . . . began each year with a game between its married and single members: E. H. Tobias, sixteen-part history of baseball in St. Louis to 1876 that appeared in *Sporting News* in 1895 and 1896, especially the second part, which appeared on November 9, 1895.

111 "there was considerable expense . . .": Major Julius G. Rathbun, "Baseball Here Forty Years Ago," unidentified article, circa 1907, *Chadwick Scrapbooks*.

111–112 "the great game—the game which added much to the reputation . . .": Major Julius G. Rathbun, "Baseball Here Forty Years Ago," unidentified article, circa 1907, *Chadwick Scrapbooks*.

112–113 "The technicalities of the game . . .": *French Scrapbooks*, article in unspecified Washington paper, circa 1867.

113 "There were few uniforms in the rural nine . . .": Clarence Deming, "Old Days in Baseball," *Outing*, June 1902, 358.

113 "a rural club composed of men with long, flowing beards . . .": Joe Weiss, interviewed in the *Detroit Free Press*, January 13, 1889.

114 "Not far away from the truth . . .": Clarence Deming, "Old Days in Baseball," *Outing*, June 1902, 357. The narrator of attorney Clarence Darrow's autobiographical 1904 novel similarly recollected that "each boy had about as much to say as any of the rest. This was especially true when the game was on. Not only did each player have a chance to direct and advise, in loud shouts and boisterous words, but the spectators joined in all sorts of counsel, encouragement, and admonition. When the ball was struck particularly hard, a shout went up from the gathered multitude as if a fort had fallen after a hard-fought siege. Then every player on the field would shout directions,—how many bases should be run, and where the fielder ought to throw the ball,—until the chief actors were so confused by the babel of voices that they entirely lost their heads" (Clarence Darrow, *Farmington*, 214).

114 "an eccentric character . . .": Robert S. Pierce, in a ten-part history of baseball in Cleveland in *Cleveland Press*, part one, 1908, from the *Chadwick Scrapbooks*.

114 "as the 'terrible hayseed.'. . .": F. X. White, *Bismarck Daily Tribune*, July 7, 1891.

114 "inscribed the suggestive word 'Practice'": *Chicago Times*, June 29, 1866.

115 the Rustlers of Cherry Valley and the Plowboys of Stillman Valley: *New York Times*, April 12, 1896.

115 "th' Forest Citys bate th' Pecatonica Blues . . .": Finley Peter Dunne, syndicated column, *Detroit Free Press*, March 8, 1914.

116 "a mere country club": *French Scrapbooks*, unspecified article; the "mere country club" in question was the Irvingtons of Irvington, New Jersey, which beat the Atlantics 23-17 with a roster that included future greats Rynie Wolters, Andy Leonard, and Charley Sweasy.

116 gained the informal nickname of the Haymakers of Troy: *Oliver Optic's Magazine* explained on August 1, 1868: "The nickname 'Haymakers' belongs to the Union Club of Lansingburgh, N.Y. The fact that many of the nine are well-posted in this branch of farm-work is the probable cause of this name being applied to them."

116 "The Haymakers were nine grotesque country lads . . .": *Chicago News*, reprinted in *Cleveland Plain Dealer*, June 9, 1888.

118 "an old-fashioned hayrick . . .": *Chicago Inter-Ocean*, April 24, 1887. No game in Marshall D. Wright's *The National Association of Base Ball Players, 1857–1870* closely matches the details provided, increasing the likelihood of exaggeration.

119 "fairly taken from us our hard-earned laurels": *Chicago Tribune*, July 31, 1867.

119 Brian Turner and John S. Bowman demonstrated: Brian Turner and John S. Bowman, *Baseball in Northampton, 1823–1953*, 14–15.

119 "to withdraw [rather] than to have it on record that they were black-balled": Michael E. Lomax, *Black Baseball Entrepreneurs, 1860–1901*, 23.

119 "to keep out of the Convention the discussion": *The Ball Player's Chronicle*, December 19, 1867; reprinted in Dean Sullivan, ed., *Early Innings*, 68–69.

120 "to eloquently explain the why wherefore . . .": Henry Chadwick, "Old Boys," *Brooklyn Eagle*, December 2, 1877, 1.

120 the "patience of hope": See Peter Morris, *Baseball Fever*, Chapter 8, for additional details. The phrase itself originated in 1 Thessalonians 1:3 but received fresh currency in the 1860s from an inspirational work by Dora Greenwell.

121 to rise at 5 A.M. or earlier to squeeze in practice: The *Boston Journal* of March 6, 1905, recalled that 5 A.M. practices were often held at the Boston Common in the 1850s. A Detroit club that was aptly named the Early Risers started practice as early as 4:30 in the summer months, helped, according to the *Detroit Free Press* of March 25, 1928, by steaming-hot coffee from a vendor. And the Nassau and Charter Oak Clubs of Brooklyn scheduled three 1857 games at 5 A.M. (*Porter's Spirit of the Times*, July 4, 1857; cited in Carl Wittke, "Baseball in Its Adolescence," *Ohio State Archaeological and Historical Quarterly*, vol. 61, no. 2 [April 1952], 119, and on the Protoball website.)

7. Club Life

122 "the sport then was earnest work . . .": Henry Chadwick, "Old Boys," *Brooklyn Eagle*, December 2, 1877, 1.

123 "the honor of Lake View was at stake . . .": *Chicago Tribune*, February 4, 1906.

124 "one representing the silk stocking district . . .": *Chicago Tribune*, February 4, 1906.

124 Early baseball clubs in the New York City area: *Chadwick Scrapbooks*, unspecified article circa 1878, apparently from *Spirit of the Times*.

124 Philadelphia boasting a club of clergymen: *Chadwick Scrapbooks*, unspecified article circa 1879.

124 Chicago having one made up of the employees of the McCormick Harvester works: *Chicago Tribune*, February 3, 1923.

124 "oul man Rogers and Sam Storer's fish chowder nine": *Brooklyn Eagle*, August 5, 1897, 5, July 28 letter from G. Smith Stanton.

124 "young shipbuilders who were employed . . .": *Brooklyn Eagle*, April 12, 1896, 8; see also *Brooklyn Eagle*, January 18, 1891, 16, though Henry Chadwick erroneously refers to the shipbuilder as "John" Eckford in both articles.

124 "a tournament of baseball teams . . .": B. J. Griswold, "A Pictorial History of Fort Wayne," *Fort Wayne Sentinel*, August 29, 1914.

124–125 "the base ball and fire engine were . . .": *Brooklyn Eagle*, December 3, 1877.

125–126 "That esteemed member of the Atlantic Club . . .": *French Scrapbooks*, unspecified article, circa 1865.

126–127 badges were also popular enough: *Spirit of the Times*, March 24, 1860.

127 "You should have seen the Bower city nine . . .": *Janesville Daily Gazette*, February 8, 1905, 5.

128 "one of the last things a club should . . .": *National Chronicle*, March 20, 1869.

128 a club in Burlington, Wisconsin: *Sporting Life*, December 11, 1897.

128 An 1896 description of the "cozy" rooms: *Brooklyn Eagle*, April 12, 1896, 8.

129 early member Jack Chapman expressed great concern: *Chadwick Scrapbooks*, 1905 article in the *Brooklyn Eagle*. The exact date of the article is not provided, but Chapman's letter was dated December 1, 1905, and was in response to an article that appeared November 3.

129 the Spalding Collection of the New York Public Library: James L. Terry, *Long Before the Dodgers*, 77.

129 "was neatly furnished and adorned . . .": E. H. Tobias, first of sixteen-part history of baseball in St. Louis to 1876, *Sporting News*, November 2, 1895, 5.

129 Chicago's leading club of the late 1860s: *Chicago Tribune*, December 19, 1866.

129 "the headquarters for the ball fraternity . . .": *French Scrapbooks*, unspecified article from the end of the 1866 season; the player was R. A. Cronin of the National Club of Washington, and his cigar store was located at 238 Pennsylvania Avenue.

130 fielding junior nines: For example, in May 1868 a Washington writer observed: "The Junior Nationals include among their number several promising young players, and the Washington Clubs could not do better than to organize a junior nine for each club to form a *corp de reserve* to replace retired stagers who may become played out" (*French Scrapbooks*).

130 "proved a success in every respect . . .": E. H. Tobias, second of sixteen-part history of baseball in St. Louis to 1876, *Sporting News*, November 9, 1895, 5.

130 The Atlantic Club of Brooklyn also sponsored an annual off-season ball: see "Old Chalk" [Chadwick], "Base Ball Reminiscences," *Brooklyn Eagle*, June 7, 1891, 16, for a lengthy account.

130 "continued as a debating and singing society": B. J. Griswold, "A Pictorial History of Fort Wayne," *Fort Wayne Sentinel*, August 29, 1914.

130 matches on ice: see the *Spirit of the Times*, February 9, 1861, for one of many examples. My *A Game of Inches*, vol. 2, pp. 235–236, includes many more.

131 formal notifications of their nomination and election: For example, the
Chadwick Scrapbooks include a letter to Chadwick dated February 6,
1863, that reads: "Dear Sir: You were proposed for honorary membership in the Star Base Ball Club, by Mr. William W. Skaats and an election
being held at a Meeting of the Club, held on Thursday the 5th day of February 1863, you were declared by the President to be Duly Elected. Re-
spectfully yours, Bruce A. Charlton, Secretary."

131 "The meetings were occasionally noisy . . .": *Kent Base Ball Club By-
Laws and Constitution*, unpublished log book, Grand Rapids Public Library.

131 "played ball merely to work off the effects of rich dinners . . .": *Brooklyn Eagle*, August 5, 1897, 5, a July 28 letter from G. Smith Stanton of
Great Neck, New York.

132 "we had a good time while the organization was going": Sheriff John
McNamee, quoted in John Clark, "From Milan," *Brooklyn Eagle*, January 14, 1876, 2.

132 the club's "base ball suppers": *Brooklyn Eagle*, May 19, 1879, 2.

132 "The old Pastime Club used to do things up in style . . .": Henry Chadwick, "Old Boys," *Brooklyn Eagle*, December 2, 1877, 1; another account
appeared in an obituary of Quevedo in the *Eagle*, October 16, 1887.

132 "healthy, enjoyable exercise": "Old Chalk" [Henry Chadwick], "Base
Ball in Its Infancy," *Brooklyn Eagle*, December 15, 1889, 4. It appears that
most club members focused on cricket in the years before the baseball
furor—as members of the Long Island Cricket Club—and then turned to
harness racing after the Civil War. But there may well have been some
overlap. The *Brooklyn Eagle* had articles about their harness racing activities on June 3, 1865, June 4, 1866, April 26, 1873, and December 23, 1888.

133 "It was for just such enjoyment . . .": "Old Chalk" [Henry Chadwick],
"Base Ball in Its Infancy," *Brooklyn Eagle*, December 15, 1889, 4.

133 "But didn't we have fun though on our practice days?": William Barre,
quoted in Henry Chadwick, "Old Boys," *Brooklyn Eagle*, December 2,
1877, 1.

133 "the City Hall Club": John Clark, "From Milan," *Brooklyn Eagle*, January 14, 1876, 2.

134 "the base ball section of the club dropped away": *Brooklyn Eagle*, April
12, 1896, 8.

8. Intercity Competition and Civic Pride

135–136 "no such ball playing . . .": *Brooklyn Eagle*, July 9, 1860; quoted in
James L. Terry, *Long Before the Dodgers*, 31.

136 "It was not thought that the Baltimore Club . . .": William Ridgely
Griffith, *The Early History of Amateur Base Ball in the State of Maryland*;
reprinted in *Maryland Historical Magazine*, vol. 87, no. 2 (Summer
1992), 204.

136 "done more to advance the popularity of the game . . .": Charles Peverelly, *The Book of American Pastimes*; in John Freyer and Mark Rucker, ed., *Peverelly's National Game*, 106.

136 the "evil" of "gadding around the country . . .": *Chadwick Scrapbooks*, article from the *Philadelphia Mercury*, exact date not provided, but context makes clear that it was from before the 1867 season.

137 "Off we started . . .": "B. P.," "'Nassau vs. Star'—The Trip of Our Nine," *Nassau Literary Magazine*, March 1863 [23,6], p. 6.

137–138 "On Tuesday last . . .": *Kalamazoo Gazette*, June 14, 1861.

138 During their three-thousand-mile journey, the Nationals: see the chapter entitled "When We Went Westward Ho!" in William Ryczek's *When Johnny Came Sliding Home*.

138 "joy when it became known . . .": E. H. Tobias, third of sixteen-part history of baseball in St. Louis to 1876, *Sporting News*, November 16, 1895, 5.

139 "It was a trip that proved of incalculable value . . .": *Chadwick Scrapbooks*, unspecified article, circa 1907.

139–140 "would fill volumes if the mishaps . . .": *Chadwick Scrapbooks*, unspecified article.

140–141 "I was one of the hardy patriots . . .": *Chadwick Scrapbooks*, unspecified article.

142 "a large delegation received them at the depot . . .": Charles Peverelly, *The Book of American Pastimes*; in John Freyer and Mark Rucker, ed., *Peverelly's National Game*, 60.

142 "having successfully demonstrated that it was cock of the home walk . . .": E. H. Tobias, second of sixteen-part history of baseball in St. Louis to 1876, *Sporting News*, November 9, 1895, 5.

143 "I missed the train . . .": Patrick W. Purtell, circa 1906 article in the *Binghamton Press*, describing a game against a club from Norwich, from the *Chadwick Scrapbooks*.

143 "there was no barge to be found . . .": *Boston Globe*, March 19, 1900.

143 "A dinner after the game . . .": Clarence Deming, "Old Days in Baseball," *Outing*, June 1902, 358.

143–144 "When we went to an outside town . . .": Jerome Trowbridge, quoted in "Ball Tossers of Olden Days," *Kalamazoo Gazette*, February 11, 1906; Kalamazoo and Jackson are about sixty-five miles apart.

144 "a frenzy for the game swept the land . . .": Clarence Deming, "Old Days in Baseball," *Outing*, June 1902, 357.

144 "The whole country . . .": *Hudson* (Mich.) *Gazette*, July 28, 1866.

144–145 "We had got friendly with the Tri Mountains . . .": Archie McDonald of the Chemungs of Stoughton, *Boston Globe*, June 27, 1909.

145 "The day was wet and disagreeable . . .": *Iowa North West* [Fort Dodge], exact date not given, approximately September 26, 1866; quoted in John Liepa, "Baseball Mania Strikes Iowa," *Iowa Heritage* 87:1 (Spring 2006), 6.

145 One of the first was held at the 1865 Michigan State Fair: *New York Clipper*, August 8, 1865.

146 At one in Fenton, Michigan: see Peter Morris, *Baseball Fever*, p. 255 for more on this tournament, and throughout for the limitations of tournaments.

146 "ten noble bands of young men . . .": *Chicago Times*, June 27, 1866.

147 "had on a sweater and an undershirt . . .": *Brooklyn Eagle*, August 5, 1897, 5, July 28 letter from G. Smith Stanton.

147 "when a point of play occurred . . .": "Old Stand Bys," *Brooklyn Eagle*, November 18, 1877.

147 "Then there was some excitement . . .": Jerome Trowbridge, quoted in "Ball Tossers of Olden Days," *Kalamazoo Gazette*, February 11, 1906.

149 "in the late fall of 1870, a ball club at Elkhorn . . .": *Janesville Daily Gazette*, February 22, 1905, 2.

149 "One chief reason, why the people of Brooklyn . . .": *Brooklyn Eagle*, November 5, 1868.

150 "composed of only home talent . . .": *Detroit Advertiser and Tribune*, June 13, 1868.

150 "What gave great interest . . .": *Brooklyn Eagle*, August 5, 1897, 5, July 28 letter from G. Smith Stanton, emphasis added.

150 "caused the General's election as an honorary member . . .": "Paid Players: Amateur Ball Began to Wane in 1869," E. H. Tobias, seventh of sixteen-part history of baseball in St. Louis to 1876, *Sporting News*, December 14, 1895, 5.

151 "We left Fort Wayne, full of enthusiasm . . .": "'Bob' Fisher Talks of Old Kekiongas," *Fort Wayne News*, April 1, 1908, 7.

9. The Civil War

152 "we youngsters used to hear with bated breath . . .": *Elizabethtown Post and Gazette*, May 28, 1903, letter from Peter Flint of New York City about baseball in Port Henry, New York, in the late 1860s.

154 Pratt enlisted in Pennsylvania's 193rd Infantry Regiment in 1864: Pratt's military service has been gleaned from pension and regiment records, and is also mentioned briefly in *Sporting Life*, April 15, 1905.

154 Pratt also learned the game of baseball: *Sporting News*, March 23, 1895.

154 used a great deal of rhetoric and very few facts to attribute the game's spread to the war: Albert Goodwill Spalding, *America's National Game*, 92–93.

155 "absorbed every other interest during the summer . . .": *Chadwick Scrapbooks*, 1879 article from the *Cincinnati Enquirer*.

155 The Daybreak Club of Jackson, Michigan: *Detroit Advertiser and Tribune*, June 7, 1862.

155 "enlisted in their country's cause . . .": B. J. Griswold, "A Pictorial History of Fort Wayne," *Fort Wayne Sentinel*, August 15, 1914.

155 "In the spring of 1861 . . .": Charles Peverelly, *The Book of American Pastimes*; in John Freyer and Mark Rucker, ed., *Peverelly's National Game*, 108.

155 three cheers were offered: *Brooklyn Eagle*, June 7, 1862.

155 More typical was St. Louis, where five clubs were thriving when the hostilities began: E. H. Tobias, first of sixteen-part history of baseball in St. Louis to 1876, *Sporting News*, November 2, 1895, 5.

157 accounts of the more flexible games of bygone days reemerging: Peter Morris, *Baseball Fever*, 80.

157 "patriotically went to the war in '61 . . .": *Chadwick Scrapbooks*, unspecified article about Simon Burns of the Mutuals of New York City.

158 the gentlemanly Knickerbockers, Excelsiors, and Pastimes all ceased to schedule match games: The *Brooklyn Eagle* of August 23, 1865, 2, noted that the Excelsior Club would no longer "play any 'Champion' games"; by then the other two clubs had already taken the same course.

158 "succumbed to the war . . .": *Detroit Advertiser and Tribune*, May 2, 1867.

158 senator John S. Newberry: Peter Morris, *Baseball Fever*, 80–81.

158 Fred Benteen: E. H. Tobias, second of sixteen-part history of baseball in St. Louis to 1876, *Sporting News*, November 9, 1895, 5; Benteen's obituary in the *Atlanta Constitution*, June 23, 1898, provides additional details.

159 "We are not or . . .": *French Scrapbooks*.

159 "Just why this special hostility . . .": *Chadwick Scrapbooks*, unspecified article, circa 1907.

159 the club's first baseman had enlisted in the Confederate army during the war and been expelled: *Brooklyn Eagle*, August 23, 1865, 2; the player was Dr. Aleck Pearsall.

10. Competitiveness and Professionalism, and What They Wrought

161 "Until the club became ambitious of winning matches . . .": "Old Chalk" [Henry Chadwick], "Base Ball in Its Infancy," *Brooklyn Eagle*, December 15, 1889, 4.

162 disquieting upsets of well-established clubs by much younger ones: E. H. Tobias, fifth of sixteen-part history of baseball in St. Louis to 1876, *Sporting News*, November 30, 1895, 5. In Janesville, Wisconsin, Frank L. Smith organized a junior club in 1867 and, as he later described, "As the big fellows were inclined to ridicule our efforts we challenged them to a game." To everyone's surprise the junior club won (*Janesville Daily Gazette*, February 9, 1905, 5). Several other shocking upsets during these years in which teams made up primarily of teenagers defeated ones of adults are described in my *Baseball Fever*, 146–148.

162 "hot time of it": *Chadwick Scrapbooks*, 1886 article from unspecified source, quoting Charles Coon.

162–164 "in those days, membership in a club . . .": E. H. Tobias, first of sixteen-part history of baseball in St. Louis to 1876, *Sporting News*, November 2, 1895, 5.

164 "The great national game is indebted . . .": *Brooklyn Eagle*, August 5, 1897, 5, July 28 letter from G. Smith Stanton.

164 "350 members who each paid . . .": Stanley B. Cowing, quoted in the *Kalamazoo Evening Telegraph*, March 26, 1906.

164 "never participated in the game but . . .": E. H. Tobias, first of sixteen-part history of baseball in St. Louis to 1876, *Sporting News*, November 2, 1895, 5.

164–165 "furnished the players with uniforms and . . .": Robert S. Pierce, ten-part history of baseball in Cleveland in *Cleveland Press*, part three, 1908, from the *Chadwick Scrapbooks*.

165 "the ball-players of this place . . .": *Kalamazoo Weekly Telegraph*, October 3, 1866.

166 "the grounds, extensive as they will be . . .": *Brooklyn City News*, April 14, 1862. The three clubs that initially used it were the Eckford, Constellation, and Putnam.

167 "gradually became used to the idea": James Wood, as told to Frank G. Menke, "Baseball in By-Gone Days," part three, syndicated column, *Indiana* (Pa.) *Evening Gazette*, August 17, 1916.

167 "generally had an aversion to making . . .": *New York Clipper*, November 1, 1879.

167–168 "It would be a good investment in any city . . .": *The Ball Player's Chronicle*, June 6, 1867.

168 "it is always better for a club . . .": *The Ball Player's Chronicle*, June 27, 1867.

168 The most likely candidate to have been the first paid player was Jim Creighton: On July 16, 1873, the *Brooklyn Eagle* referred to "the noted Excelsiors, who in 1859 practically inaugurated the professional system by their engagement of Creighton."

169 "Give us part of the gate receipts or . . .": James Wood, as told to Frank G. Menke, "Baseball in By-Gone Days," part three, syndicated column, *Indiana* (Pa.) *Evening Gazette*, August 17, 1916.

169 "accumulated little of this world's goods": *Brooklyn Eagle*, August 5, 1897, 5, July 28 letter from G. Smith Stanton.

170 Even the best clubs were not drawing salaries until around 1866: Joe Start later said that in the early to mid-1860s when the Atlantics of Brooklyn were dominating the game, "We didn't get any salaries, I remember very well, for three or four years. . . . [They were introduced] about 1866, as near as I remember" (*Sporting Life*, November 16, 1895).

170 "we are charged with having secured professional players . . .": *New York Clipper*, June 19, 1869.

170 Henry Burroughs of New Jersey: see *Baseball Fever*, especially page 191, for details.

170 "We don't blame Detroit for thus . . .": *University Chronicle*, June 22, 1867.

170–171 "The Mutuals of New York City were under control . . .": E. H. Tobias, "Paid Players: Amateur Ball Began to Wane in 1869," seventh of sixteen-part history of baseball in St. Louis to 1876, *Sporting News*, December 14, 1895, 5.

171 "Upon inquiry we ascertained . . .": *Chicago Tribune*, January 26, 1890.

171–172 "It is a singular fact that . . .": *French Scrapbooks*.

173 "they don't play ball nowadays as they used to": Pete O'Brien (writing as "Old Peto Brine"), *American Chronicle of Sports and Pastimes*, January 9, 1868.

173 "When we heard of the professional game . . .": Clarence Darrow, *The Story of My Life*, 171–178. Darrow was born in 1857, placing this in the late 1860s or early 1870s. Similarly, in his autobiographical 1904 novel *Farmington*, Darrow's narrator remarks, "The hired players of to-day are no more players than mercenary troops are patriots. They are bought and sold on the open market, and have no pride of home and no town reputation to maintain. Neither I nor any of my companions could any more have played a game of base-ball with Hartford against Farmington than we could have joined a foreign army and fought against the United States. And we would have scorned to hire mercenaries from any other town. We were not only playing ball, but we were fighting for the glory and honor of Farmington" (pp. 209–210).

173–174 "Extra provisions were made to guard against . . .": *Janesville Daily Gazette*, February 18, 1905, 2.

174 "The idea of making money . . .": unspecified New York paper, quoted in *Brooklyn Eagle*, August 16, 1867.

174 Some clubs tried to become "semi-professionals": The *Chicago Tribune* later recalled: "In 1869 the Excelsior Ball Club of Chicago, by hiring [Harry] Lex and one or two other outside players, made themselves virtually a professional organization—or, as we should say now-a-days, a 'semi-professional club'" (*Chicago Tribune*, September 27, 1876). The Excelsiors were lambasted in the local press for their lack of success, as were other clubs such as the Detroit Base Ball Club and the Forest Citys of Cleveland that attempted to pursue "semi-professionalism."

174 the silver ball that John Lowell offered to the champion team of New England: *New England Base Ballist*, August 13, 1868; *New England Base Ballist*, November 5, 1868; see my *A Game of Inches*, vol. 2, pp. 293–296, for more details on these and similar efforts.

174 bands were often hired: Troy Soos, *Before the Curse*, 23.

175 the original ball was melted down: *Boston Journal*, February 20, 1905.

175 "to abolish the committee on nines . . .": *Brooklyn Eagle*, April 2, 1864, describing the Star Club of Brooklyn.

175 "his fidelity to his club . . .": *Chadwick Scrapbooks*, unspecified 1868 article describing David Birdsall.

176 "There was considerable feeling because . . .": Robert S. Pierce, ten-part history of baseball in Cleveland in *Cleveland Press*, part three, 1908, from the *Chadwick Scrapbooks*.

176 the Atlantics of Brooklyn announced plans: *American Chronicle of Sports and Pastimes*, January 2, 1868.

176 the tour was eventually canceled: *American Chronicle of Sports and Pastimes*, February 13, February 27, March 5, 1868.

176–177 "made the name of the club . . .": *Grand Rapids Daily Eagle*, July 22, 1871.

177 When the Unknowns unexpectedly won the tournament, considerable controversy ensued: See Peter Morris, *Baseball Fever*, 163–170.

177 scheduling games so that the title never left the New York City area: William Ryczek, *When Johnny Came Sliding Home*, especially 157–161 and 214–216.

178 "The receipts of the afternoon were . . .": *New York Clipper*, November 1, 1879.

178 "used to play ball every afternoon and . . .": *Philadelphia Times*, reprinted in *Sporting Life*, October 24, 1891.

178 "subscriptions from the members . . .": *New York Clipper*, November 1, 1879.

179 "In those good old times there was . . .": *New York Clipper*, November 1, 1879.

179 "to confine their nine to Philadelphians in the future . . .": *French Scrapbooks*, unspecified article from the end of the 1866 season.

179–180 "We wish to draw attention to another matter . . .": *Chadwick Scrapbooks*, article from the *Philadelphia Mercury*, before the 1867 season.

180–181 "Gentlemen of the Athletic Club . . .": *Brooklyn Eagle*, July 17, 1867.

181 "kept clear from such innovations . . .": "Paid Players: Amateur Ball Began to Wane in 1869," E. H. Tobias, seventh of sixteen-part history of baseball in St. Louis to 1876, *Sporting News*, December 14, 1895, 5.

181–182 "It was early developed in 1868 that . . .": E. H. Tobias, fourth of sixteen-part history of baseball in St. Louis to 1876, *Sporting News*, November 23, 1895, 5.

182 "what the originators of the game . . .": E. H. Tobias, fourth of sixteen-part history of baseball in St. Louis to 1876, *Sporting News*, November 23, 1895, 5.

182–183 "on the ground that the umpire . . .": E. H. Tobias, fourth of sixteen-part history of baseball in St. Louis to 1876, *Sporting News*, November 23, 1895, 5.

183 "satisfied with its two leading clubs and . . .": E. H. Tobias, fifth of sixteen-part history of baseball in St. Louis to 1876, *Sporting News*, November 30, 1895, 5.

183 In Mansfield, Ohio: John C. Carrothers, "Early Base Ball: The Game as Played Here in the '60's with Straight Pitching," *Mansfield News*, June 3, 1895, 5.

183 Similarly dramatic changes gripped the ball clubs of Michigan and West Virginia in 1868: Peter Morris, *Baseball Fever*, Chapter 16; William Akin, *West Virginia Baseball: A History, 1865–2000*, 12. Likewise the leading club in Syracuse, New York, passed a resolution after the 1868 season "declaring that their club is strictly an amateur organization, kept up for the purpose of social pleasure upon the ball field, and that it is not their intention to participate in any matches for championship [in 1869]" (*Detroit Advertiser and Tribune*, May 11, 1869).

183 "by 1868 . . . no one was bearing any defeats gracefully": William Ryczek, *When Johnny Came Sliding Home*, 166.

11. The Cincinnati Base Ball Club and the Red Stockings

185 Some historians have tried to suggest that the club was the first all-salaried one: See my *A Game of Inches*, vol. 2, pp. 181–182, for a discussion of the claim.

186 "We really had no athletic sport . . .": *Cincinnati Commercial*, August 21, 1870.

186 "published a challenge . . .": *Cincinnati Commercial*, August 21, 1870.

187 One of the new clubs was comprised mostly of local lawyers: "Early Base Ball Days," *Chadwick Scrapbooks*, circa 1890; *Cincinnati Commercial*, August 21, 1870.

187 "The players were prompt in attendance . . .": *Cincinnati Commercial*, August 21, 1870.

187 "in the use of strong words": *Cincinnati Commercial*, August 21, 1870.

187 "consisted of a room in Blymyer's foundry": "Early Base Ball Days," unspecified article in the *Chadwick Scrapbooks*, circa 1890.

187 The first was the need to mow the grass: *Cincinnati Commercial*, August 21, 1870.

187 "the mud proved too formidable an obstacle": "Early Base Ball Days," unspecified article in the *Chadwick Scrapbooks*, circa 1890.

187–188 "Holmes Hoge was chosen as Captain . . .": *Cincinnati Commercial*, August 21, 1870.

188 "was found to be short . . .": *Cincinnati Commercial*, August 21, 1870; Glassford's background comes from an obituary in the *New York Times* of April 12, 1900.

188 the club adopted a name: "Early Base Ball Days," unspecified article in the *Chadwick Scrapbooks*, circa 1890.

189 "Scanlan, Fry, Wulsin and Glassford . . .": *Cincinnati Commercial*, August 21, 1870.

190 "unique uniform . . .": *French Scrapbooks*, description of a game in October of 1868 from an unidentified source.

190 the ball club became unofficially but universally known as the Red Stockings: *Chadwick Scrapbooks*, letter by "an Old Member" to the *Cincinnati Commercial*, February 23, 1871.

192 "a feeling of goneness . . .": *Cincinnati Commercial*, August 21, 1870.

192 "adherents were of the rougher elements . . .": *Chadwick Scrapbooks*, circa 1879 article from the *Cincinnati Enquirer.*

192–193 New Yorker John Hatfield "was secured . . .": *Cincinnati Commercial*, reprinted in the *Chicago Tribune*, April 13, 1879.

193 "created more excitement than . . .": *Chadwick Scrapbooks*, circa 1879 article from the *Cincinnati Enquirer.*

193 "Since Saturday there has . . .": *Chadwick Scrapbooks*, unspecified local paper, reprinted in the same circa 1879 article from the *Cincinnati Enquirer.*

195 printed a transcript of the proceedings: *Cincinnati Base Ball Club v. John V. B. Hatfield*; in the *Chadwick Scrapbooks.*

196 never lost a game: There is confusion about the club's exact record. It played about seventy games in all, but Wright considered only fifty-seven to be matches and the others exhibitions. One game was tied when the opposing team walked off the field. Wright could by rights have considered this a victory but preferred to consider it a tie.

196 "They've done something to add to the glory of our city!": *Cincinnati Commercial*, July 2, 1869; quoted in Stephen D. Guschov, *The Red Stockings of Cincinnati: Base Ball's First All-Professional Team*, 68.

198 "Though beaten not disgraced": Greg Rhodes and John Erardi, *The First Boys of Summer: The 1869–1870 Cincinnati Red Stockings*, 99.

198 "the facts prove that he has not been well treated . . .": *Cincinnati Commercial*, November 27, 1870.

200 "very much as though some old gentleman . . .": *Spirit of the Times*, November 26, 1870; quoted in William J. Ryczek, *When Johnny Came Sliding Home*, 237.

200 "are paid by the government of the United States to play baseball": Greg Rhodes and John Erardi, *The First Boys of Summer: The 1869–1870 Cincinnati Red Stockings*, 136.

200–201 "Mr. George B. Ellard, now a resident of this city . . .": *Cincinnati Commercial*, February 23, 1871, letter from "an Old Member," *Chadwick Scrapbooks.*

12. Looking Backward

202 George Wright eventually retired: *Forest and Stream*, April 8, 1880.

202 Leonard Bergen: "Old Stand Bys," *Brooklyn Eagle*, November 18, 1877, 3.

202 Rowing became the sport of preference for many of West Virginia's early baseballists: William Akin, *West Virginia Baseball: A History, 1865–2000*, 21.

202 four ballplayers from Hillsdale, Michigan: *Detroit Post and Tribune*, July 17, 1879; *Hudson Gazette*, July 18, 1879.

203 Richard Fyfe: *Detroit News*, October 28, 1931.

203 "as much of a fan as ever": Dorothy Jordan, "The Old Home Town," *Decatur Daily Review*, July 17, 1921, 9.

203 "I'm still an enthusiastic fan . . .": William H. McMullen, letter to the *Fort Wayne News*, April 11, 1908.

203 H. Clay Sexton: *St. Louis Post-Dispatch*, May 19, 1883.

203 "never lost his interest in the game . . .": *Chadwick Scrapbooks*, circa 1899 account in unnamed newspaper provided by Thomas Taylor.

204 "The question with our young people . . .": *Boston Journal*, March 6, 1905.

204 "When the Pastimes broke up . . .": Sheriff John McNamee, interviewed by John Clark in "From Milan," *Brooklyn Eagle*, January 14, 1876, 2.

204 Charley Smith: *Sporting News*, February 24, 1894.

204 "Frank would have nothing to do . . .": Henry Chadwick, "Old Chalk's Reminiscences: The True Story of the Old Eckford Club," *Brooklyn Eagle*, January 18, 1891, 16.

204 "they don't play ball nowadays as they used to": Pete O'Brien (writing as "Old Peto Brine"), *American Chronicle of Sports and Pastimes*, January 9, 1868.

204–206 "On September 16, 1865 . . .": *Brooklyn Eagle*, April 12, 1896.

206 "Among those who display . . .": *Grand Rapids Daily Democrat*, May 18, 1883.

206 "Loving cups are presented to . . .": *Brooklyn Eagle*, August 5, 1897, 5, July 28 letter from G. Smith Stanton of Great Neck, New York.

206 "A fine lot of rules they are": *Chicago Inter-Ocean*, April 24, 1875.

206–207 "We used to think then that base . . .": *The Galaxy: A Magazine of Entertaining Reading*, July 15, 1866, 561.

207 "The game of base ball, which long ago . . .": "The Moral of Base Ball," *Forest and Stream*, July 31, 1879.

207 "never missed a ball nor struck out": *Brooklyn Eagle*, August 5, 1897, 5, July 28 letter from G. Smith Stanton of Great Neck, New York.

207–208 "as famous as a baseball pitcher as . . .": *Decatur Daily Review*, August 11, 1905.

208 "was known as the Babe Ruth of Central Illinois . . .": Dorothy Jordan, "The Old Home Town," *Decatur Daily Review*, July 17, 1921, 9, describing J. C. McQuigg.

208 Jimmy Foran made all three outs: *Chadwick Scrapbooks*, unspecified article, circa 1879.

208 "Even if they played after a hard day's work . . .": *Newport Daily News*, May 22, 1914.

208 "Here's to the memory of . . .": *Boston Journal*, March 6, 1905.

208–209 "There are but few left who can tell of . . .": "Ball Tossers of Olden Days," *Kalamazoo Gazette*, February 11, 1906.

209 "old flow of language, especially when baseball is the topic": *Chadwick Scrapbooks*, unidentified article by Henry Chadwick, circa 1906.

209 "with celerity and tackled his favorite topic of base ball with avidity": *Detroit Free Press*, January 13, 1889.

210 "Yet may the *laudator temporis acti* . . .": Clarence Deming, "Old Days in Baseball," *Outing*, June 1902, 360.

210–211 "Upon such occasions we readily recall . . .": *Elizabethtown Post and Gazette*, May 28, 1903.

211 "What a magician time is . . .": "Old Boys," *Brooklyn Eagle*, December 3, 1877, 2.

212 "the days of our youth, when you and I . . .": *Chadwick Scrapbooks*, unspecified article, circa 1907.

18. Moving Forward

213–214 "I recollect that the [early] game was played . . .": Charles McCulloch, quoted in B. J. Griswold, "A Pictorial History of Fort Wayne," *Fort Wayne Sentinel*, August 15, 1914.

214 "In most of our ballclubs the brunt . . .": *Chadwick Scrapbooks*, unspecified article.

214 "It seems to me now . . .": Melville McGee, "The Early Days of Concord, Jackson County, Michigan," *Michigan Pioneer and Historical Collections* 21 (1892), 430.

214 "We played ball; we did not work at the trade of amusing people": Clarence Darrow, *Farmington*, 210.

215 "It became customary last season . . .": *Chicago Times*, November 27, 1870; quoted in Robert Pruter, "Youth Baseball in Chicago, 1868–1890: Not Always Sandlot Ball," *Journal of Sport History*, Spring 1999.

216 as a "second rate man" instead of a "second nine man": *Detroit Post*, September 25, 1867.

217 "one of the most noted games ever played in St. Louis": E. H. Tobias, fifth of sixteen-part history of baseball in St. Louis to 1876, *Sporting News*, November 30, 1895, 5.

218 An account of a muffin game in Connecticut: Major Julius G. Rathbun, "Baseball Here Forty Years Ago," article in *Chadwick Scrapbooks*, circa 1907.

218 "But one fly was taken . . .": *The Ball Player's Chronicle*, July 11, 1867.

218–219 "the Heavies were sent blowing . . .": *Chadwick Scrapbooks*, October 1868 clipping.

219 "I haven't played ball for ten years . . .": *Golden Age*, reprinted in the *Marion* (Ohio) *Star*, August 12, 1880, 2.

219 "an agile but near-sighted muffin . . .": *Chadwick Scrapbooks*, unidentified clipping.

219 "a B.C. (behind the catcher)": Major Julius G. Rathbun, "Baseball Here Forty Years Ago," article in *Chadwick Scrapbooks*, circa 1907.

219 "all who have any knowledge . . .": *Detroit Advertiser and Tribune*, October 26, 1867.

219 "muffin soup": Major Julius G. Rathbun, "Baseball Here Forty Years Ago," article in *Chadwick Scrapbooks*, circa 1907.

220 "as most of them wished . . .": *Saginaw Daily Courier*, September 12, 1879.

220 "Hail! Order of Muffins . . .": *Chadwick Scrapbooks*, unidentified clipping.

220 "would undoubtedly have secured . . .": *The Ball Player's Chronicle*, July 11, 1867.

220–221 a batter could count two runs if he completed the circuit of the bases on his own hit and then made it back to first base again: An instance is described in the *Detroit Advertiser and Tribune*, October 12, 1866. Aptly, this account used a different term, calling the play a "double tally."

221 "The gyrations of the players . . .": *Louisville Courier*, reprinted in *New York Herald*, July 26, 1869.

221–222 "Your committee to whom was referred the inquiry . . .": *Chadwick Scrapbooks*, unidentified clipping.

222 "to use a slang expression . . .": Major Julius G. Rathbun, "Baseball Here Forty Years Ago," article in *Chadwick Scrapbooks*, circa 1907.

224 "Dr. Neil is one of the most noted players . . .": *Chadwick Scrapbooks*, original in the *New York Sun*, circa 1889.

224 parading in uniform through the center of the town: For example, the *Philadelphia Inquirer* of June 23 and 25, 1888, described a parade that, in spite of showers, featured more than one hundred clubs in Philadelphia. And the *Chicago Inter-Ocean* of September 2, 1891, reported on a similar number of Chicago amateur ballplayers who paraded "in military alignment."

224–225 "I pitched for the town team . . .": Lawrence S. Ritter, *The Glory of Their Times*, 155.

Selected Bibliography

This book relies upon my perusal of thousands of accounts, both contemporaneous and retrospective. Listing all of them would be of little use to researchers, especially since specific sources are always noted in the footnotes. So here I have restricted myself to books and articles with substantial descriptions of early baseball.

Primary Sources (works by eyewitnesses or consisting largely of firsthand accounts)

Dr. Daniel L. Adams (early Knickerbocker), interview, *Sporting News*, February 29, 1896, 3.

Aetna Base Ball Association Constitution and By-Laws (unpublished logbook; Burton Collection, Detroit Public Library).

Adrian C. "Cap" Anson, *A Ball Player's Career* (1900; reprint: Mattituck, N.Y., n.d.).

"Ball Tossers of Olden Days," *Kalamazoo Gazette*, February 11, 1906.

"Base Balls," *Brooklyn Eagle*, February 3, 1884, 7.

"'Bob' Fisher Talks of Old Kekiongas," *Fort Wayne News*, April 1, 1908, 7.

"B. P.," "'Nassau vs. Star'—The Trip of Our Nine," *Nassau Literary Magazine*, March 1863 [23,6], 6.

John C. Carrothers, "Early Base Ball: The Game as Played Here in the '60's with Straight Pitching," *Mansfield News*, June 3, 1895, 5.

Henry Chadwick, *The American Game of Base Ball* (aka *The Game of Base Ball. How to Learn It, How to Play It, and How to Teach It. With Sketches of Noted Players*) (1868; reprint: Columbia, S.C., 1983).

"Old Chalk" [Henry Chadwick], "Base Ball Reminiscences," *Brooklyn Eagle*, June 7, 1891, 16.

"Old Chalk" [Henry Chadwick], "Base Ball in Its Infancy," *Brooklyn Eagle*, December 15, 1889, 4.

Chadwick Scrapbooks.

Henry Chadwick, *Beadle's Dime Base-Ball Player* (1860) (reprint: Morgantown, Pa., 1996).

Selected Bibliography

Henry Chadwick, *Haney's Base Ball Book of Reference for 1867* (aka *The Base Ball Player's Book of Reference*) (New York, 1867).

Henry Chadwick, "Old Boys," *Brooklyn Eagle*, December 2, 1877, 1, and December 3, 1877, 2.

Henry Chadwick, "Old Chalk's Reminiscences: The True Story of the Old Eckford Club," *Brooklyn Eagle*, January 18, 1891, 16.

Seymour R. Church, *Base Ball: The History, Statistics and Romance of the American National Game from Its Inception to the Present Time* (1902; reprint: Princeton, N.J., 1974).

Cincinnati Base Ball Club v. John V. B. Hatfield, book printed by the club to describe the evidence for expelling Hatfield, in the *Chadwick Scrapbooks*.

John Clark, "From Milan," *Brooklyn Eagle*, January 14, 1876, 2 (interview with John McNamee by Clark, himself a former baseball player of some prominence).

William A. Cochran, "The Olympians," *The Round Table*, April 22, 1898 (reprinted on Beloit College website: http://www.beloit.edu/~lib-home/Archives/papers/olympians.html).

T. Z. Cowles, multipart series on early Chicago sports history, *Chicago Tribune*, May 26, June 2, June 16, June 30, 1918.

Clarence Darrow, *Farmington* (Chicago, 1904).

Clarence Darrow, *The Story of My Life* (1932; reprint: New York, 1996).

Clarence Deming, "Old Days in Baseball," *Outing*, June 1902, 357–360.

"The First Detroit Base Ball Club Formed in the Free Press Office Twenty-Seven Years Ago," *Detroit Free Press*, April 4, 1884.

Edmund F. French Scrapbooks, Historical Society of Washington, D.C.

Richard Fyfe, letter to Clarence Burton, Burton Collection, Detroit Public Library.

William Ridgely Griffith, *The Early History of Amateur Base Ball in the State of Maryland*; reprinted in *Maryland Historical Magazine* 87, no. 2 (Summer 1992), 201–208.

"How Baseball Began—A Member of the Gotham Club of Fifty Years Ago Tells About It," *San Francisco Examiner*, November 27, 1887, 14 (interview with William Wheaton).

Kent Base Ball Club By-Laws and Constitution, unpublished logbook, Grand Rapids Public Library.

Gene Kessler, "Deacon White, Oldest Living Player, at 92 Recalls Highlights of Historic Career That Started in 1868," *Sporting News*, June 22, 1939, 19.

R. M. Larner, "Old-Time Baseball in the White Lot," *Washington Post*, June 26, 1904, S4.

R. M. Larner, "Beginning of Professional Baseball in Washington," *Washington Post*, July 3, 1904, S3.

Dave Larson, *Wide Awakes, Invincibles and Smokestackers: Early Baseball in Tall Timber Country, 1869–1905* (Minneapolis, 2006).

Selected Bibliography

Connie Mack, "Memories of When the Game Was Young," *Sporting Life* (monthly), June 1924.

Melville McGee, "The Early Days of Concord, Jackson County, Michigan," *Michigan Pioneer and Historical Collections* 21 (1892).

"An Old Member," letter to the *Cincinnati Commercial*, February 23, 1871, in the *Chadwick Scrapbooks*.

James O'Rourke [assumed], "Forty Two Years of Base Ball: Wonderful Life Story of Jim O'Rourke," (multipart series) *Kalamazoo Evening Telegraph*, February 24, 25, 26, March 1, 2, 3, 1910.

Charles Peverelly, *The Book of American Pastimes*; in John Freyer and Mark Rucker, ed., *Peverelly's National Game*.

Robert S. Pierce, ten-part history of baseball in Cleveland, *Cleveland Press*, February 11–21, 1908.

Protoball website, at www.retrosheet.org/Protoball/

Major Julius G. Rathbun, "Baseball Here Forty Years Ago," unidentified clipping from a Hartford newspaper, circa 1907, *Chadwick Scrapbooks*.

Harry Slye, "Early Days of Baseball in Baraboo," *Baraboo* (Wisc.) *Daily News*, June 25 and 26, 1925.

Frank L. Smith, twenty-part history of baseball in Janesville, Wisconsin, *Janesville Daily Gazette*, February 8–May 4, 1905.

Albert Goodwill Spalding, *America's National Game: Historic Facts Concerning the Beginning, Evolution, Development, and Popularity of Base Ball, with Personal Reminiscences of Its Vicissitudes, Its Victories, and Its Votaries* (1910; reprint: Lincoln, Nebr., 1992).

Alfred H. Spink, *The National Game* (1911; reprint: Carbondale, Ill., 2000).

G. Smith Stanton, letter, *Brooklyn Eagle*, August 5, 1897, 5.

Dean Sullivan, ed., *Early Innings: A Documentary History of Baseball, 1825–1908* (Lincoln, Nebr., 1995).

E. H. Tobias, sixteen-part history of baseball in St. Louis to 1876, *Sporting News*, November 2, 1895–February 15, 1896.

"Tri-Mountain," three-part series on early baseball in Boston, *Boston Journal*, February 20 and 22, March 6, 1905.

Richard Weddle, 1901 letter to Henry Chadwick, *Sporting News*, January 19, 1901.

"When D. M. Ferry Played Ball," *Detroit Free Press*, June 14, 1903.

James Leon Wood, Sr. (as told to Frank G. Menke), "Baseball in By-Gone Days," syndicated series, *Indiana* (Pa.) *Evening Gazette*, August 14, 1916; *Marion* (Ohio) *Star*, August 15, 1916; *Indiana* (Pa.) *Evening Gazette*, August 17, 1916.

Secondary Sources

Melvin L. Adelman, "The First Baseball Game, the First Newspaper References to Baseball, and the New York Club: A Note on the Early

History of Baseball," *Journal of Sport History* 7, no. 3 (Winter 1980), 132–135.

Melvin L. Adelman, *A Sporting Time: New York City and the Rise of Modern Athletics, 1820–70* (Urbana, Ill., 1986).

William Akin, *West Virginia Baseball: A History, 1865–2000* (Jefferson, N.C., 2006).

Thomas L. Altherr, "A Place Leavel Enough to Play Ball," reprinted in David Block, *Baseball Before We Knew It* (Lincoln, Nebr., 2005), 229–251.

Priscilla Astifan, "Baseball in the Nineteenth Century," *Rochester History* LII, no. 3 (Summer 1990); "Baseball in the Nineteenth Century Part Two," *Rochester History* LXII, no. 2 (Spring 2000); "Baseball in the Nineteenth Century, Part 3: The Dawn of Acknowledged Professionalism and Its Impact on Rochester Baseball," *Rochester History* LXIII, no. 1 (Winter 2001); "Rochester's Last Two Seasons of Amateur Baseball: Baseball in the Nineteenth Century, Part Four," *Rochester History* LXIII, no. 2 (Spring 2001); "Baseball in the Nineteenth Century, Part V: 1877—Rochester's First Year of Professional Baseball," *Rochester History* LXIV, no. 4 (Fall 2002).

The Barry Halper Collection of Baseball Memorabilia (New York, 1999).

Phil Bergen, "Lovett of the Lowells," *National Pastime* 16 (1996), 62–68.

David Block, *Baseball Before We Knew It* (Lincoln, Nebr., 2005).

Randall Brown, "How Baseball Began," *National Pastime* 24 (2004), 51–54.

Patricia Cline Cohen, *The Murder of Helen Jewett: The Life and Death of a Prostitute in Nineteenth-Century New York* (New York, 1998).

W. Harrison Daniel and Scott P. Mayer, *Baseball and Richmond: A History of the Professional Game, 1884–2000* (Jefferson, N.C., 2006).

Paul Dickson, ed., *The New Dickson Baseball Dictionary* (New York, 1999).

Alice Morse Earle, *Child Life in Colonial Days* (1899) (reprint: Stockbridge, Mass., 1993).

Harry Ellard, *Base Ball in Cincinnati: A History* (1907) (reprint: Jefferson, N.C., 2004).

Federal Writers' Project, *Baseball in Old Chicago* (Chicago, 1939).

John B. Foster, "The Evolution of Pitching" (part 1), *Sporting News*, November 26, 1931, 5; "The Evolution of Pitching" (part 2), *Sporting News*, December 10, 1931, 6; "The Evolution of Pitching" (part 3), *Sporting News*, December 24, 1931, 6; "The Evolution of Pitching" (part 4), *Sporting News*, January 7, 1932, 6.

Stephen Fox, *Big Leagues: Professional Baseball, Football, and Basketball in National Memory* (New York, 1994).

Warren Goldstein, *Playing for Keeps: A History of Early Baseball* (Ithaca, N.Y., 1989).

B. J. Griswold, "A Pictorial History of Fort Wayne," *Fort Wayne Sentinel*, August 29, 1914.

John H. Gruber, multipart series on baseball rules and customs under a variety of headings, weekly series in *Sporting News*, November 4, 1915–April 6, 1916.

Stephen Guschov, *The Red Stockings of Cincinnati: Base Ball's First All-Professional Team and Its Historic 1869 and 1870 Seasons* (Jefferson, N.C., 1998).

Stephen Hardy, *How Boston Played: Sport, Recreation, and Community, 1865–1915* (Boston, 1982).

Robert W. Henderson, *Ball, Bat, and Bishop: The Origin of Ball Games* (1947) (reprint: Urbana, Ill., 2001).

Frederick Ivor-Campbell, "When Was the First Match Game Played by the Knickerbocker Rules?," *Nineteenth Century Notes* 93:4 (Fall 1993), 1–2.

George B. Kirsch, *The Creation of American Team Sports: Baseball and Cricket, 1838–72* (Urbana, Ill., 1991).

Peter Levine, *A. G. Spalding and the Rise of Baseball: The Promise of American Sport* (New York, 1985).

John Liepa, "Baseball Mania Strikes Iowa," *Iowa Heritage* 87:1 (Spring 2006).

Michael E. Lomax, *Black Baseball Entrepreneurs, 1860–1901: Operating by Any Means Necessary* (Syracuse, 2003).

Angus Macfarlane, "The Knickerbockers: San Francisco's First Baseball Team?", *Base Ball* 1:1 (Spring 2007), 7–21.

William A. Mann, "The Elysian Fields of Hoboken, New Jersey," *Base Ball* 1:1 (Spring 2007), 78–95.

Tom Melville, *Early Baseball and the Rise of the National League* (Jefferson, N.C., 2001).

Peter Morris, *Baseball Fever: Early Baseball in Michigan* (Ann Arbor, Mich., 2003).

Peter Morris, "From First Baseman to Primo Basso: The Odd Saga of the Original Pirate King (Tra La!)," *NINE* 15:2 (Spring 2007), 46–65.

Peter Morris, *A Game of Inches: The Stories Behind the Innovations That Shaped Baseball: Volume 1: The Game on the Field* (Chicago, 2006).

Peter Morris, *A Game of Inches: The Stories Behind the Innovations That Shaped Baseball: Volume 2: The Game Behind the Scenes* (Chicago, 2006).

Peter Morris, *Level Playing Fields: How the Groundskeeping Murphy Brothers Shaped Baseball* (Lincoln, Nebr., 2007).

Robert A. Nylen, "Frontier Baseball," *Nevada*, vol. 50, no. 2 (March/April 1990), 27–29, 56.

Preston D. Orem, *Baseball (1845–1881) from the Newspaper Accounts* (Altadena, Calif., 1961).

Harold Peterson, *The Man Who Invented Baseball* (New York, 1969).

Greg Rhodes and John Erardi, *The First Boys of Summer* (Cincinnati, 1994).

Francis C. Richter, *Richter's History and Records of Base Ball* (1914) (reprint: Jefferson, N.C., 2005).

Lawrence S. Ritter, *The Glory of Their Times* (1966) (reprint: New York, 1984).

Mark Rucker, *Base Ball Cartes: The First Baseball Cards* (Saratoga Springs, N.Y., 1988).

William J. Ryczek, *Blackguards and Red Stockings: A History of Baseball's National Association, 1871–1875* (Jefferson, N.C., 1992).

William J. Ryczek, *When Johnny Came Sliding Home: The Post-Civil War Baseball Boom, 1865–1870* (Jefferson, N.C., 1998).

Robert H. Schaefer, "The Lost Art of Fair-Foul Hitting," *National Pastime* 20 (2000), 3–9.

P. David Sentance, *Cricket in America, 1710–2000* (Jefferson, N.C., 2006).

Harold Seymour, *Baseball: The Early Years* (New York, 1960).

Tom Shieber, "The Evolution of the Baseball Diamond," originally printed in the *Baseball Research Journal* 23 (1994), 3–13; reprinted in an expanded version in *Total Baseball IV*, 113–124.

John Shiffert, *Base Ball in Philadelphia: A History of the Early Game, 1831–1900* (Jefferson, N.C., 2006).

Robert Smith, *Baseball* (New York, 1947).

Troy Soos, *Before the Curse: The Glory Days of New England Baseball, 1858–1918*, rev. ed. (Jefferson, N.C., 2006).

James L. Terry, *Long Before the Dodgers: Baseball in Brooklyn, 1855–1884* (Jefferson, N.C., 2002).

George A. Thompson, Jr., "New York Baseball, 1823," *National Pastime* 21 (2001), 6–8.

Robert L. Tiemann and Mark Rucker, eds., *Nineteenth Century Stars* (Kansas City, 1989).

Brian Turner and John S. Bowman, *Baseball in Northampton, 1823–1953* (Northampton, Mass., 2002).

Jules Tygiel, *Past Time: Baseball as History* (New York, 2000).

David Quentin Voigt, *American Baseball: From the Gentleman's Sport to the Commissioner's System* (Norman, Okla., 1966).

Marshall D. Wright, *The National Association of Base Ball Players, 1857–1870* (Jefferson, N.C., 2000).

Joel Zoss and John Bowman, *Diamonds in the Rough: The Untold History of Baseball* (New York, 1989).

Index

Connecticut clubs. *See* Bristol,
Collinsville, Hartford,
Litchfield, Middletown, New
Haven, New London,
Norwich, Springfield, and
Waterbury
Cope, Elias, *163*
Craver, William, 116, *117*, 118
Creighton, Jim, 10, 69–72, 105,
137, 168, 250, 259
Cricket. *See* rival bat-and-ball
games
Cronin, R. A., 254
Curry, Duncan, 23, 27
Custer, Gen. George, 158
Cuthbert, Ed, *163*
Cyclone club. *See* St. Louis

Dakin, Thomas, 69
Darrow, Clarence, 43–44, 173,
214, 242, 248, 252, 260
Davenport, Iowa, ball clubs, 20
Davis, J. W., 34
Daybreak club. *See* Jackson,
Michigan
Dayton, Kentucky, ball clubs,
186
DeBost, Charles, 33
Decatur, Illinois, ball clubs, 42,
207–208
De Coster, Billy, 16
De la Vergne, Ben, 245
Delmar, County Clerk, 211
Deming, Clarence, 58–60, 77,
79–80, 84, 113–114, 210
Detroit, Michigan, ball clubs,
21–22, 50, 82, 86, 107, 113,
157–158, 177, 202–203, 216,

219, 226; Cass club, 95, 209;
Detroit Base Ball Club, 170,
260; Early Risers club, 95, 253;
Franklin club, 40–41, 53, 158
Dick, Billy, *163*
Dickens, Charles, 5
District of Columbia. *See*
Washington, D.C.
Dockney, Patsy, 178–179, 192
Doolittle, W. J., 46
Doubleday, Gen. Abner, 3,
227–228
Doubleday, Abner Demas,
227–228
Doubleday, Bill, 114
Dowagiac, Michigan, ball clubs,
138
Dunderberg club. *See* Peekskill,
New York
Dunne, Finley Peter, 115
Dupignac, Ebenezer, 6
Durkee, John, 244

Eagle club. *See* Florence,
Massachusetts, New York City
Earle, Alice Morse, 13
Early Risers club. *See* Detroit
Easton, Col. A. R., 150–151
Eaton Rapids, Michigan, ball
clubs, 102
Eckford club. *See* Brooklyn
Eckford, Henry, 124
Edgerton, Elisha W., 82
Elizabeth I, 13
Elizabeth, New Jersey, ball
clubs, 43
Elizabethtown, New York, ball
clubs, 43, 50, 210–211,

A NOTE ON THE AUTHOR

Peter Morris has established himself as one of the foremost historians of early baseball in America. His *A Game of Inches: The Stories Behind the Innovations That Shaped Baseball* (2006) was the first book ever to win both the coveted Seymour Medal of the Society for American Baseball Research and the Casey Award from *Spitball* magazine as the best baseball book of the year. Mr. Morris has also written *Catcher: How the Man Behind the Plate Became an American Folk Hero; But Didn't We Have Fun?*, an informal history of baseball's pioneer era; *Level Playing Fields*, about the early days of groundskeeping; and *Baseball Fever*, the story of early baseball in Michigan. A former national and international Scrabble champion, he lives in Haslett, Michigan. For more information, see his website: www.petermorrisbooks.com.